teach yourself...

PageMaker 6.5

for Macintosh and Windows

David D. Busch

MIS:
PRESS

A Subsidiary of
Henry Holt and Co., Inc.

A Subsidiary of
Henry Holt and Co., Inc.

MIS:Press
A Subsidiary of Henry Holt and Company, Inc.
115 West 18th Street
New York, New York 10011
http://www.mispress.com

First Edition—1997

Library of Congress Cataloging-in-Publication Data

ISBN 1-55828-539-3

10 9 8 7 6 5 4 3 2 1

Associate Publisher: *Paul Farrell*   **Production Editor:** *Anne Incao/Gay Nichols*
Managing Editor: *Shari Chappell*   **Technical Editor:** *Deb Hiett Borgia*
Editor: *Rebekah Young*   **Copy Editor:** *Suzanne Ingrao*

CONTENTS

v

Introduction

1

This book is about *PageMaker*, a page-composition software program that automates all the steps in developing a printed document. *Composition* is the process of laying out text and graphics—typography, lines, boxes, pictures, drawings, and colors—on a page. PageMaker is considered by many industry experts, and by many users, to be one of the most functional, expert systems available for the design and composition of documents. I think it is also the easiest, most intuitive page-composition software to learn. PageMaker is taught in high schools and colleges, art schools, trade schools, and vocational centers (it's probably offered in some advanced elementary schools). It is used by graphic designers and artists, technical writers and illustrators, corporate communications departments, marketing groups, newspapers, magazines, and book publishers. The beauty of PageMaker is that it can be simple to use for those who want just the basic resources, yet it is highly sophisticated for creating complex, four-color designs. Its long-document capabilities are better than the best word processors while still presenting a simple, friendly workplace for the novice.

The Highlights of Version 6.5

Although Adobe added only a half of a "release point" in enhancing PageMaker from 1995's Version 6.0 to the 1996 Version 6.5, the improvements in this latest edition are just as significant as those of the previous upgrade. The sixth major release of PageMaker had improved color controls, up to 256 different Master Pages per document, a new Guide Manager, Photoshop filter compatibility, as well as HTML (Web page) and Adobe Acrobat export capabilities. Now, 6.5 adds to that document-wide layers and a host of other professional-level features.

Document Layers

Layers allow you to place elements on different overlay "sheets" that you can make visible or invisible anytime you like. These layers can be used for creating multiple versions, adding annotations, or simply hiding an element you temporarily don't want to see or use. Photoshop users have had layers for several years. Now PageMaker users have them, too.

Easier Layouts

PageMaker 6.5 adds frames, which can hold any kind of text or image, and has new capabilities for reflying text into columns when you change layouts, or resizing images. PageMaker has long been praised for its free-form layout capabilities, and now becomes even more flexible with its frames and text controls.

Better Integration

Adobe has modified all its flagship applications, from PageMaker to Photoshop to Illustrator, so they all work more alike, with standard menus, interactive tabbed palettes, and the ability to drag and drop images and elements directly from one of these applications to the other. You'll find that many keyboard shortcuts also work exactly the same between applications and across Windows and Mac platforms.

Color Controls

PageMaker 6.5 builds on the improvements of the last release with new color technologies, including PANTONE's Hexachrome six-color process for high-fidelity color. A new desktop color separation tool is available, and the Kodak Color Management System introduced in 1995 now supports the International Color Consortium standard for sharing device profiles.

Internet Awareness

The previous release of PageMaker came when the Internet was still a new and largely misunderstood realm to the masses. Today, the World Wide Web has become an integral part of our lives, and Version 6.5 includes improvements that reflect that. In this release, *hierarchical text markup language (HTML)* creation has been enhanced. You can create Web pages in PageMaker, and export finished HTML pages with links preserved and any included image files converted to the JPEG and GIF formats required for the Internet. PageMaker's color library includes the 216 "standard" colors that browsers usually default to. You can now drag and drop links directly from browsers into PageMaker. If your Web pages need more sophisticated layout than HTML provides, you can export PageMaker documents in Adobe Acrobat format. Most browsers can use the Acrobat Reader plug-in to display these pages exactly as you created them.

DESKTOP PUBLISHING: HOW IT ALL STARTED

Many in professional publishing today worked back in the good old days, before the advent of personal computers, or even digital typesetters. Back then, newspaper pages were designed by layout editors who marked up dummies of each page of the paper, told reporters how many lines of copy each story had to be, and fit the advertisements around the stories. The dummy was the layout specification for the newspaper page. Writers had little idea of how the stories would look or of their location until the page was ready to be printed. If a story needed to be added at the last minute, it would often involve the entire remake of the page, which means that the page had to be completely redesigned and the type reset.

The dummies and typed stories were sent to composing, where *hot lead typesetting* machines literally set the type in melted lead, one justified line at a time (the line came out in a slug, or strip of lead). If a word was misspelled in the line, the entire line had to be reset. The machines were gigantic, hot, noisy, and smelly. There were a dozen or more in most composing rooms. Several were always shut down for repairs.

At that time, these machines were still considered pretty much state-of-the-art for a large newspaper. Working with hot lead was a lot faster than working with *cold type*. Cold type meant that the lead characters were already cast, and you had to manually arrange the type in a galley tray, set as the mirror image of the printed page (that is, backward and reading right to left). The classified ad pages were all set in cold type. Sometime in 1460, Johann Gutenberg had popularized the printing from movable type. There was very little difference between setting want ads at most daily newspapers in 1970, and the way Gutenberg set the type for his Bible in 1465—in both instances the type was cast individually in lead and placed by hand in a galley.

ALONG CAME THE MAC (AND, EVENTUALLY, THE PC)

Regardless of the method for setting type, page composition remained a completely manual process for the most part, until the mid-1980s, when small, personal laser printers were invented, the PostScript page description language for laser printers was refined, and a graphics-based personal computer called the *Apple Macintosh* was introduced. The Mac could run a most unorthodox program called PageMaker, which displayed a page laid out exactly as it would be printed—a radically new concept called *What-You-See-Is-What-You-Get*, or *WYSIWYG* (pronounced "wizzy wig"). Until the Macintosh, most personal computers were generally character-based systems, like the IBM PC, which could not display the shapes of typeset characters or graphic symbols—

they weren't WYSIWYG. The Mac, PageMaker, and the Apple LaserWriter were the impetus for a new computer-designed, computer-generated graphic composition industry that came to be known as desktop publishing.

It took quite a few years for the PC to catch up to the Macintosh in graphics capabilities, and it wasn't really until Windows 95 was introduced in August 1995 that both platforms became roughly equal in terms of usability for layout work. Starting with PageMaker 6.0, introduced at about the same time as Windows 95, Adobe began providing twin versions of its layout program, with virtually identical features, dialog boxes, and menus. So, if you learn the program on one computer, you can move over to the other and immediately begin doing productive work. You may have to remember that the **Ctrl** key on the PC is the **Command** key on the Mac (although the Mac also has a **Ctrl** key, to confuse things a little), and that the **Option** key on the Mac is the same as the **Alt** key on the PC. But, generally, the move between platforms should be seamless and easy.

WHAT THIS BOOK IS ABOUT

This book does exactly what its title says: It helps you to teach yourself PageMaker 6.5. If you're like me, you're probably standing in a bookstore, reading this introduction, trying to decide whether this is the book to buy. I'll tell you a secret: If you start Chapter 2, "A Weekend Tour of PageMaker," on Saturday morning, by Monday you'll understand PageMaker. This book covers all of the basic functions of PageMaker in depth, and in most cases, gives you an overview of PageMaker's high-powered functions. It is arranged to introduce you to capabilities in the order in which you will probably need them. That is, it explains how to install the software before telling you how to use it, covers how to create a basic document before telling you how to print it, and so forth.

WHO SHOULD READ THIS BOOK

You won't need to know very much about computers, software, or your computer's operating system to understand this book. It is a basic text on PageMaker: It starts at the beginning and assumes you know very little. Since the chapters are arranged functionally, if you already know what I'm talking about in a section, feel free to jump ahead. You will also find a comprehensive reference section (Appendix B) explaining each command on each pull-down menu, arranged in the left-to-right order of the menus across the top of the PageMaker window.

If You Work in the Graphic Arts

While you don't necessarily need to know anything about art, design, typography, or composition, if you are a graphic artist, you will continually be surprised at how simple it is to do so many repetitious, hand-worked chores in PageMaker. I use examples of documents in this book to fit the beginner's as well as the expert's needs. If you are a graphic designer, or at least have some creative juices, you will find that PageMaker can accomplish in seconds things that would take hours manually. All of the graphic artists to whom I have introduced PageMaker (and there have been quite a few over the years) have taken to it immediately. PageMaker is a natural extension of their fingertips.

If You Are a Writer or Editor

If you write for a living, you will be pleasantly surprised at how easy it is to develop copy for manuals, brochures, and fact sheets in PageMaker. You'll find it equally easy to import stories from your favorite word processor, and graphics from Macintosh and Windows graphics programs. You will find yourself looking forward to laying out and composing the page as much as you did to writing the page. And you'll learn that it is indeed painless to try out new ideas and experiment with graphic designs.

TO SUM UP

I first saw PageMaker demonstrated in 1985. It was running on a Macintosh hooked up to a Linotronic typesetter. The typesetter was actually printing out typesetting that had been composed on the Mac in PageMaker—unbelievable! I was exuberant. I had waited for such a marvelous invention for many years, and I was hungry for it. Those of us who worked in graphic arts and publishing before the advent of desktop publishing know how time-consuming, restrictive, and difficult manual page composition could be. Just as computers and computer users have matured over the past few years, so has PageMaker. It is now an extremely powerful publishing and graphics tool, made even more significant by the latest generation of Macintosh and Pentium-based computers.

CHAPTER 1

Getting Started

- ✦ The PageMaker advantage
- ✦ The OS advantage
- ✦ Installing PageMaker
- ✦ A quick primer
- ✦ To sum up

Desktop publishing is undergoing an exciting revitalization. Improvements in technology—600-dpi printers have become a virtual standard—have made desktop publishing more practical. Anyone can produce high-quality documents right on their desktop with enough resolution for razor-sharp text and rich-looking photographic images. In addition, the dramatic explosion in the number of Web pages has created a huge demand for transferring documents created with programs such as Adobe PageMaker into HTML files or Adobe Acrobat files for distribution. Burgeoning intranets also need this type of document. Even competing vendors have helped: low-cost, sub-$100 publishing programs are great for simple jobs but tend to quickly create a thirst among serious users for more powerful programs like PageMaker.

If there is one central advantage to PageMaker over these alternatives, it is creative freedom. PageMaker and graphical operating systems like those found on both PCs and Macintoshes allow users to push their creative limits. Turn on your computer, open PageMaker, and before you realize it, you're using commands and tools without referring to this book or Adobe's documentation—PageMaker and its tools make logical sense and just seem to feel right. Documents that communicate are developed from creative skill that comes, in part, with having the freedom to explore a palette of ideas and discard those that don't work. PageMaker frees you to experiment, buying you time to try more ideas. And, with PageMaker, documents can continue to evolve as they are designed, written, laid out, revised, and printed.

THE PAGEMAKER ADVANTAGE

PageMaker makes your work more efficient and your time more productive. Over the course of the ten years that I've used PageMaker, I've found that an hour working in PageMaker can equal as many as twelve hours of handwork. For the graphic designer, layout artist, or draftsperson, such repetitive tasks as inking lines, pasting down type, painstakingly searching for typos, aligning art to page frames, even drawing crop marks and registration bullets are gone. You can put away your razor blades and artist's tape. PageMaker gives you better things to do with your time. The writer or editor, accustomed to turning in typed stories to a graphic arts group, can now design documents and carry that design through to a finished, camera-ready mechanical that is ready to print.

PageMaker is a splendid vehicle for playing "what if?" You can use some of your newfound time to play with ideas. As shown in Figure 1.1, creating rough layouts for an ad can be easy and creative.

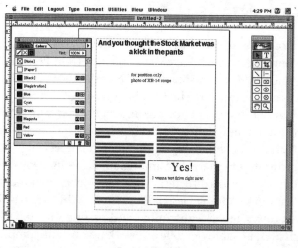

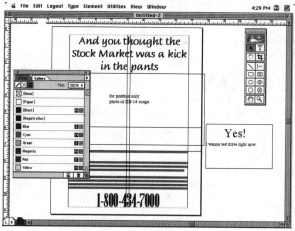

Figure 1.1 *Different layouts for the same ad.*

One important benefit to designing and producing documents in PageMaker is the ease with which you can revise them. Instead of storing documents in stacks of art boards, mechanicals, and negatives, you can store them on your hard drive or a few floppies. Making changes is simply a matter of opening the file, editing it, and saving the file. And, if you save the file under a different name, you will have both your original document and a second, changed document. When you've perfected your document, you can save it as a template. Templates, covered in Chapter 5, are master copies of any document you might want to duplicate in the future.

THE OS ADVANTAGE

PCs and Macintoshes both use an operating system, or OS, to provide the rich graphical environment in which PageMaker operates. On PCs, that operating system is usually Windows 95; on the Macintosh, it's called Mac OS (the new name for the Macintosh System software). The OS also gives PageMaker the ability to share data with other applications on your system. PageMaker supports object linking and embedding capabilities. Called *OLE* (like what the spectators shout to the bullfighter ... or the bull) for short, object linking and embedding allows Macintosh and Windows computers to share data among applications—you can literally plant the data from other programs directly in your PageMaker documents (OLE is fully explained in Chapter 4, "Adding Design Elements"). When used with PageMaker's powerful import filters, along with cutting and pasting with the Clipboard, OLE gives you the greatest possible flexibility in working on your computer with different software. When combined with the inherent power of PageMaker, your Macintosh or PC becomes an automated publishing system capable of supporting your creative efforts and your imagination.

INSTALLING PAGEMAKER

On the Macintosh, PageMaker 6.5 requires a 68030 or 68040 Macintosh or a Power PC–based Power Macintosh system. You'll need Mac OS 7.1 or later and 16 MB of RAM. Approximately 8 MB of memory must be available for PageMaker (12 MB on a Power Mac). Adobe recommends a CD-ROM drive to access the provided utilities, including Acrobat Distiller. You'll also need 26 MB of hard disk space.

On the PC, PageMaker 6.5 requires an Intel 486 or Pentium processor, Microsoft Windows 95 or Windows NT 4.0 or later, a CD-ROM drive, 8 MB of RAM for Windows 95 or 16 MB of RAM for Windows NT, and 26 MB of hard disk space.

If your system meets all these requirements and you haven't already installed PageMaker 6.5 on your system, you can do so now, by following these steps:

Macintosh users: Depending on the number and types of Control Panels or Extensions (sometimes still referred to by their earlier term, *inits*) you have loaded and the amount of free memory on your Mac, you may have to reboot without loading these startup files to free up enough memory to install PageMaker. To do so, hold down the **Shift** key while restarting your computer. Then follow the installation steps.

1. Insert the CD-ROM for PageMaker 6.5 installation in your computer's CD-ROM drive (or the floppy in the drive). On a PC, an installation screen will pop up automatically and offer the option to install PageMaker. If it doesn't, use the Windows 95 Explorer to find the **Pm6_5** folder. Open it and double-click **SETUP**. On a Mac, open the **Adobe PageMaker 6.5** folder and double-click the **Install Adobe PageMaker 6.5** icon. In the introductory screens, you'll be asked to choose a preferred language, from U.S. English, Canadian English, or International English (I selected **U.S. English**) and consent to Adobe's licensing agreement. In a moment or two you will see the Adobe Installer main window, similar to the examples in Figure 1.2.

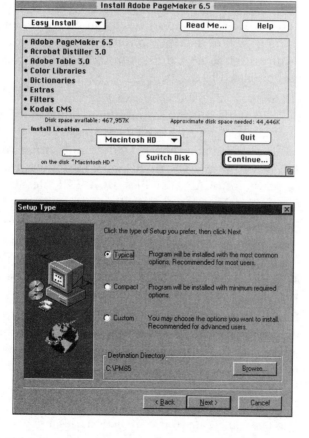

Figure 1.2 *The Adobe Installer main window (both Mac and Windows shown) allows you to customize your installation of PageMaker.*

2. Use the Installer main window to select which of the PageMaker components you'd like to install with the PageMaker program:

   a. Mac users can choose from **Easy Install** or **Custom Install**. **Easy Install** installs everything; a typical installation requires about 26 MB of space.

   b. PC users can select from **Typical** (which is the same as **Easy Install** for the Mac), which deposits about 26 MB of files on your hard disk, or **Compact**, which is a minimal configuration. You might select this option if you have limited space on your hard disk. You can also select **Custom**.

   c. For both Mac and PC users, the **Custom** choice lets you select among options such as these:

      + **Tutorial files**. The tutorial is an interactive, computer-based learning system that speeds you through many of PageMaker's features. You'll get hands-on instruction and work with actual files prepared by Adobe.

      + **Filters**. PageMaker comes with a variety of import filters. You can add all the filters to your system, but they will take up a lot of room. Instead, click the **Filters** option and click **Setup** to see the list of available filters. Choose only those you will need. You'll see quite a few listed, including filters for ANSI CGM graphics, AutoCAD DXF files, DCA/RFT files, PC PaintBrush, Excel, WriteNow, Word, WordPerfect, and Kodak Photo CD.

      + **Plug-ins**. Plug-ins (called *Additions* in previous versions of PageMaker) are programs that Adobe and third-party developers have created to do certain chores in PageMaker. You can install additions by clicking the **Plug-ins** option. You will find them as PageMaker Plug-ins within the Utilities menu.

      + **Printer files**. Choose this option to install PostScript printer description (PPD) files for the printers you have and those you will be creating print-to-disk files for (such as the high-resolution image setter your service bureau uses).

      + **Dictionaries**. If you have ordered foreign-language dictionaries, you will install them as an option in this dialog box. PageMaker 6.5 also lets you create your own dictionaries, but you don't need to do that now.

3. When you are finished, click the **Install** button.

The Adobe installation program will ask you to enter the serial number of your software package. You will find the number on the registration card. Enter the number exactly as you see it, including dashes between sets of numbers; but without any alphabetic characters.

N O T E

Remember to fill out and return the license registration card included in the PageMaker package. Doing so entitles you to a one-year subscription to Adobe Magazine and 90 days of technical support from Adobe.

N O T E

As the installation program copies programs and files onto your hard disk, if you're installing from floppy disks (we hope not!) it will ask you to insert the various installation disks in the floppy drive, based on what items you chose to install. When the installation is complete, you will see the Adobe PageMaker 6.5 window. To start PageMaker, double-click the **PageMaker 6.5** icon.

A QUICK PAGEMAKER DESKTOP PRIMER

Macs and PCs present a creative, graphical environment that allows you to use your software in much the same way that you work at your desk or drawing board. Applications display text and graphics very close to the way they will look when printed: typefaces are shown in their actual sizes and styles, and graphics and scanned images look realistic. Your operating system gives a natural, intuitive feel to programs and allows you the personal flexibility to:

✦ Use the mouse to pick up and move graphic elements or to stretch, shrink, and otherwise resize graphics. You select commands and menus directly with the mouse instead of having to remember complicated keyboard commands.

F   Arrange programs on your computer screen in much the same way that you arrange work on your desk. The blank screen is known as the desktop. You can open many different programs simultaneously, arranging them on the desktop any way you like to help optimize your work. An example of this is shown in Figure 1.3.

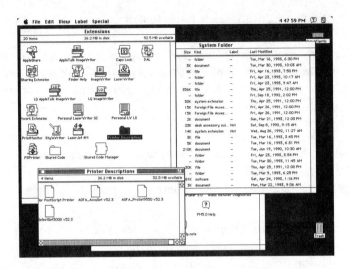

Figure 1.3 *You can open multiple windows on the desktop.*

✦ Exchange information between programs. For example, you can analyze financial data in your spreadsheet and import the results into a
financial report written with your word processor. You can also create
a graphic in a paint program and import it directly into PageMaker to
use as part of a page layout or copy information from one program
and paste it into another, without worrying about inconsistent formatting or data incompatibility.

The Windows 95 and Macintosh operating systems provide a standardized operating environment for different programs. All well-designed applications work with
your monitor and printer in exactly the same way, with the following benefits:

✦ You don't have to load different printer drivers for different programs
or define your display monitor differently for different software. Every
program shares the same printers and offers the same high-quality
video resolution; there's never a question of incompatibility. Use the
PC Printer Control Panel or Mac Chooser to select the printer you'd
like to use.

✦ Installing a new printer is simple. Make the change, and all your applications will recognize the new printer.

The operating system provides standardized commands for applications. Most applications share the same commands to activate similar functions. For example, you can always press **Command/Ctrl+X** to cut, **Command/Ctrl+C** to copy, and **Command/Ctrl+V** to paste. Pressing **Command/Ctrl+S** saves the document you're working on, while **Command/Ctrl+Q** usually quits the program you're in. Once you've learned the keyboard shortcuts for one application, you're well on your way to learning any other program on the same platform. These common features make it possible to create programs like PageMaker that operate virtually identically on both PC and Macintosh systems (once you get used to substituting the **Command** or **Ctrl** and **Option** or **Alt** keys that have the same functions but different names between the platforms).

Using the Mouse

The mouse is the most important feature of any graphical interface like Windows 95 or the Macintosh OS. If you've never used a Macintosh or a Windows computer before, you might initially find the mouse a bit awkward; many PageMaker functions can be activated with the keyboard, but the mouse is your most important tool. Once you get used to it, you'll wonder how you ever managed to work without it.

Clicking

When you see the word *click*, it means press quickly on the left mouse button with a PC mouse, or the primary button on a Macintosh mouse. (Most Mac mice have only one button, but there are multibutton mice that can be used with the Macintosh.) You can think of clicking as the keyboard equivalent of pressing the **Return** or **Enter** key in that it activates commands, but it also does a lot more. Clicking the mouse button twice quickly is called *double-clicking*. To highlight a word in PageMaker, double-click anywhere in the word. The word and the space following it will be highlighted. Pressing the mouse button quickly three times, or *triple-clicking*, highlights all the words and spaces up to the next hard return code (created by pressing the **Return** key at the end of a paragraph). Triple-clicking could highlight a line, a group of lines, or a full paragraph of text.

Selecting

In PageMaker, you select graphic elements by clicking the element with the mouse. Place the mouse pointer within the area of the graphic element and click once. PageMaker will display sizing handles around the object, as shown in Figure 1.4. To cancel the selection, click anywhere outside the graphic element.

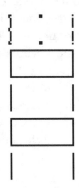

Figure 1.4 *A selected graphic element in PageMaker.*

When you have stacked graphics on top of one another, clicking the mouse will usually just select the topmost graphic. To see and select graphics underneath, hold down the **Command CTRL** key and click on the top graphic. With each click, the next layer of graphics will rotate to the top for you to select. You'll learn how to work with graphics in Chapter 4.

Highlighting

In PageMaker, there are two ways to choose a block of text: select it with the Pointer tool or highlight it with the Text tool. Selecting text with the Pointer tool selects the entire text block, as shown in Figure 1.5. The text block can then be copied, cut, or deleted; or it can be stretched by dragging a sizing handle. Working with text blocks is covered in Chapter 2 (the "Entering Text" section) and Chapter 3 (the "Threading and Unthreading Text" and "Selecting Text" sections).

Figure 1.5 *A text block selected with the Pointer tool.*

Highlighting text with the Text tool marks only the words you highlight, as shown in Figure 1.6. Highlight text when you want to change the specifications of type, indents and tabs, color, or style. You can also cut, copy, or delete highlighted text. To highlight text, position the Text tool insertion point before the first letter of the first word you want to highlight. Hold down the mouse button and pull the mouse to the right. As the insertion point moves over the words, they will be marked with a black highlight bar (the characters will be reversed in white). Pulling the mouse down will highlight a line from your insertion point forward.

Figure 1.6 *A text block highlighted with the Text tool.*

Understanding Dialog Boxes

The dialog box is the standard way PageMaker and other applications display command choices and options. A typical dialog box is shown in Figure 1.7.

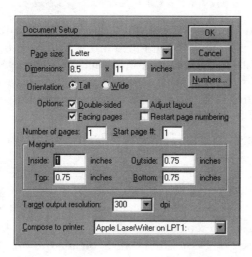

Figure 1.7 *PageMaker's Document Setup dialog box.*

Dialog boxes can be simple or complex; they can offer a list of choices, options, text boxes to type into, or buttons that lead to more dialog boxes. Let's look at some of the characteristics of dialog boxes:

✦ Pop-up lists inside dialog boxes display numerous items from which to choose. Press and hold down the mouse button to pop open the list box and drag the highlight bar up or down the list to select the item you'd like. The Colors palette's Tint pop-up list, shown in Figure 1.8, allows you to choose from a list of percentages for a particular color.

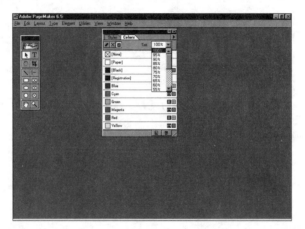

Figure 1.8 *The Colors palette's Tint pop-up list.*

✦ Command buttons activate whatever command or function is printed on them. The most common buttons in dialog boxes are **OK** and **Cancel**. Click the **OK** button to activate whatever choices you've selected in the dialog box and return to your document. Click the **Cancel** button to ignore the choices you've made and return to your document. The button with the heavier border is considered the *default* button. Pressing the **Return** or **Enter** key on the keyboard will automatically activate the default button.

✦ Text boxes usually show a current value. To change the value, position the insertion point in the box and type the new value. The Inside Margin text box, for example, appears in the Page Setup dialog box.

✦ Check boxes present options or choices that can be toggled on and off. A check box containing an **X** means the option is on. Select it again to remove the **X** and toggle the option off. Check boxes may be dimmed (and unavailable) at times, based on other selected options in a dialog box.

✦ Radio buttons present choices that are mutually exclusive. Only one in a list of radio buttons can be selected at a time. When an option is selected it has a black dot in the center. Often, radio buttons will be tied to text boxes; choosing a certain radio button enters corresponding values in nearby text boxes. For example, in the Print Setup dialog box you can select one of two page orientations with the Orientation radio buttons. Choosing the other orientation reverses the page dimensions in the Page Dimensions text boxes.

Understanding Scroll Bars

The scroll bars, shown in Figure 1.9 along the bottom and right edges of the window, are used to move the contents of the window up and down and left and right when the page size is larger than the window. Scroll bars operate similarly in Windows 95 and Macintosh environments.

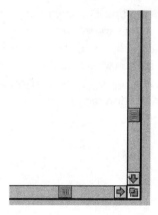

Figure 1.9 *Scroll bars.*

Moving in Small Steps

To move about the page in relatively small steps, position the mouse pointer over the appropriate arrow at the end of one of the scroll bars and click the mouse button. Each time you click the arrow, the document page will scroll in the opposite direction. For example, if you click the **Right arrow** once, the scroll box will jump slightly to the right, which scrolls the page slightly to the left.

Moving in Larger Steps

To move in larger steps, position the mouse pointer over the scroll box and depress the mouse button. You will see a dotted outline of the scroll box. Hold down the mouse button and drag the scroll box outline in the direction you want to move the page. Release the mouse button. The scroll box will jump to the new position indicated by the outline, and the page will be repositioned in the direction you want. You can also reposition the page in larger steps by clicking on the gray part of the scroll bar in the direction you want to move. The further along the scroll bar (away from the scroll box) you click, the more the page will move.

Moving in Giant Steps

To move the page in very large steps, position the mouse pointer on the scroll bar very near the arrow that points in the desired direction. Hold down the mouse button, and the scroll box will rapidly move toward the mouse pointer.

Arranging Windows

The Windows menu arranges multiple documents on your desktop. The menu allows you to organize document windows in cascaded or tiled order. *Cascaded* windows are stacked one on top of another, with the title bars of each window visible, as shown in Figure 1.10. Click on the title bar you want to make active, and that document moves to the front. Click **Cascade** to arrange the documents so you can see them all or choose the document you want from the Window menu.

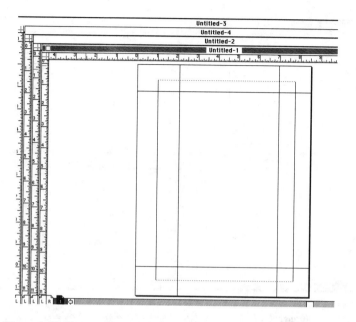

Figure 1.10 *Four newly created documents arranged in a cascaded stack.*

Tiled windows are positioned side by side, like tiles on a floor, as shown in Figure 1.11. The more windows you add to the tiled arrangement, the smaller each tile is. In other words, with three documents open, individual tiled windows will be larger than with six documents open.

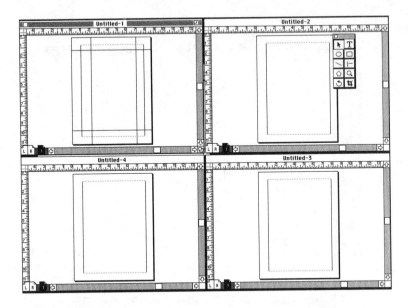

Figure 1.11 *The same four documents arranged as tiles.*

To Sum Up

If you have limited experience with applications, you will find PageMaker very easy to learn. If you are a veteran, you'll have absolutely no trouble getting up to speed with PageMaker. Once you have gained some experience, PageMaker's natural feel and intuitive commands will have you thinking of new ways to use the software and to produce finished work in a fraction of the time it previously took.

In the next chapter, you'll walk through a tour of PageMaker that will have you using the program before you realize it.

CHAPTER 2

A Weekend Tour of PageMaker

This chapter gives you a solid overview of using PageMaker and provides a number of useful examples. I called this chapter "A Weekend Tour of PageMaker" because, in just two days, you will be working comfortably and confidently with PageMaker. If you left work Friday night not knowing PageMaker and vowing to do something about it, well, here's your chance. This chapter walks you through the basics of designing, laying out, and preparing to print a document—everything you need to know to become productive in PageMaker. So grab a cup of coffee and get comfortable, because we're going to cover a lot of ground.

If you haven't already started up your Macintosh or PC, do so now. In a moment you'll see the icon representing your system's hard disk. Double-click on the icon to display the main folders in your system, then open the **PageMaker 6.5** folder. To start PageMaker, move the mouse pointer over the **PageMaker** program icon, and double-click it. PageMaker begins loading, and in a few moments you see the main PageMaker title bar and a blank document window, as shown in Figure 2.1.

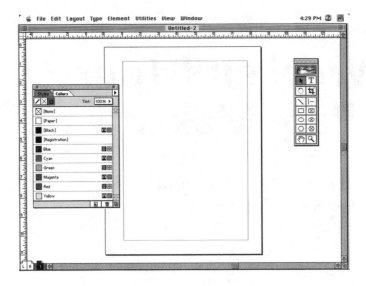

Figure 2.1 *PageMaker's unadorned interface.*

SHORTCUT

If you use PageMaker frequently, you'll probably want to make it easy to load. Windows 95 users can open the **Windows>Programs>Start Menu** folder, then use the Windows Explorer to find the PageMaker program. Right-click on its icon, and drag to the **Start Menu** folder. You can access it from the

Start>Programs menu. Mac users can do something similar by including PageMaker in your Apple menu. Select the **PageMaker 6.5** application in its folder, and click **File: Make Alias** (or press **Command-M**). Then drag the new alias to the System Folder's Apple Menu Items subfolder. You can rename the alias to something else if you like, such as "PM6."

COMPONENTS OF THE PAGEMAKER WINDOW

The PageMaker window is the working space for creating and producing documents. Let's take a brief look at all of the components in the window, since they are similar in both the Mac and PC environments. I'll cover them in greater detail later in this chapter and in the chapters that follow.

+ **Title bar**. Across the top of the screen is the PageMaker application's title bar. When the size of the window is less than the maximum size, you can move the entire window by clicking on the title bar and dragging the mouse to a new position.

+ **Close box**. The box at the upper-left side of the document's title bar on the Mac is called the *Close box*. In Windows 95, a similar box is located at the far right of the document's title bar, with an X in it. Click the **Close** box once to close the active window.

+ **Size box**. The Size box in the lower right-hand corner lets you resize the height and width of the active window. Click in the **Size** box and drag it diagonally to create the size window you want. PC users can also resize a window by dragging the right, left, top, or bottom margins of a window.

+ **Zoom box**. The Zoom box, in the upper right-hand corner of the Mac window increases the window to maximum size. Clicking the **Zoom** box again reduces the window back to the size it was. Under Windows 95, this control is to the left of the Close box, and will be represented by a miniature box with title bar (maximized) or a pair of small overlapping boxes (less than maximized.)

+ **Pull-down menus**. The main pull-down menus control all PageMaker functions. Click on a menu title in the menu bar to pull down the menu. Pull-down menus contain five types of commands:

    + **Commands with ellipsis (...)**. Clicking a command with an ellipsis (such as **Save As...**) displays a dialog box. Command dialog boxes require you to enter more information, or they present you with more choices.

- ✦ **Commands with arrows**. A right-pointing arrow means there is a second-level menu (called a *submenu*) to follow. For example, clicking **Font >** displays a font submenu showing all the currently installed fonts in your system.
- ✦ **Commands with check marks**. A check mark beside a command means the command is toggled on (turned on). Clicking a command with a check mark removes the mark and toggles the command off. The check mark beside the **Guides** command means that guides are displayed. Click the **Guides** command again to remove the check mark and hide the guidelines.
- ✦ **Commands that are dimmed**. A dimmed command is not currently available. Often you must select or highlight some text before dimmed commands will darken and become available.
- ✦ **Commands with keyboard shortcuts**. Sometimes a keyboard equivalent is displayed to the right of the command. Pressing the keys gives you the same result as selecting the command indicated from the menu.

To pull down menus, position the mouse pointer over the pull-down menu name you want to activate, and press and hold down the mouse button (Windows 95 users don't have to hold down the button). The menu drops down. To see a submenu or invoke a menu command, drag the mouse pointer over the menu command title (a right-facing arrow points to another level of menus), and a submenu will open. To pull the menu back up, simply release the mouse button if you have a Mac, or click outside the menu area if you are using Windows 95.

CREATING A NEW DOCUMENT

Creating a new document is similar to taping a clean sheet of paper to your drawing board. Before you can begin to work, you must tell PageMaker some things about the paper, such as the margin specifications, paper size, and how many pages long your document will be. Follow these steps to create a new document:

1. Move the mouse pointer to the File pull-down menu and open it.

2. Move the pointer to select **New**. PageMaker displays the Document Setup dialog box, shown in Figure 2.2.

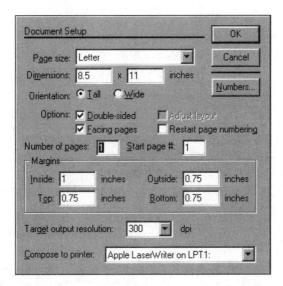

Figure 2.2 *Use the Document Setup dialog box to begin specifying a new document.*

Use the Document Setup dialog box to set the initial specifications for your paper, including:

✦ **Page**. Indicates the size of paper for this document, based on the printer you have selected.

✦ **Page dimensions**. Indicates the overall width and height of the paper specified in the Page List box. Enter your own dimensions here to define a custom page size.

The default measurement system in PageMaker is inches. Chapter 3 tells you how to change the measurements to another standard, such as picas or millimeters.

N O T E

✦ **Orientation**. The default orientation is tall (also called *Portrait*). *Wide* orientation turns the page 90° (also called *Landscape*). Depending on the page dimensions you enter above, PageMaker selects the **Tall** or **Wide** orientation automatically. If you click on the opposite orientation, the values you entered in the dimension text boxes are switched.

✦ **Start page #**. This command indicates which number to start numbering the pages with (for example, if you want your first page number to be 7 and your second page to be 8, and so on, enter **7** in the text box).

✦ **Options**. If you will be printing on both sides of the page, click the **Double-Sided** check box. If your document will be bound on the left side, and you want PageMaker to compensate for the binding or hole punch, click the **Facing Pages** check box.

✦ **Margins**. The default margins for a new document are displayed. You can change the margins if you wish.

Changing the margins after formatting one or more pages of text may produce some unexpected results. Save the document before changing the margins. Then, if you wish to change your mind, simply close the current document without saving it and reopen the version of the document you saved before changing the margins.

Setting the Margins

For many types of documents, including reports, proposals, stationery, business forms, fact sheets, and flyers, the default margin settings may be satisfactory. But you can change the margin size and the page size to suit practically any need. Remember, the page size is the overall size of the printed page. Margins are the inner boundaries of that page, which normally designate where the printer prints text and graphics. To change the margin settings:

1. Position the mouse pointer in the Margin Measurement text box you want to change, and click the mouse button to highlight the current entry.

2. Type the new margin value. If the default margins are in inches and you want to enter a pica value, simply type **P** after the value. When you click **OK** or press **Return** to leave the dialog box, PageMaker converts the pica measurement to equivalent inches (for example, 7 picas are converted to 1.167 in.).

N O T E

PageMaker also recognizes millimeters (mm) and ciceros (c). See the "Changing Design Preferences" section, in Chapter 3.

3. Press **Tab** to move to the next margin text box you want to change.

4. When you have finished, click **OK** or press **Return** to display the new document window.

Setting the Page Size

PageMaker comes configured with standard paper sizes, based on the capability of your laser printer. You can't print a larger page size than your printer can physically handle, but you can always specify a smaller size. Why would you want to? Because PageMaker prints crop marks, based on the page-size dimensions, that indicate the trim size of the finished page. To change the page-size dimensions:

1. Position the mouse pointer over the first dimension text box and click the mouse button to highlight the current dimension.

2. Type the new dimension. If the default dimensions are in inches and you want to enter a pica value, simply type **P** after the value. When you click **OK** or press **Return** to leave the dialog box, PageMaker converts the pica measurement to equivalent inches (for example, 51 x 84 picas is converted to 8.5 x 14 in.).

3. Press **Tab** to move to the second dimension text box. Enter its value.

4. When you're finished, click **OK** or press **Return** to move to the new document window.

N O T E

Using the **Tile** option in the Print dialog box, you can print pages larger than the physical size of the paper by printing tiles that fit together to form the larger size. You'll learn more about tiling in Chapter 7, "Printing."

N O T E

Using printed crop marks helps your commercial printer align, print, and trim your PageMaker documents, saving you time and thus saving you money.

Changing the Page Orientation

If you find after setting a different page size that the page width is actually the height because you entered the page dimension values in the wrong order, you can easily change the orientation without re-entering the page dimensions. Here's how:

1. From the document window, click on the **File** pull-down menu and select **Document Setup** to display the Document Setup dialog box.

2. To change a tall document to a wide document, click the **Wide** radio button. To change wide to tall orientation, click the **Tall** radio button.

Notice that the page dimensions switch text boxes when you change their orientation.

3. Click **OK** or press **Return** to return to the document window. You can change page orientation at any point while composing a page, but doing so may disturb the placement of text and graphics. It is a good idea to settle the orientation issue before you begin work.

Setting Page Numbers

When you create a new document, PageMaker sets the number of pages to 1 and highlights the text box. You can enter any number of pages up to 999. To change the number of pages (assuming all else is correct in the dialog box), simply type the number of pages and click **OK** or press **Return**. Follow these steps:

1. If you want the page numbers to start with a number other than 1, place the insertion point in the Start Page # text box, and click the mouse button.

2. Type the new beginning page number. Press **Tab** to move to the # of Pages text box.

3. Alternately, if you only want to increase the number of pages, type the number in the highlighted text box.

It's safer to break up extremely large documents into individual chapters. PageMaker runs faster when working with smaller files. See Chapter 9, "Developing Long Documents," for more information about the Book and Link features.

4. Click **OK** or press **Return** to move to the new document window. For multipage documents, you needn't be concerned with setting the correct number of pages—you can add more pages or delete excess pages at any time. See the "Inserting and Removing Pages" section, in Chapter 3.

You cannot change the page size, orientation, or page margin values for a single page within a multipage document. Any changes to the dialog box are global, and therefore, affect all pages of the document.

Changing the Page Size View

PageMaker offers a number of perspectives, or views, of your document pages. You can shrink the image to see the whole page, or see varying enlargements of the page up to 400% of actual size. When a new document is created, it is initially displayed in the Fit in Window view, shown in Figure 2.3. You see the whole page and the edges of the PageMaker pasteboard at each side of the page. This perspective is ideal for seeing the overall design of your page. Body copy 16 points or smaller is represented by gray bars; type 17 points and up is readable in this view.

Figure 2.3 *Major components of the PageMaker document window, displaying a document in the Fit in Window view size.*

You can change views of the page at any time. To increase the size of your page, choose the **Layout** pull-down menu and select the **View** command to display the View submenu. Then choose one of the following page view options:

✦ **Fit in Window (Command/Ctrl+0)**—Shows the full size of the page, no matter how large, as in Figure 2.3.

✦ **Show pasteboard (Command+Option/Ctrl+Alt+0)**—Shrinks the page to a postage-stamp size, and shows the entire width (and contents) of the pasteboard. If you're sure you moved something to the pasteboard, but can't seem to find it, choose this view and you'll see it right away. You can see this view in Figure 2.4.

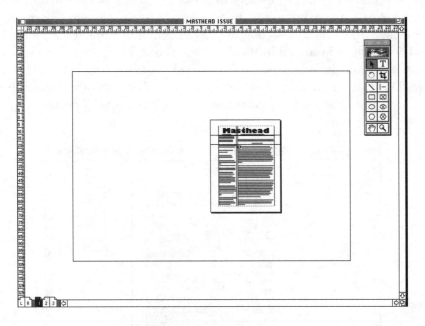

Figure 2.4 *A pasteboard view size shows a thumbnail layout of the page.*

✦ **50% size** (**Command+5**)—Displays a half-size view of the page, as shown in Figure 2.5. Normal body copy is greeked (displayed in gray lines) below 13 points, but there is good definition to larger headings and graphics.

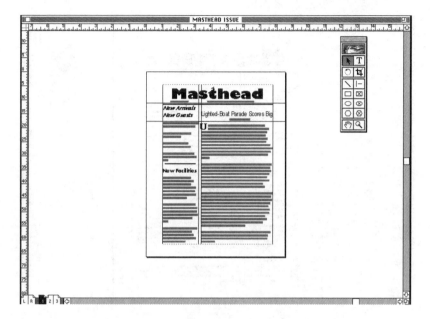

Figure 2.5 *A 50% view size of the same page.*

✦ **75% size** (**Command+7**)—Displays body copy clearly, as shown in Figure 2.6. In this view, the full width of an 8-in. page is visible. It takes very little movement of the scroll box to move to the top or bottom of the page. Of course, if you have a big full- or dual-page display, you can see everything in the Actual Size view.

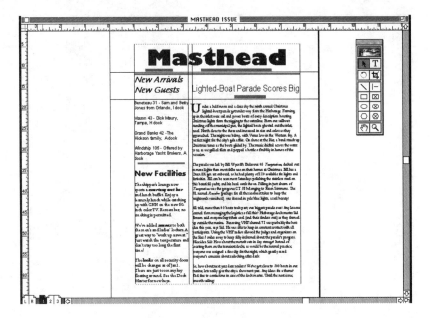

Figure 2.6 *A 75% view size of the same page.*

✦ **Actual size** (**Command+1**)—Shows an exact one-to-one representation of the page, as shown in Figure 2.7. Use this perspective when adjusting lines, text, or graphics, or when typing text on the page.

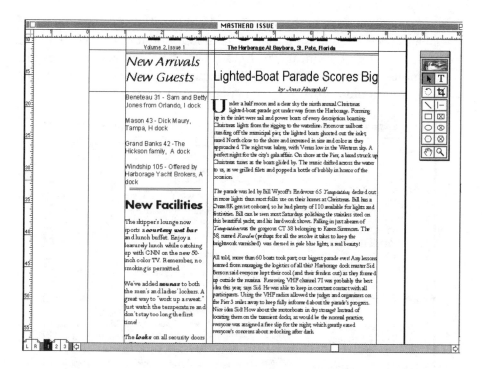

Figure 2.7 *Actual view size of the same page.*

✦ **200% size** (**Command ctrl+2**)—Doubles the actual view size, as shown in Figure 2.8, giving you very fine control over the placement of text and graphics. You may find it awkward using the scroll boxes to move around the page in this view. If so, hold down the **Command ctrl** key and press the mouse button. The mouse pointer changes to a hand icon. While continuing to hold down the **Command ctrl** key and mouse button, push the page in the direction you want it to move, just as you would push a piece of paper on your desk.

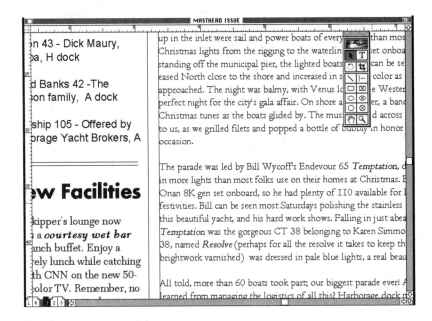

Figure 2.8 A 200% view size of the same page.

✦ **400% size** (**Command ctrl+4**)—Again doubles the size of the page, as shown in Figure 2.9. At this perspective, you're seeing less than a 2 x 2-in. area of the page—great for extra-fine work, but it may take your computer a moment to refresh the screen when you move the page with either the hand icon or the scroll boxes.

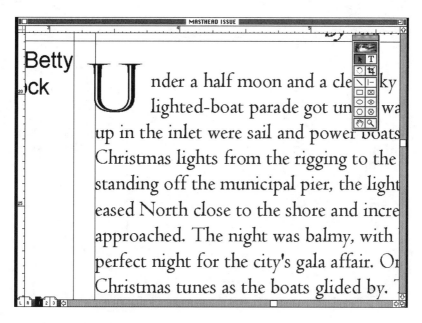

Figure 2.9 *A 400% view size of the same page.*

NEW DOCUMENT WINDOWS

When you leave the Document Setup dialog box, PageMaker displays a new document window, shown in Figure 2.10. Page 1 is displayed in the Fit in Window view, with rulers along the top and left edges. At the left side are the *Colors* and *Styles* palettes, which we'll explore shortly. In the upper-right corner is the Toolbox palette. The Toolbox contains all the tools you need to compose your page. When you click the mouse pointer on a tool, the mouse changes to that tool when you move the pointer outside the boundaries of the Toolbox. The tools (shown in the toolbox in Figure 2.10) included in the left-hand column are:

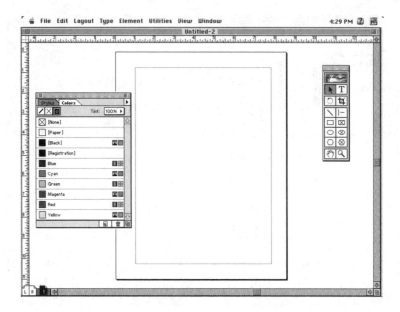

Figure 2.10 *A newly created document, displayed in the Fit in Window view.*

✦ **Pointer tool**. Use the pointer to select any kind of object on the page, including blocks of text, lines, boxes, circles, and imported graphics. When selected, the objects display sizing handles, as shown in Figure 2.11. Moving text is covered later in this chapter. See Chapter 3 for more information about selecting and moving text, and Chapter 4 concerning resizing and moving graphic objects and images.

Figure 2.11 *Selected objects are sized by their handles.*

✦ **Rotating tool**. This tool allows you to rotate a selected item to any of 360° of rotation in 0.01° increments. To use the tool, first click the item you want to rotate with the Pointer tool. Then click the **Rotating** tool. Move the crosshairs to the center of rotation for the item, press and hold down the mouse button, and draw a line with the crosshairs in the direction you want to rotate. Pretend that the line is the rotating lever, and while still holding down the mouse button, position the crosshairs at the outboard end of the lever and drag the lever clockwise or counterclockwise. When you have established the degree of rotation you want, release the mouse button. You can force the rotation to 45° increments by holding down the **Shift** key while you drag the rotating lever.

✦ **Diagonal Line tool**. Use this tool to draw diagonal lines. You can select a diagonal line with the Pointer tool and click on either handle to resize the line or change its angle.

✦ **Box tool**. This tool draws square-cornered boxes. Click the mouse button to position the upper-left corner of the box and drag the Box tool icon to the right and down to create the box. Holding down the **Shift** key while drawing creates a perfect square.

✦ **Oval tool**. Use this tool to draw circles and ovals. You draw ovals much like boxes: start in the upper-left side and drag toward the lower right. Holding down the **Shift** key while drawing creates a perfect circle.

✦ **Polygon tool**. Use this tool to draw regular-sided (i.e., all the sides have the same length) polygons. You can change the degree of inset, so that a pentagon can be transformed into a five-pointed star. When you install PageMaker, the default polygon shape is a pentagon, which you can change to another value by double-clicking on the **Polygon** tool icon in the Toolbox. You can edit the object's properties by clicking the **Elements: Polygon Settings...** menu choice.

✦ **Hand tool**. Use this tool to move the entire image around on the screen.

NOTE

In PageMaker 6.5, you can change the preferences of any tool in the Toolbox by double-clicking on the tool's icon, and setting the new values in the dialog box that pops up.

NOTE

If you save a publication in PageMaker 5.0 format, any polygons created with the Polygon tool are removed.

In the right-hand column, you'll find these tools:

+ **Text tool**. Clicking the **Text** tool changes the pointer to an insertion point for typing and highlighting text.

+ **Cropping tool**. Use this tool to *crop* (reduce the image area of) graphics and scanned photos.

+ **Perpendicular Line tool**. This tool draws vertical and horizontal lines. You can shorten or lengthen the lines with the Pointer tool by clicking on either handle.

+ **Box frame tool**. Use this tool to create rectangular frames into which you may place text or pictures.

+ **Oval frame tool**. This tool creates oval and circular frames for text or images.

+ **Polygon frame tool**. This tool creates multisided frames for text and pictures.

+ **Zoom tool**. This tool is used to change the magnification of your page view.

Other screen elements include:

+ **Master page icons and page number icons**. In the lower-left corner of the window are the Master Page icons (discussed in Chapters 4 and 5) and the page icon, displaying the page numbers. You'll learn how to use the page icons to move around the document later in this chapter. Master pages can also be controlled from the Master Pages palette (not shown on the screen.) We'll look at this palette in Chapter 4.

+ **Other palettes**. Only the Colors and Styles palettes were displayed in Figure 2.10. Other palettes are available to control additional PageMaker features. These include the Layers, Hyperlinks, Scripts, and Libraries palettes, which will be discussed later in this book.

Displaying the Rulers (Ctrl/Command+R)

If rulers are not displayed in the document window, you can activate them by pressing **Ctrl/Command+R**. The default measurement system for the rulers is inches, but you can change to any of several systems at any time. To save time, you might want to use the PageMaker keyboard shortcut **Ctrl/Command+R** to toggle the display of rulers on and off.

Changing the Ruler Measurement System

By default, the rulers are calibrated in inches. However, you can change PageMaker's measuring system at any time by following these steps:

1. Click the **File** pull-down menu and click **Preferences>General** to display the Preferences dialog box, shown in Figure 2.12.

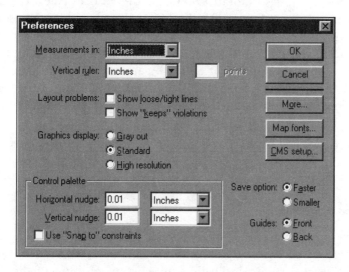

Figure 2.12 *Use the Preferences dialog box to change the ruler measurement system.*

2. In the Measurement in area, click the pop-up list to see the measurement system choices:

   ✦ **Inches**—This is the default measurement system.

   ✦ **Decimal inches**—The rulers display 10 tick marks (when the page view allows) to the inch, and values are entered in decimals.

   ✦ **Millimeters**—25.4 millimeters equal 1 inch.

   ✦ **Picas**—There are 12 points to the pica and 6 picas to the inch; the length of a text line (known as the *line measure*) is traditionally specified in picas.

   ✦ **Ciceros**—A *cicero* is slightly larger than a pica; there are 5.58 ciceros to an inch.

3. Select the measurement system you want. Your choice is displayed in the top ruler and in all dialog text boxes requiring a measurement

value. For example, if you select **Picas** as the measurement system, the top ruler displays picas, and the margin values you originally set up in inches are converted to picas.

4. Next, click the **Vertical Ruler** pop-up list to see your choices. Notice that the same measurement choices are displayed, with the addition of **Custom**.

5. Choose a measurement system for the vertical ruler. It can be the same as your selection for the Measurement system text box (which controls the top, horizontal ruler), or you can choose a different system. Click **Custom** if you'd like to establish point-measurement tick marks on the vertical ruler that equal the amount of leading for your type. Then, if you click **Snap to Rulers** in the Guides and Rulers submenu (from the Layout menu), the baselines of the text align to the tick marks on the vertical ruler.

6. If you clicked **Custom** in step 5, enter the number of points of leading in the Points list box. Click **OK** to return to your document.

Using the Rulers

The rulers give you accuracy in laying out a page. As you move the mouse pointer or tool icon across the page, reference marks also move on the horizontal and vertical rulers, indicating the current position of the mouse, as shown in Figure 2.13.

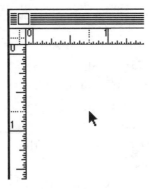

Figure 2.13 *The mouse pointer reference marks indicate the current position on the rulers (0.75 in. to the right and 0.75 in. down from the zero point).*

You may find it helpful at times to reset the zero point of either ruler to measure a specific area of the page. For example, you add a line to a page and want to place it exactly 1 in. from the bottom margin. You can gauge the measurement on the vertical ruler (although you may have to change the measurement system to inches first), or you can pull down the zero point of the vertical ruler to be even with the bottom margin. To reset the vertical ruler's zero point:

1. Position the page in the chosen work area. Consider enlarging the page view to get a more accurate picture.

2. Place the pointer in the junction of the two rulers (upper-left corner of the document screen) and do one of the following:

    ✦ To pull the horizontal ruler's zero point down the page, click in the **Ruler Junction** box, hold down the mouse button, and drag the pointer down the vertical ruler to the position you want. When you release the mouse, the new zero point is established. To accurately position the box in the example above, drag the zero point down until it is even with the bottom margin. Then position the box at the 1-in. tick mark on the ruler.

    ✦ To pull the vertical ruler's zero point across the page, click in the **Ruler Junction** box, hold down the mouse button, and drag the pointer along the horizontal ruler to the position you want.

    ✦ To reposition both zero points, click in the **Ruler Junction** box, hold down the mouse button, and drag both zero points off the rulers onto the page to the position you'd like. As you drag the zero marks out of the rulers, you see a pair of intersecting lines extend down and across the page, like crosshairs, to help you align the ruler's zero points accurately on your page.

    ✦ Although you can change the zero points of the rulers at any time, you may want to lock a particular adjustment, so that the points can't be accidentally moved. To do so, click the **View** pull-down menu and click the **Zero Lock** to toggle the option on (you will see a check mark by the option if you click the menu again). To unlock the zero points, simply click the **Zero Lock** option again, toggling it off.

Using Guidelines

A fundamental aid to page layout is the *grid*, which helps you visualize the basic symmetry of a page and provides an accurate reference for positioning text and graphics. On a drawing board, you drew grids with a T-square and a blue pencil. In PageMaker it's much simpler: position the mouse pointer on either ruler and click and drag a horizontal or vertical guideline onto the page. *Guidelines* are the equivalent of nonreproducible blue pencil lines (on a color monitor, the guidelines are displayed in blue) and, just like the nonreproducible pencil lines, do not print. They are used for alignment only.

Positioning Guidelines

Guidelines are a basic building block of PageMaker's design and layout capabilities. You can use as many of them as you need, and each page can contain a unique arrangement of guidelines. You can also set up master guidelines that are the same for all pages.

To position a unique set of guidelines on an individual page:

1. Select the page view needed to accurately position the guideline. You can begin in the Fit in Window size (press **Ctrl/Command+W**) to see the overall page, position the guideline in the general area, then select **Actual Size** (**Ctrl/Command+1**) or **200%** (**Ctrl/Command+2**) to finalize the guideline's position.

2. Regardless of which toolbox tool you are using, move it onto the horizontal ruler if you need a horizontal guideline, or onto the vertical ruler if you need a vertical guideline. Once inside the ruler, the tool icon changes to a pointer.

NOTE   You can click anywhere on the ruler to grab a guideline, except in the Junction box of the two rulers. Clicking there repositions the zero points.

3. Hold down the mouse button. The pointer changes to a two-headed arrow, indicating you have grabbed a guideline. Now drag the arrow onto the page. As soon as the arrow moves out of the boundary of the ruler, you'll see a guideline the width or height of the displayed page

size. Continue dragging the guideline to the position you'd like. As you drag the guideline, the guideline reference mark moves an equal amount on the ruler, indicating the guideline's position.

4. Release the mouse button to fix the guideline's position. You can adjust the guideline at any time by clicking it with the Pointer tool. The pointer changes back to the two-headed arrow. Drag the arrow to reposition the guideline.

N O T E   You may have noticed that guidelines do not appear on the PageMaker paste-board. If you need a guideline on the pasteboard, position the guideline on the page in relation to where you want it on the pasteboard. Then click the **Perpendicular Line** tool and draw a line over the guideline, but continue it off the page. Unless you specifically want the line leading off the page to print, delete it or shorten it so that it is completely on the pasteboard before printing.

Adding Guidelines to Master Pages

Each PageMaker document includes a set of master pages that are used to contain document-wide text, graphics, and formatting. The *Master Pages* feature is explained in detail in Chapters 4 and 5—but let's look at it briefly now to see how guidelines work with it. To set up master guidelines that are the same for all of the pages in your document:

1. The **Master Pages** icon is located beside the **Pages** icon at the lower-left corner of the document window. Click the **Master Pages** icon to display the master pages window. If you clicked **Double-Sided** pages in the Document Setup dialog box, you will see a blank, two-page spread consisting of the left and right master pages. Anything added to the left page is added to all left pages (usually the even-numbered pages). Anything added to the right page is added to all right pages (usually the odd-numbered pages).

   For example, let's say you wanted to add a logo in the top margin of both pages of a two-page document, to be printed on the front and back. By positioning the logo on the right master page, it automatically is displayed on the front page of the document, locked in position. By adding an additional logo to the left master page, the logo is also displayed on the back of the page (p. 2). You don't have to manually position the logo on each page in exactly the same spot. Similarly, if you add more pages to your document, the logos are displayed automatically on every page. Finally, if you decide you really want the logo in the bottom margins, all you have to do is click on the **Master Pages** icon and move the two logos to the bottom of the pages. The logos are then automatically repositioned throughout your document.

2. Move the mouse pointer to the ruler, grab a guideline, and drag it onto the master page. Position the guideline exactly where you want it. Add as many guidelines as you'd like. You can add more, or remove some, at any point.

3. When you've finished, click on the appropriate page number, beside the Master Pages icon, to move back to that page of your document. You will see the guidelines you just added to the master pages. Notice that you can't move these guidelines. You must go back to the Master Page feature to adjust them. PageMaker 6.5 has a plug-in called *Grid Manager* that lets you create libraries of grids and guidelines that you can open and apply to a publication.

Aligning to Guidelines

Guidelines make it easy to align text and graphics. It's even easier if you turn on the **Snap To** guides feature. *Snap* means that if you get the object you're aligning close to the guideline and release the mouse button, that object automatically jumps to the guideline, giving you perfect alignment (within 1/2880-in.). To turn on the **Snap To** feature:

1. Click the **View** pull-down menu; then click **Snap To Guides**. Click the menu again to see a check mark next to **Snap To Guides**, indicating the feature is toggled on. Select it again to toggle the feature off.

2. You can differentiate between guides and rulers with the Snap To feature. Notice that the View menu allows you to set the **Snap To** feature differently for both guides and rulers.

When the **Snap To** option is on, it is in effect for all pages in your document.

Displaying Guidelines

Sometimes you may want to see guidelines, other times you might want to hide them. The View menu controls the display of guidelines. Follow these steps:

1. Click the **View** pull-down menu.

2. Click **Show Guides** to toggle the display of guidelines on and off. A check next to the option means the option is on. Select the option again to toggle it off. You can also use **Command+;** (semicolon).

You may also want to change whether guidelines are displayed over the top of items on the page or behind items. Each mode has its advantages. I like to display the guide on top of items so that I'm sure the items align to the guides; however, some people find the guides annoying when they are visible in front of text and graphics. Just click the option you prefer. The relationship can be changed at any time without affecting what is aligned to the guidelines.

Locking Guidelines

Once the guidelines are positioned correctly, it's a good idea to lock them in place. To lock guidelines:

1. Click the **View** menu.

2. Click **Lock Guides** to lock the guidelines on the pages of your document. A check mark means the guides are locked. Select the option again to remove the check mark and unlock the guides.

ENTERING TEXT

There are two things to remember about entering text in PageMaker: First, click on the **Text** tool. Second, position the text insertion point where you'd like to begin typing and click the mouse. Let's try entering some text on your new document page. This is also a good time to learn about PageMaker's new *Frames* capability.

1. Move the pointer to the **Box Frame** tool (it's the fourth tool down in the right-hand column), and click to activate it.

2. Move the cursor over to the document page. As soon as the pointer leaves the toolbox, it changes to a crosshair. The *midpoint* of the crosshair is the point at which the frame you'll create starts.

3. Hold down the mouse button and drag down and to the right to create a frame. You can place a picture in the frame, or just type text, as we'll do next.

4. Move the pointer to the toolbox and click on the **Text** tool. The Text tool icon darkens, indicating that it is active.

5. Move the pointer onto the document page. As soon as the pointer leaves the toolbox, it changes to an insertion point. Position the insertion point where you'd like to begin typing within the frame you just created, and click the mouse.

NOTE   You may notice that if you click in the middle of the document, the insertion point and your typing skip to the left margin. Clicking the insertion point in the document invokes whatever page formatting is currently in effect—in this case, PageMaker defaults to left justification. Overriding current type alignment is discussed later in this chapter.

Before starting to type text, let's get a closer view of your work. To change the view of this page from Fit in Window to the full-size view:

1. Move the mouse up to the View menu. Notice that the Text tool insertion point changes back to the mouse pointer when it leaves the boundaries of the document.

2. Click **Actual Size**. The document resizes to a one-to-one perspective, and the rulers automatically recalibrate to actual size. Hold a real ruler up to the PageMaker ruler and compare them if you like; you will see that they're the same.

3. Use the scroll bars to reposition that portion of the page you want to work in.

4. Move the pointer back onto the page—the pointer changes back to the Text tool insertion point—and click where you want to begin typing.

Whatever you type is displayed in the PageMaker type default style and font. We'll cover changing the type specifications shortly, but first let's learn how to place the text where you'd like it, instead of where PageMaker wants it.

Opening a Text Block

In PageMaker, text is actually typed in text blocks or frames, not on the "paper" of the document window. A text block is always rectangular in shape, while a frame can be rectangular, round, or a polygon. Text blocks are defined by the amount of text and the margins of the page. Think of typing in a text block as typing onto one or more windowshades: It is normally as wide as the column or margins, and it unrolls as you add more text. When selected with the Pointer tool, you see handles at the top and bottom of each windowshade, as shown in Figure 2.14. Use the handles to roll the windowshade up and down, covering up, or revealing more text.

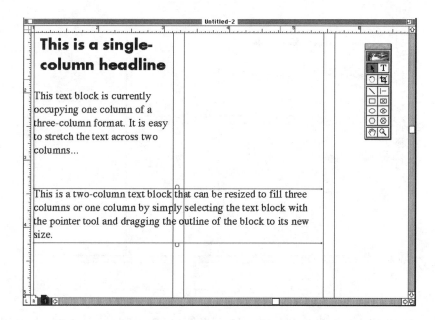

Figure 2.14 *A selected text block shows its top and bottom windowshade handles.*

Windowshade handles are also used to thread text blocks together, as explained in Chapter 3.

NOTE

Because text blocks and frames have their own identity in PageMaker, you can move them like any other graphic object or image. When typing in a text block, you can continue adding text right off the bottom of the page. You can click on a text block and drag it off the page as easily as you might move a piece of type off to the side of the drawing board. Text blocks, like all other objects in PageMaker, have sizing handles that allow you to resize their width. You can easily stretch a one-column text block across two columns by simply clicking and dragging a text block handle. When you do this, the text inside the box is rearranged to fit the new width—the size of the type is not affected. Figure 2.15 shows some examples of resized text blocks.

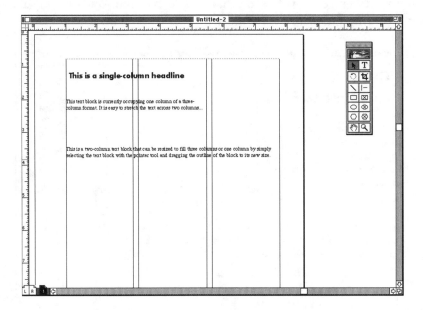

Figure 2.15 *Text blocks that have been resized.*

You can open a text block without creating a frame, as you did earlier. To open a new text block positioned where you want:

1. Click on the **Text** tool from the toolbox. Place the insertion point where you want to type.

2. Press the mouse button and drag the insertion point to the right, the width that you want the line of text. As you drag, you'll see a box open. This box defines the boundaries of your text block.

3. When you have opened the box to the correct size, release the mouse button. The insertion point snaps to the beginning of the new, now invisible, text block.

4. Begin typing. The text moves to the right until it reaches the right edge of the text block you defined, and then wraps back to the next line, as shown in Figure 2.16.

You can see the boundaries of the text block by clicking it with the Pointer tool.

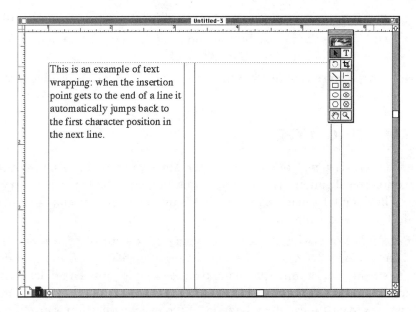

Figure 2.16 *Text typed in a newly created text block wraps automatically to the next line when it reaches the right-hand boundary of the text block.*

Moving a Text Block

To move a text block:

1. Click on the **Pointer** tool and click anywhere inside the text block. The windowshade and sizing handles are displayed.
2. Position the pointer anywhere inside the block, other than on one of the four-corner sizing handles.
3. Hold down the mouse button—the pointer changes to the positioning icon—and drag the text block to a new position.
4. When you are sure of the new position, release the mouse button.

Resizing a Text Block

To resize the width of a text block:

1. Click on the **Pointer** tool and click anywhere inside the text block. The windowshade and sizing handles are displayed.

2. Position the Pointer tool over one of the four corner sizing handles.

3. Hold down the mouse button and drag the handle to a new location, stretching or shrinking the text block.

4. When you release the handle, the text refills the newly sized text block.

FORMATTING TYPE

When you create a new document in PageMaker, it contains a set of default formatting specifications, which may, or may not, be suitable to what you want to do. The default format is easily changed, and once it is, the change remains in effect for that document.

PageMaker offers highly accurate typographic control of letters, words, lines, and paragraphs. One of the advantages of PageMaker is that you don't have to spend a lot of time specifying type for simple jobs. The default specifications do nicely for many designs. Other documents might require only a few changes to customize the type or layout to exactly what you want. In more complex projects, you can get as picky as you like.

With PageMaker, you are free to experiment with different formats. You can make as many changes as you'd like in the format of a document. Each page of a brochure could contain text in a number of columns, for example, set in different typefaces (although I don't think this type of design would be attractive). Only two things cannot change within a document: the size of the page and the width of the margins.

Changing Font Families

A *font family* consists of the basic typeface and (usually) bold, italic, and bold italic styles of the face. Some typefaces have extra light, extra bold, condensed, and extended versions as well. An example of a font family is Helvetica, one of the standard fonts that comes installed on all PostScript printers. You could define a letter, word, sentence, paragraph, or an entire document with any combination of Helvetica, Helvetica Bold, Helvetica Italic, and Helvetica Bold Italic, and remain within the Helvetica family. (Additionally, there are a number of Helvetica downloadable fonts that you can buy, including Helvetica Black, Condensed, Compressed, Extended, Light, Rounded, and Narrow.)

To change font families in a document, follow these steps:

1. If you are not in the Actual Size page view, select it by pressing **Ctrl/Command+1**.

2. Now, let's create some personalized stationery for you. Position the Text tool in the upper-left corner of the page, and type your name on the document page.

3. Highlight the name by placing the Text tool anywhere on it and quickly clicking the mouse button three times. Double-clicking a word in a text block highlights the word. Triple-clicking a word highlights that word and all the words around it until a paragraph code (made when you press the **Enter** or **Return** key) is encountered. Normally, this means that the entire paragraph is highlighted.

4. Move the mouse to the Type menu and click **Font**. The system displays a submenu of available font families. You will see a check mark beside the family for the currently selected font.

5. Move the mouse pointer down the submenu, or scroll down the submenu with the Down arrow to select a new family. Click the mouse button on the new family name, or press **Return**. Notice that the selected text is now formatted in the font you just picked.

6. Now, position the Text tool to the right of the last letter in your last name, and press **Return** to move down to a new line in the text block. Type your street address, press **Return** to move down another line, and then type your city, state, and zip code. Move down one more line with the **Return** key and add your phone number.

Changing Font Sizes

PostScript, TrueType, and HP LaserJet PCL fonts are *scalable*, meaning that you can display and print type in any size from 4 to 650 points. PageMaker comes set with a default type size of 10 points, but you can change the size as often as you like. To change the size of your type, do the following steps:

1. Position the insertion point anywhere in your name on the first line of the letterhead. Select the entire line by quickly clicking the mouse button three times.

2. Choose the **Type** pull-down menu and click **Size** to display the Size submenu. You can choose any size from this list, or click **Other** to enter a different size. Clicking **Other** displays the other point size dialog box for you to enter the type size you want. Click **OK**.

When you return to your document, the new size is in effect for the selected type.

Changing Typeface Styles

Styles are changed as easily as sizes. There are eight different styles for any typeface. They include:

✦ **Normal** (**Command/Ctrl+Shift+Spacebar**)—The look of the font without any styles added. If you'd like to undo styles that you've added to text, just redefine the text as Normal.

✦ **Bold** (**Command/Ctrl+Shift+B**)—Adds blackness and thickness to the type.

✦ **Italic** (**Command/Ctrl+Shift+I**)—Slants the type to the right. It is generally accepted that the first italic typeface was developed in Venice, Italy, around the turn of the fifteenth century by a printer named Aldus Manutius. The italic face he designed was called Chancery, but became known throughout Europe as italic. Aldus Corporation, which created PageMaker and was absorbed by Adobe several years ago, derives its name from this famous Italian printer and font designer. Chancery is still one of the most popular and beautiful italic typefaces.

✦ **Underline** (**Command/Ctrl+Shift+U**)—Underlines text and spaces between words, if the spaces are included in the text selected to be changed.

✦ **Reverse** (**Command/Ctrl+Shift+V**)—Reverses the color of the type from black to white (to see reversed type you must color the background).

✦ **Strikethru** (**Command/Ctrl+Shift+S**)—Draws a horizontal line through the middle of each letter selected. This style is often used in legal correspondence and contracts to indicate text changes.

✦ **Shadow** (**Command/Ctrl+Shift+W**)—Adds a distinctive drop shadow behind all the characters in the chosen font.

✦ **Outline** (**Command/Ctrl+Shift+D**)—Creates a lined outline of the shape of the characters in the font you choose, while leaving the center of the characters white.

You can change any highlighted text to all caps by pressing **Command/Ctrl+Shift+K**, and to all small caps by pressing **Command/Ctrl+Shift+H**.

You can undo any style by pressing the keyboard shortcut a second time. For example, if you highlight several words and press **Command/Ctrl+Shift+B** to make them bold, pressing the same key combination again toggles the style off. Alternately, you can always press **Command/Ctrl+Shift+Spacebar** to undo the style.

You can combine any or all of the styles in one font to create a custom look. For example, if you click both **Reverse** and **Bold**, you will have a white, bold type that must be placed on a black or colored background. This creates the striking effect shown in Figure 2.17.

Figure 2.17 An example of reversed, bold type on a black background.

To change the font style of text:

1. Position the insertion point of the Text tool in the name portion of the letterhead you just created.

2. Highlight the entire line by quickly clicking the mouse button three times.

3. Click on the **Type** pull-down menu, click **Type Style**, and select the style you want. In this case, click **Bold**.

4. When you return to your document, the new bold style is in effect for the selected text.

CHANGING CHARACTER SPECIFICATIONS

Occasionally you will want to change several aspects of a line of type all at once. A quick way to do so is with the Character Specifications dialog box. Let's take a look:

1. Select some text to change—in this case, select the two-line address of your letterhead.

2. Click on the **Type** pull-down menu and select **CharacterO** to display the Character Specifications dialog box, which is shown in Figure 2.18. A nice shortcut to the dialog box is to press **Ctrl/Command+T**. You can also double-click the **Type** tool to produce the same dialog box.

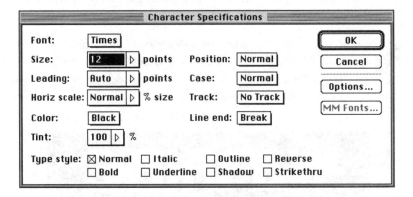

Figure 2.18 *The Character Specifications dialog box lets you choose several type attributes in one step.*

As you can see, the dialog box allows you to make all the changes to type we've just covered, plus many others. Let's look at the remaining capabilities briefly, and then use the dialog box to change the type you have selected.

✦ **Leading** (pronounced "ledding")—Constitutes the height of the font plus the space above the font, based on its size. As the font size is changed, so must the leading measurement change. The correct leading for a given size is normally about 120% of the type size (so that if the type size is 10 points, the leading is usually 12 points). PageMaker calculates leading in two different ways. Luckily, you don't normally have to worry about leading because PageMaker has an Auto feature that automatically determines and sets the correct amount of leading for you. When you change the type size, PageMaker adjusts the leading size accordingly. See the "Changing Type Leading" section, later in this chapter.

✦ **Set Width**—Changes the width of individual characters proportionally from 70 to 130% of normal. See the "Changing Character Widths" section, later in this chapter.

✦ **Color**—Assigns the selected type a color, based on the colors you have defined for this document. See Chapter 8, "Adding Color."

✦ **Position**—Used mostly in typesetting equations, this feature allows you to set type as *subscript* characters (dropped below the baseline) or *superscript* characters (raised above the baseline).

✦ **Case**—Allows you to set type in all capital letters, all small capital letters, or leave it as typed.

✦ **Track**—Tracking is similar to kerning, except tracking applies to a group of selected letters or words and the spaces between those words. Kerning applies to only certain pairs of letter combinations. The looser the tracking, the longer the line. Tighter tracking results in a shorter line. See the "Changing Tracking" section, later in this chapter.

✦ **Type style**—Gives you access to the same style features we have already discussed. It doesn't matter whether you change a type style with the Character Specifications dialog box or by clicking the **Type Styles** submenu from the Type pull-down menu.

Now let's change that address you selected:

1. Position the mouse pointer over the Case text box, and click to open the pop-up list. Notice that **Normal** is currently checked. Click on **Small Caps** to select it and close the list.

2. Click **OK**. When you return to the document window, the address is in small caps—very formal.

Changing Type Leading

Leading is the space between two lines of type. Too little leading causes the descenders of the upper line (the tails of the lowercase *g*s and *p*s, for example) to overlap the ascenders of the lower line, as shown in Figure 2.19. If there is too much space between the two lines, it is difficult for the eye to track down the page. Too little space, and the autonomy of the line is lost—again making a paragraph of such lines difficult to read. The leading measurement for a given line depends on the size of the type. The larger the type, the more leading is needed. With dedicated typesetting equipment (back in the days before PageMaker and personal computers), leading had to be specified for each type size change, just as the type size had to be specified. Fortunately, PageMaker makes it a lot easier for us. Just click the **Auto** option, and PageMaker adjusts the leading automatically each time you change the size of the type.

| Leading for these lines is set correctly with the Auto option in the Type Specifications dialog box. The correct amount of leading lets the type breathe and helps your eyes read a line at a time. | Leading for these lines is set too tightly: there is not enough space between the lines of type, so it seems to run together and is very difficult to read. You probably find the words on these lines jumbled together and more difficult to follow. |

Figure 2.19 *An example of correct versus incorrect leading.*

PageMaker defaults to the **Auto Leading** option, in which leading is automatically adjusted based on the size of the type. But there may be instances where you deliberately want to adjust the leading manually, as shown in Figure 2.20.

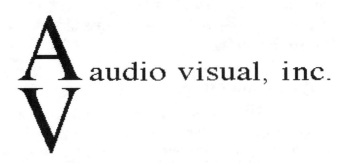

Figure 2.20 *Drastically reduced leading produces a company logo.*

To adjust leading manually:

1. Click on the **Type** pull-down menu and click **Character** (or press **Command+T**). PageMaker displays the Character Specifications dialog box.

2. Click the **Leading** text box arrow. Notice that **Auto** is selected.

3. Select a specific leading value: Remember, the rule for the correct amount of leading is generally to use 120% of the type size for leading. For example, 12-point type needs about 14.5 points of leading. Or, as in the example in Figure 2.20, you can select a specific value to gain a special effect.

4. Click **OK** to return to the document window.

Changing Character Widths

Character width (like leading) is something you generally don't think about with PageMaker. However, for special effects, very bold headlines, or designing a unique logo, changing the character width can help you achieve a special look. The default width of all characters is normal, or 100% of the width. You can change the percentage of the width value from 5% to 250% of normal in as small as 0.1% increments.

To change the character width:

1. Use the Text tool to highlight your name on the first line of the stationery.

2. Click on the **Type** pull-down menu and click **Character** (or press **Command+T**) to display the Character Specifications dialog box.

3. Click the **Set Widths** text box arrow, and select **130%**.

4. Click **OK**, and return to your document. Notice that the name is now considerably wider than before.

Changing Tracking

Tracking stretches or squeezes text. Tracking is similar to kerning in that it adjusts the space between letters, but kerning only adjusts the space between certain pairs of letters and does not affect the spacing between words. On the other hand, tracking adjusts the spaces between letters and words in equal proportion; if you select a headline to squeeze, everything in the headline shifts toward the margin to which the text is aligned. Figure 2.21 shows an example of the effects of tracking.

Figure 2.21 *The same headline with* **Very Tight** *(top),* **No Track** *(middle), and* **Very Loose** *(bottom) tracking.*

To adjust the tracking of selected text:

1. Highlight the address and phone number portion of your letterhead with the Text tool.

2. Click on the **Type** pull-down menu and click **Character** (or press **ctrl Command+T**) to display the Character Specifications dialog box.

3. Click the **Track** pop-up list and click **Loose**.

4. Click **OK** to return to your document.

Notice that the address lines appear longer, and that there is slightly more space between the letters and words.

Changing Type Options

The Type Options dialog box contains little-used options for altering the look of small caps, superscript characters, and subscript characters. Their default values are fine for most documents, but if you wish to change the proportional size of these type styles, do this:

1. Click on the **Type** pull-down menu and click **Character** (or press **ctrl Command+T**) to display the Character Specifications dialog box.

2. Click the **Options** button to display the Character Options dialog box, which is shown in Figure 2.22.

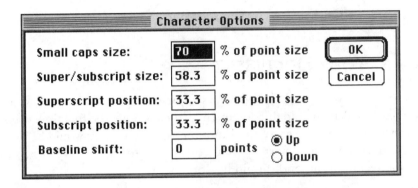

Figure 2.22 The Character Options dialog box.

Use the dialog box to adjust the size of these special type styles:

✦ **Small caps size.** To change the size of the small caps, enter a different percentage in the text box. The percentage you enter is proportional to the type size. For example, if you enter **60%**, and the typeface was set at **24 points**, then the small cap size would be about 14.5 points.

✦ **Super/subscript size, position.** Superscript characters are positioned above the normal baseline of the type (like a footnote in-text reference). Subscript characters drop below the baseline. To change the size of these characters, enter a different percentage in the text box, that is, above or below the baseline, relative to the surrounding type. In other words, the default value of 33.3% means that a superscript character is 33.3% of the character's *em* size above the baseline of the surrounding type. (The *em size* is the width of the letter *m* in the size and typeface you have selected.) You can also specify separately the positions for super- and subscript.

✦ **Baseline shift**. The *baseline* is an invisible line on which all type rests. If you were to specify points for the vertical ruler to align the tick marks on the ruler to the leading value of your text, the invisible baselines would actually be aligned to the ruler. To shift the baseline is to move the baseline for selected type up or down. Enter the amount of shift you want in the Points text box, in as small as 0.1 point values. Then click either the **Up** or **Down** radio button to tell PageMaker in which direction you want to shift the baseline.

When you have finished, click **OK** to return to your document.

SAVING YOUR DOCUMENT

Up to this point you haven't saved your sample letterhead document. You also haven't assigned a name to the document, which is done the first time you save it. If you were to lose power to the computer right now, there would be no hint that the document ever existed when you restart the system. Clearly, saving your work is important and should be done often.

How often you save your work really depends on the complexity and importance of the document you are creating. Saving your work once an hour means you risk losing only an hour's work. I generally save every ten minutes, more often if I'm working on a very complex document. Luckily, PageMaker realizes the possibility of a power failure and automatically saves a miniature version of the file whenever any one of a number of certain tasks is performed. These tasks include adding or removing pages from the document, switching to the Story Editor, switching back to the document window, printing, copying, and changing the Page Setup options.

If you lose power and lose some of the work you entered prior to saving, you may be able to recover the work by opening the miniversion using the **Revert** command. If you lost power before assigning a file name to the new document, the miniversion of the document is saved as a temporary file in the **Rescued Items** folder inside the Trash Can. The file is named **xxxTMP01** and numbered sequentially. Double-click on the file to open it and assign a proper document name.

Saving a New Document

The first time you save your document, use the Save dialog box to assign a file name and directory path. To save your new document, do this:

1. From the File pull-down menu, click **Save** to display the Save Publication As dialog box, shown in Figure 2.23. The shortcut key for this command is **Ctrl/Command+S**. The Windows 95 version is similar.

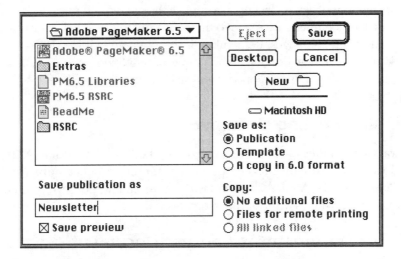

Figure 2.23 *The Save Publication As dialog box.*

2. The insertion point is positioned in the Name text box. Type a descriptive file name for this document.

3. The default folder for the dialog box is **Adobe PageMaker 6.5**, where PageMaker's programs are located. To change the folder, click the drive or folder you'd like using the Mac's list box or Windows 95's standard Save dialog box.

4. Click on the **Save as: Publication** radio button (or choose **Publication** from the drop-down list provided instead in Windows 95.) If you click the **Save as: Template** radio button (or from the Windows 95 drop-down list), your document will be saved as a *template* (templates are covered in

Chapter 5). You'll notice that an option is also present to save in the older PageMaker 6.0 format, if you need to share this publication with someone using the earlier version.

5. Mac users can create a preview of the document that is displayed in Adobe Fetch by clicking the **Save Preview** check box.

6. Click **OK** to return to your document.

You assign a file name only once to a new document. Each subsequent time you open the document, you in fact open a copy of the document. Any changes made to the opened document are made to the copy until it is saved, then the original is updated with the changes. Remember, if you open an existing document and make some changes you don't like, the simplest thing to do is just close the document without saving it, then reopen it and start again.

Saving an Existing Document

It's always a good idea to save your work often; it takes only a moment. To save your document, click on the **File** pull-down menu and click **Save** (or press **Ctrl/Command+S**). After a while you will get into a habit of saving often—by pressing the shortcut—without thinking about it.

Saving a Document As Another Document

An easy way to try different ideas as you develop a document is to save it as an experimental file; then you can try your idea and see if it flies. If it doesn't, you haven't altered the original document—just close the test document and reopen the original. If your idea works, simply rename the experimental document with the name of the original document to replace the original. For example, as illustrated in the table, suppose you are working on a newsletter called *Jones Newsletter* and want to try a tabloid size instead of the 8.5 x 11-in. size. Use the **Save As** command to save Jones Newsletter as **Jones Newsletter1**. PageMaker opens a duplicate of the file name for you to work in. Nothing has happened to the original file, and if the tabloid layout doesn't work, nothing will be lost (except the duplicate, experimental file). If it does work, you can use the **Save As** command again to save the experimental files as **Jones Newsletter** and continue with your work.

To use the **Save As** command:

Start with this:	New Save As name:	To get this:
Original file	**Jones newsletter 1**	Duplicate test **Jones newsletter** file
Duplicate test file	**Jones newsletter**	Duplicate test **Jones newsletter 1** file renamed as original

1. Choose the **File** menu and click **Save As** to display the Save Publication As dialog box.

2. The name of the current document is highlighted in the text box. Type a new name for the document.

3. Click **OK** to save the new document and return to the document window.

PageMaker saves the old document and closes it, makes a copy of the document with the new assigned name, and opens the new document in the document window. Notice that the title bar of the document window now reflects the new document's name.

Another way of protecting the original version of a document is to save it as a template. Then you can open as many versions of it as you like. See Chapter 5 for more information on templates.

N O T E

Reverting to a Previously Saved Version

Sometimes the easiest way to fix a problem is to revert to an earlier version of your document, which is what the **Revert** command does: It takes the document back to the way it was the last time it was saved and deletes everything you have done since the last save (another reason to save often!). Using **Revert** is easy—simply click it on the File pull-down menu. The rest is automatic.

DEVELOPING PARAGRAPHS

There are three ways to type copy in PageMaker: (1) type copy on your laid-out page on the pasteboard or a frame, (2) type copy using the *Story Editor* (the Story Editor is covered in Chapter 9), or (3) type copy using a word processing program and import the file into PageMaker (importing files, called *placing*, is covered in Chapter 4.

Typing Text

You can type in your document in much the same way you type in your word processor:

1. Click on the **Text** tool from the toolbox. Position the insertion point where you want to begin typing, and click the mouse button.

2. Type the text as you normally would. If the page view size is too small, enlarge the view of the page by clicking on the **Page** pull-down menu and selecting a different view.

3. Press the **Spacebar** once after periods. Press the Tab key if you wish to move the insertion point more than one space to the right. At the end of a line, the insertion point automatically wraps to the next line (don't press the **Return** key at the end of the line as you would press the carriage return key on an electric typewriter).

N O T E

It's a good idea not to use the **Spacebar** in formatting columnar or indented text in PageMaker. While you can't see spaces, each time you press the **Spacebar** you insert a hidden code in your document. Although the text may look aligned properly on your screen, it may not print correctly. Instead, press the **Tab** key if you wish to move the insertion point more than one space forward. Similarly, if you are typing your text in a word processor to place in PageMaker, press the **Tab** key, not the **Spacebar**.

Adding Special Characters to Text

PageMaker has a number of special characters available to insert in your text, such as copyright and trademark symbols, em and en dashes, open and close quotation marks, and many others. The following table details the 20 most common special characters and the keyboard shortcuts that insert them. You'll find a complete list in Appendix A of your PageMaker manual.

To insert this:	Press this:	You'll see this:
Nonbreaking hyphen	**Command/Ctrl+Option/Alt+-**	-
Nonbreaking slash	**Command/Ctrl+Option/Alt+/**	/
Em dash	**Option/Alt+Shift+=**	—

En dash	**Option/Alt+=**	-
Open double quote	**Option/Alt+[**	`"`
Close double quote	**Option/Alt+Shift+[**	`` `` ``
Open single quote	**Option/Alt+]**	'
Close single quote	**Option/Alt+Shift+]**	`
Auto page numbers	**Command/Ctrl+Option/Alt+P**	LM RM
Bullet	**Option/Alt+8**	*f*
Trademark	**Option/Alt+2**	‡
Registered trademark	**Option/Alt+r**	®
Copyright	**Option/Alt+g**	©
Paragraph marker	**Option/Alt+7**	¶
Section marker	**Option/Alt+6**	§
Discretionary hyphen	**Command/Ctrl+-**	-
Em space	**Command/Ctrl+Shift+M**	
En space	**Command/Ctrl+Shift+N**	
Thin space	**Command/Ctrl+Shift+T**	
Fixed space	**Option/Alt+Spacebar**	

Aligning Text

Aligning text determines how the text will be oriented in columns, pages, and headlines (see Figure 2.24). There are five text alignment orientations: centered, aligned left, aligned right, justified, and force justified.

This is an example of left-aligned text. The left edge of the text block is even, and the right edge is ragged.	This is an example of center-aligned text. Each line is centered, creating ragged left and ragged right edges to the text block.	This is an example of right-aligned text. The right edge of the text block is even and the left edge is ragged,

Figure 2.24 *Examples of left-, center-, and right-aligned text.*

✦ **Align left** (**Ctrl/Command+Shift+L**). Lines up the left edge of the text evenly. The right edge is not aligned (this unaligned edge is called a *ragged-right* edge). Left-aligned text is commonly used in personalized letters, informal newsletters, and the body text in many books.

✦ **Center** (**Ctrl/Command+Shift+C**). Centers text between the left and right margins, or within columns. Centered text is often used for headlines in ads and for headings in newsletters and brochures. Several centered lines of text can be difficult to read because neither edge is even, making it difficult for the eye to track down the page.

✦ **Align right** (**Ctrl/Command+Shift+R**). Lines up the right edge of text evenly, producing a ragged-left edge. Right-aligned text (if used sparingly) can produce a refreshing change to body copy. Right-aligned heads in a brochure can contribute to a fresh, unusual look.

✦ **Justified** (**Ctrl/Command+Shift+J**). Lines of text are even on both edges, made so by adjusting the internal spacing of letters and words in the line, as shown in Figure 2.25. To reduce increased spaces in the line, justified text is normally hyphenated, that is, words are broken at the ends of lines that would normally be too short or long for the line, thus equalizing the spacing.

This is an example of justified text, not hyphenated. Notice that there are many overly wide spaces as PageMaker adjusts the right margin, without being able to break long	This is an example of justified text, that is hyphenated. Notice that the number of overly wide spaces is eliminated because as PageMaker adjusts right margin, it gets to break long words across lines of text.

Figure 2.25 *Example of justified text not hyphenated and hyphenated; note the difference in internal word spacing.*

✦ **Force justify** (**Ctrl/Command+Shift+F**). Stretches a word or words across a line (forcing it to be justified). Force justification is normally used to add spaces to the letters of a word, as shown in Figure 2.26.

Figure 2.26 *A force-justified word stretched evenly across a column.*

The default alignment for text in PageMaker is align left. To change the alignment:

1. Click on the **Text** tool to highlight the text you want to change. If you are about to type new text, click on the **Text** tool and then click on the page where you want to begin typing.
2. Click on the **Type** pull-down menu and click **Alignment** to display the Alignment submenu.
3. Click the alignment orientation you want; a check mark next to the alignment choice indicates that it is in effect.

The keyboard shortcuts in the following table allow you to select an alignment orientation without using the pull-down menus.

ORIENTATION	SHORTCUT
Align left	**Command/Ctrl+Shift+L**
Align center	**Command/Ctrl+Shift+C**
Align right	**Command/Ctrl+Shift+R**
Justify	**Command/Ctrl+Shift+J**
Force Justify	**Command/Ctrl+Shift+F**

FORMATTING PARAGRAPHS

Paragraph formatting includes setting indent values in paragraphs, specifying the space above and below a paragraph, setting the text alignment orientation, and controlling how paragraphs split among columns and between pages. To make formatting changes to a paragraph, follow these steps:

1. Determine what paragraph text you want to format:

    ✦ To change the format of a series of paragraphs, but not the whole document, highlight the paragraphs with the Text tool and click on the **Type** pull-down menu.

    ✦ To change just one paragraph, click the **Text** tool anywhere in the paragraph and click on the **Type** pull-down menu.

    ✦ To change the paragraph default settings for this document, do not click in the document, just click on the **Type** pull-down menu.

2. Click the **Paragraph** command (or press **Ctrl/Command+M**) to display the Paragraph Specifications dialog box, which is shown in Figure 2.27.

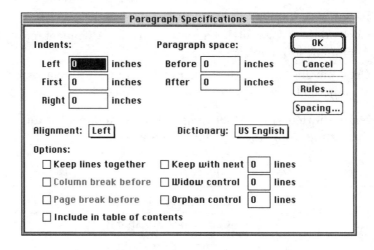

Figure 2.27 The Paragraph Specifications dialog box.

Changing Indents

To change the indent specifications for a paragraph:

1. Change the left indent amount by clicking in the **Left** text box and entering a value. The left margin of the paragraph is indented by the amount of the value entered, as shown in Figure 2.28.

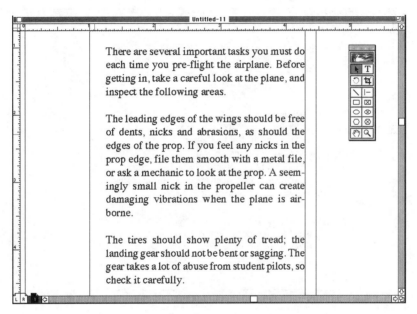

Figure 2.28 *Entering a value of .25 in the Left text box indents the left margin of the paragraph 1/4 inch.*

2. Change the first line indent amount by clicking in the **First** text box and entering a value. If a value has been entered in the Left text box above, entering a negative value here outdents the first line by the amount of the negative value entered, while the remaining lines of the paragraph are indented the amount entered in the Left text box, as shown in Figure 2.29.

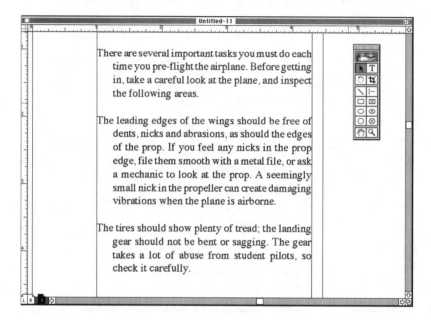

There are several important tasks you must do each time you pre-flight the airplane. Before getting in, take a careful look at the plane, and inspect the following areas.

The leading edges of the wings should be free of dents, nicks and abrasions, as should the edges of the prop. If you feel any nicks in the prop edge, file them smooth with a metal file, or ask a mechanic to look at the prop. A seemingly small nick in the propeller can create damaging vibrations when the plane is airborne.

The tires should show plenty of tread; the landing gear should not be bent or sagging. The gear takes a lot of abuse from student pilots, so check it carefully.

Figure 2.29 *The negative number in the First text box outdents the first line of the paragraph. The rest of the lines are indented the 0.25 in. specified in the Left text box.*

3. Change the right indent amount by clicking in the **Right** text box and entering a value. The right edge of the paragraph is indented by the amount of the Right value entered, as shown in Figure 2.30.

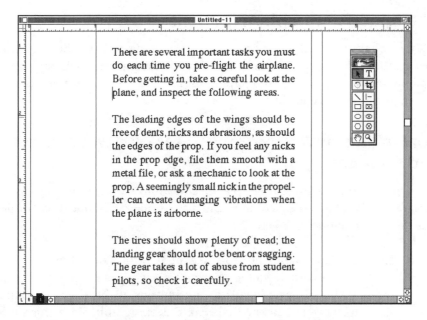

Figure 2.30 *Both left and right edges of the paragraph are indented 1/4 inch by entering .25 in the Left and Right text boxes.*

Changing the Space Around Paragraphs

The Paragraph Specifications dialog box gives you the option of adjusting the amount of space above and below paragraphs. The default amount of space is zero, meaning no extra space. Instead of double-spacing after each paragraph, you can use the **Paragraph Space** option to enter a space value above, below, or both above and below the paragraph.

Enter the amount of space you want in the Before and After text box(es). Once values are entered in either of these text boxes, you should only press the **Return** key once between paragraphs. Pressing the key twice enters twice the amount of space you specified in the text boxes.

Changing Paragraph Alignment

You can change the alignment of text in a paragraph in the Paragraph Specifications dialog box, instead of using the **Alignment** command on the Type pull-down menu. Click the pop-up list to make your choice of left, right, center, justify, or force justify.

Controlling How Paragraphs Break Between Pages and Columns

The Options area of the Paragraph Specifications dialog box controls how paragraphs are affected by column and page breaks. Choose those options that suit your document's needs:

✦ **Keep lines together**. Click to place an X in this check box to keep all the lines in a paragraph together on the same page or in the same column. If the paragraph falls at the bottom of the page or column, PageMaker would normally break the paragraph. With this option checked, all lines are kept intact, and the whole paragraph is moved to the next page or column. This option is useful if you have formatted a table that you don't want to break between pages or columns. In formatting a table to be kept on the same page, press **Shift+Return** instead of **Return** to move the insertion point down for each new line.

N O T E

If the paragraph is longer than the column it's in, PageMaker breaks the paragraph at the bottom of the column even if this option is checked.

✦ **Column break before**. Click to place an X in this check box to force a paragraph to start at the top of a new column. Check this option if you have a heading that you'd always like to start a new column.

✦ **Page break before**. Click to place an X in this check box to force a paragraph to start on a new page. Check this option if you have a heading (a new chapter title, for example) that you'd like always to start a new page.

✦ **Keep with next _ lines**. Click this check box to designate that high-lighted text be kept on the same page with the next one to three lines of text. This option is used mostly to keep headings connected to the first couple of lines (you can specify 1, 2, or 3 lines) of the paragraph that follows, so that a page break won't fall between the head and its body copy. In Chapter 6, you'll learn how to create a style that automatically designates this option for heads and body copy.

✦ **Widow control _ lines**. A *widow line* is the last line of a paragraph isolated at the top of the next page or the next column, all by itself. Enter **1**, **2**, or **3** in this text box to indicate the number of lines of the paragraph to keep together at the top of a page to prevent widowing.

✦ **Orphan control _ lines**. An *orphan line* is the opposite of a widow. An orphan is the first line of a paragraph left at the bottom of a page or column, with the rest of the paragraph continuing on the next page or at the top of the next column. Enter **1**, **2**, or **3** in this text box to indicate the number of lines of the paragraph to move to the beginning of the next page to prevent the orphan.

Adding Lines above or below Your Paragraphs

One way of emphasizing a paragraph is to add one or more lines (called *rules*) above and below the paragraph. For example, a *pull quote* is often added to relieve the visual monotony of a long column of text. A pull quote is a sentence, or part of a sentence, taken from the column of text, that is treated as a graphic to add visual interest and act as a teaser to get the reader's attention. Figure 2.31 contains an example of a pull quote.

I'm standing on the end of my bowsprit with sweat dripping off my nose into the water. I'm in the process of installing a Hood roller furling system on my old Bristol and busier than a one-armed paper hanger. It's not the sort of job to take on without some able-bodied help, and in the middle of all this a pleasant looking older gentleman strolls my way and asks if sailing is a lot of trouble.

Here I am juggling 70 or 80 pounds of gyrating aluminum luff extrusion, and this yahoo asks if sailing is hard work. I refrain from commenting as I've got a clevis pin in my mouth and I'm bent almost double trying to stick the pin through the top hole in the toggle with my teeth. No, I think to myself, sailing ain't bad, it's the work in the slip that will kill you.

It turns out this fellow had a recent heart attack and was concerned that sailing might be too much for him. Then he tells me he's looking at a 38 foot sailboat for just him and his wife. When questioned a little further, I find that he must have air conditioning, a refrigerator mit ice maker, a microwave oven and God knows what else. And he's wondering if sailboats take a lot of work?

He said that with a perfectly straight face as he explained that the price of the very nautical little 27 footer we were sitting in was $89,000! Now, to be fair, the little 27 footer was built like a brick you-know-what, and

> "It's this nesting instinct, this need to turn perfectly sound sailboats into floating motor homes, that has driven the cost of boating through the roof."

fitted out to sail around the world. Down below, we were surrounded with hand rubbed, hand-fitted teak...everywhere. Teak that was much better in grade than the little boards I buy at E&B for $25.00 a pop. Teak of the quality of our Danish dinning room table that my wife's afraid to get one drop of water on. A teak interior that this broker said took 5000 manhours to build. And, while the interior was very beautiful - and true, just as the broker pointed out, the grain of all the teak bungs covering all the screws lined up perfectly with the grain of the surrounding

Figure 2.31 Example of a pull quote.

Lines above or below a paragraph are also used to create a certain style. You could add rules to a note or a caution, as shown in Figure 2.32.

from the anti-static wrapping and place next to the computer.

Warning

Remove electrical power to the computer before disassembly. Failure to follow this warning may result in injury or death.

2. After removing the top cover, unscrew the video adaptor from the backplane. Remove it by grasping firmly, and gently rocking while pulling up.

in setting the base address.

Note:
Normally the BIOS on the video adaptor will set the base address correctly. If you experience problems with the computer after installation, there may be another circuit card in an expansion slot with a competing, identical base address. If this is the case, move the jumpter at location J2 to cover posts 2 and 3, instead of the default setting.

While FASTBIOS.SYS is loading at boot up, the com-

Figure 2.32 Different-weight rules create varying degrees of emphasis.

To add rules to paragraphs, follow these steps:

1. Highlight the paragraph you'd like to change by triple-clicking the **Text** tool anywhere inside the paragraph.

2. Choose the **Type** pull-down menu, and click the **Paragraph** command to display the Paragraph Specifications dialog box.

3. Click the **Rules** button to display the Paragraph Rules dialog box, shown in Figure 2.33.

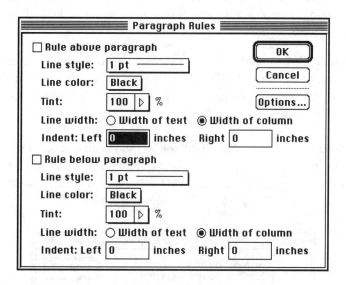

Figure 2.33 *The Paragraph Rules dialog box.*

Use this dialog box to set up a line style, line color, or line width for rules above and below your highlighted paragraph.

✦ **Changing the line style of paragraph rules**. The default Line style for paragraph rules is a one-point line. To change the weight of the line, click the **Line Style** pop-up list and choose from the styles presented.

✦ **Changing the line color of paragraph rules**. The default line color is black. To change the color, click on the **Line Color** pop-up list and choose a different color. The color choices will include any colors you have added with the Define Colors dialog box (all of the colors shown on the Color palette are available in the Line Color pop-up list).

✦ **Changing line width**. The default line width is the width of the column. To make the line width the same as the text width, click the **Width of Text** radio button.

N O T E Since a paragraph is defined as anything typed after pressing the **Return** key, paragraph headings are considered paragraphs (to type a heading you must press the **Return** key, type the heading for a new paragraph, and press the **Return** key again to begin typing the copy for the paragraph). It's easy to dress up headings by adding a line just above or below: After highlighting the heading, simply click the **Width of Text** radio button in the Paragraph Rules dialog box.

✦ **Indent**. To indent the rule from the left column or page margin, enter the amount of the indent in the Left text box. To indent the rule in from the right column or page margin, enter the amount of the indent in the Right text box.

N O T E Entering the same value in both the Left and Right text boxes centers the line over or under the paragraph. To change the amount of space between the paragraph text and the rules, click the **Option** button to display the Paragraph Rule Options dialog box, which is shown in Figure 2.34.

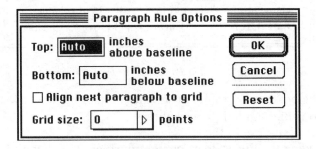

Figure 2.34 Paragraph Rule Options dialog box.

Use the Paragraph Rule Options dialog box to choose among the following:

✦ **Top**. The Auto default value aligns a rule to the top edge of the leading slug. To raise the rule higher, enter the height in this text box.

✦ **Bottom**. Again, the Auto default value places the rule at the bottom edge of the leading slug. To lower the rule, enter the value in this text box.

- ✦ **Align to grid**. If you have two or more columns on the page and are having difficulty aligning the baseline of one column to the other(s), clicking the check box aligns the selected text to PageMaker's invisible grid.

- ✦ **Grid size**. Enter the amount of leading for the type you want to align to the grid, or click the pop-up list and scroll down the list to select the leading.

- ✦ **Reset**. Resets the top and bottom values to **Auto** and unchecks the **Align to Grid** check box.

When you have finished, press **OK** to return to your document.

To Sum Up

Whew! A lot to cover in a weekend, but now you're ready to push the drawing board and light table out of the way and fire up your computer. In this chapter, you have touched on most of the basic commands of PageMaker. You've learned how to create and open documents, type text in documents, add headlines to text blocks, and change type specifications and alignment. You have also learned how to set tab stops for tabs and indents and fine-tune the look of paragraphs. You're now ready for the next step: editing your work.

In the next chapter, you'll learn how PageMaker text is threaded together and how you can change that invisible thread that connects your story's pages.

CHAPTER 3

Editing Your Work

Before I became enamored of desktop publishing and began using PageMaker, I had a desk drawer devoted to what I called my quick-fix kit. The kit contained razor blades, white tape, press-type letters and numbers, adhesive spray, little scraps of leftover type in my favorite typefaces, and a folder stuffed with page numbers printed on adhesive-backed paper. I saved the little bits of type in case I had to make a last-minute change to camera-ready copy. The sheets of numbers were cut apart into tiny, numbered squares, and carefully stuck down with the tip of an X-acto knife. (You haven't lived until you've had to renumber a long, technical document with little stick-down numbers!) When it came time to edit the work, I'd roll up my sleeves and dig out my quick-fix kit.

Editing a hand-worked mechanical is a messy affair, and it is never fun. Waxed or pasted type refuses to pull up and be moved—if you can get the type pulled up, it probably will never stick firmly again. Art boards soon take on a dirty, tattered appearance. With all of the mess and reworking, it's easy to lose sight of the design theme and overall purpose of the piece. Luckily, all of that has changed with PageMaker—my quick-fix kit drawer was cleared out years ago.

Editing a document with PageMaker is as simple and straightforward as creating a document. Open the file, make the needed changes, print out the revised version, and close the file. Proof your changes on a laser printer, and print your final mechanical either on a high-resolution laser printer or on a laser image setter at 1200 to 2500 dpi. You can edit text right on the document screen or in the story editor (explained in Chapter 10). You can grab text blocks and resize them, or drag them to new positions. In fact, you have complete control over all text and graphic elements on the page: change their position, size, or color; change margin or column settings; and change page orientation or overall page size. With a laser printer, you can instantly see the printed results of your editing.

FREE-FORM OR FRAMES?

Prior to PageMaker 6.5, text was entered into free-form text blocks, which can be created quickly by selecting the **Text** tool, positioning the cursor, and dragging a block anywhere on the page. PageMaker can also create enough text blocks to accommodate your text using its Autoflow feature on the Layout menu. You can type directly into a text block or import or place text from an external file.

Text blocks can grow to accommodate more text, and you can flow text from one text block to the next on the same page or different pages.

Frames are a new kind of "container" for text (or graphics) introduced with PageMaker 6.5 Unlike text blocks, which are always rectangular in shape, frames can be rectangles, regular polygons, irregular polygons, or ovals. Where text blocks grow to fit the text you enter, frames can be inserted and sized as you want them even if they contain no text at all. You may still type text directly in a frame, place text from a file, and reflow text between frames, just as you can with text boxes.

When to Use Free-Form Text Blocks

If you're creating a document that contains a lot of text arranged in regular columns, text blocks are the fastest way to lay out your publication. Just create the first block and start typing (or place text from a file.) This works well with books, manuals, long reports, and similar material.

When to Use Frames

Frames are great for publications that have many separate elements that you want to design and lay out carefully. Newsletters, magazines, catalogs, and similar documents all lend themselves to frames. You can insert each of the frames that will hold your text, resize and rearrange them, and design the look of your publication as much as you please, even before you have the text available. If you need an irregular shape to fit around a graphic, want to insert text into a circle or triangle, or create specialized design elements, frames will help you. A frame can have a border line around it or contain a fill. You may align the contents of the frame vertically or horizontally, and specify an amount of inset within the frame. If you wanted to create a black-bordered box containing text that is centered in the middle of the box with wide margins all around, a frame would handle this easily.

CREATING A FRAME

You already learned how to create a text block in Chapter 2. Frames are just as easy to insert in a publication, although the method is a bit different. The easiest way to create a new frame is by using one of the frame tools, shown in Figure 3.1.

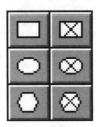

Figure 3.1 *The tools in the left column create rectangles, ovals, and polygons; the tools in the right column create frames in the same shapes.*

The frame tools correspond to the tools PageMaker already had to create rectangles, ovals, and polygons. The difference is that the other figures are simply graphics, whereas a frame can contain either text or an image. An X is shown inside the icon on the tool box, and a cyan X (which wouldn't print if you happen to print a page containing an empty frame) is displayed in an empty frame, to differentiate frames from plain graphics. To create a text frame, just follow these steps:

1. Select one of the frame tools. To get a better handle (so to speak) on what the tool is doing, you might want to activate PageMaker's Control Palette, shown in Figure 3.2, by pressing **Command/Ctrl-'** (single quote) or using **Window>Show Control Palette**.

		X	3.908 in		W	0.26 in	100%				0°	
		Y	5.246 in		H	0.236 in	100%				0°	

Figure 3.2 *The Control Palette offers updated information as you use a tool.*

N O T E

This palette offers a wealth of information you can use while using any tool. The icon at the left of the bar shows which tool is currently active. Next to it, a selection box shows the shape of the object, with the active handle presented larger than the rest. The X and Y coordinates of the cursor (in case you need to position the cursor precisely to draw a frame in a specific position) are displayed. You can click the arrows next to the coordinates to move the cursor one increment at a time. Also shown is the current width and height of the object. You can adjust the size by clicking on the arrows next to those measurements. You may also type in a percentage to enlarge or reduce the object by a fixed amount. Other icons and fields allow you to flip the object, skew it, or rotate it.

2. Position the cursor where you want to place the frame, click, and hold down the mouse button while you drag a frame of the approximate size you need. A frame can be resized at any time, either by dragging its control handles or using one of the precision methods described in the Note.

3. You can change the number of sides in a polygon by using the **Element>Polygon Settings** command. A dialog box pops up, and you can enter from 3 to 100 sides and, if you want a star-like figure, the percent each point should be inset.

Converting Other Objects to Frames

You can convert an object you've drawn with PageMaker's drawing tools into a frame (except for lines, of course). You can also convert a text block into a frame, if you decide that you need the added capabilities of frames and already have text blocks.

✦ To convert a drawn object into a frame, select the object and use **Element>Change to Frame**.

✦ To convert a text block to a frame, first create a frame. Then select the text block and the new frame (hold down the **Shift** key to select the second item) and use **Element>Frame>Attach to Frame**. The text in the text block will be added to the new frame.

An existing graphics frame cannot be converted into a text frame, nor can you add text to a frame that already has graphics. You must first delete the graphic, add the text, then attach the graphic once more.

N O T E

Threading and Unthreading Text

Once you've created a frame or text block, they are treated alike in most respects. When text blocks or text frames are selected, they are displayed as windowshades of text, with handles like windowshade pulls at the top and bottom, and sizing handles at the four corners. A text block or text frame can be so small it contains only one character (or no characters at all), or as long as the page is tall. (Effectively, the maximum size of a single text block is a little more than 20 in.

by 20 in., on a single page.) When a story in a text block or frame extends to the next or subsequent pages, it is broken up into individual page text blocks, each connected to the next, or threaded together, as this method is called in PageMaker. When text is added or deleted on one page of a threaded text block or frame, the threaded text blocks and frames on subsequent pages are reformatted automatically.

You can have more than one threaded text block or frame on a page. For example, in a two-column newsletter, Story A could fill the first column and be continued (and threaded) to the first column of page 2, and Story B could reside in the second column of page 1 and be continued (and threaded) to the second column of page 2. The newsletter contains two independent stories: Each story is made up of threaded text blocks or frames on pages 1 and 2, but the blocks are independent of each other.

The concept of threaded text blocks and frames is central to PageMaker's ability to manage long stories that flow across many pages. Threading lets you edit a story on page 1 and know that the words you add push the text forward on all of the following pages of the story. Likewise, if you delete a sentence on page 3, the pagination for all of the following pages of the story are reformatted for you.

The windowshade handles, displayed when a text block is selected, denote one of several possible conditions:

+ An empty handle indicates the beginning of a text block if it is at the top, or the end of a text block if it is at the bottom. The empty handles essentially mean there's no more text stored for this text block. All of it is displayed before you, and there are no text blocks threaded to this text block, either before or after it.

+ A plus sign in the top handle of a text block means it is connected to a story from a previous page or column. (Note that you could continue a story on page 1 to page 86, for example—the thread doesn't have to run continuously from one page to the next in sequence). If you clicked on the handle and dragged the windowshade down to reposition the top of the column of text, you would reposition all of the text in the text block, as well as in the block to which it is threaded, as shown in Figure 3.3.

Figure 3.3 *The two columns in the example on the left are each a text block, threaded together. In the example on the right, the top of column one is adjusted downward, reflowing all of the text through the threaded text blocks.*

✦ A plus sign in the bottom handle of a text block means that there is at least one more block of text that follows it. For example, if you had a three-column story, the text block for the story in the middle column would have plus signs in both the top and bottom handles, as shown in the center column in Figure 3.4.

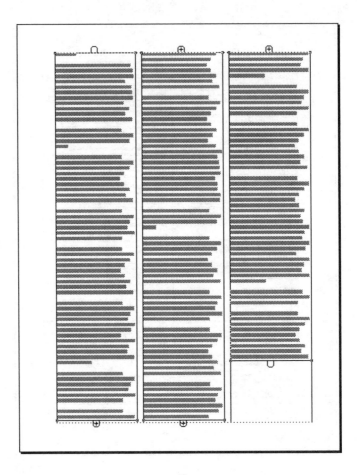

Figure 3.4 *The plus signs in the handles show how columns are threaded (the empty handles indicate either the beginning or the ending of the thread).*

✦ A down arrow in the bottom handle of a text block means that there is more text to come (the text is stored in a temporary memory area called a *buffer*). Clicking the arrow allows you to add, or thread, another text block for this story.

Threading Additional Text

Text can be flowed automatically across multiple pages when you're using text blocks. PageMaker can create as many blocks as required on multiple pages to accommodate the text remaining. If you are using text frames, you must manually create enough frames to hold all your text, and link them manually. The following description applies to text *blocks*. When the bottom windowshade displays a red arrow, indicating there is more text to come, click the arrow to thread the text to the next column or page. Here's how:

1. Click the **down arrow** in the windowshade handle, and the Pointer tool changes to a loaded-text icon.

2. Place the icon where you want the text block to start, aligning the upper-left corner of the icon with the upper-left corner of the page or column margin.

3. Click the mouse button. The text block flows down the page as it is transferred from the text block memory buffer. If you have activated the **Autoflow** control, text that would fill more than a full page auto-matically flows to as many new pages as necessary to empty the mem-ory buffer. If the Autoflow control is off, you must move to each page (or insert new pages as necessary) and manually flow the remaining text down each page.

N O T E   Flowing text using a loaded-text icon is essentially the same as placing text using the **Place** command (on the File pull-down menu), which is described in Chapter 10, "Developing Long Documents." If you decide not to place text using the loaded-text icon, you must cancel the operation correctly or you will lose the text that remains in the text block memory buffer. For example, if you placed the text and then deleted it, you would not be able to place the text again—there wouldn't be any text remaining in the buffer.

To cancel the loaded-text icon:

1. Without clicking the mouse button, position the loaded-text icon anywhere in the boundaries of the toolbox window.

2. Click the mouse button. The loaded-text icon is canceled without losing the text block that remains in the text block buffer.

To thread the additional text, you can again click the **down arrow** in the text block handle at any time after canceling the loaded-text icon.

Threading Text to a Different Page

When the bottom handle indicates that there is more text to come, you are not limited to threading that text on the same page as the selected text block or even the page immediately following it—you can thread the text to any other page in your document. For example, in a newspaper or newsletter, you might wish to continue a story to what is called a jump page (all page 1 stories might be jumped to page 14, for example). Here's how to jump a story to another page:

1. Click the **down arrow** in the text block handle. The pointer changes to the loaded-text icon.

2. Without clicking the mouse button, move the icon to the lower-left corner of the document window and click on the number of the page to which you want to move.

3. Or, move the icon up to the pull-down menu bar. The icon changes to the Pointer tool. Click on the **Layout** menu and click the **Go to Page** command (or press **Command/Ctrl+G**) to display the Go to Page dialog box. Type the page number and click **OK.**

4. When the new page is displayed, position the loaded-text icon where you want to begin flowing the text, aligning the upper-left corner of the icon to the upper-left corner of the page or column margin.

5. Click the mouse button to flow the threaded text block onto the page.

Even though you may have jumped a continued story from page 1 to page 100, and you have created 98 pages of other stories in multiple-page text blocks, the page 1 story is permanently threaded to page 100, unless you choose to unthread it.

Unthreading Text Blocks

You may wish to unthread a portion of a threaded text block, to use as a separate, related story (sometimes called a sidebar when it's positioned in a column beside the main story). It's easy to unthread the text by following these steps:

1. Select the **Text** tool and highlight the text you want to unthread.

2. Choose the **Edit** pull-down menu and select **Cut**. The highlighted text is cut from the body of the text block (the text in the text block reflows to fill the hole).

3. Position the Text tool insertion point where you want to paste the text, and choose **Paste** from the Edit menu.

What if you want to unthread a complete text block, instead of just a portion of a text block? That's just as easy. Simply use the Pointer tool, instead of the Text tool, to select the text block. Cut the selected block, and paste it back wherever you want.

Rethreading Text Blocks

Rethreading a text block is just the opposite of unthreading it. Simply cut the separate text block and paste it inside another text block. Use the **Cut** and **Paste** commands on the Edit menu. The text block readjusts itself and any affected pages are repaginated automatically.

Making Text Blocks Disappear Without Deleting Them

To clear a column of its text block without deleting the text:

1. Select the text block with the Pointer tool.

2. Click the bottom windowshade handle and roll the handle up the text block past the top handle. The column looks like the right-hand column in Figure 3.5.

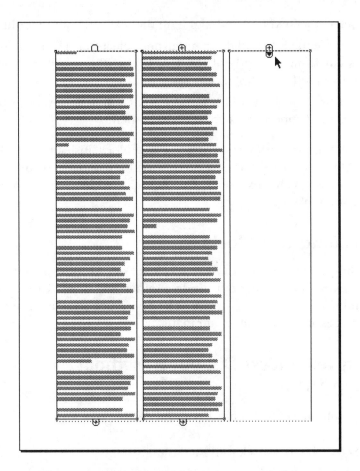

Figure 3.5 *A rolled-up text block.*

When you're ready to open the windowshade again, first choose **Select All** from the Edit pull-down menu to highlight all the text blocks on the page. Then click the bottom handle of the hidden text block and pull it down the page.

Threading Text Frames

The previous description applies to threading text blocks. The added flexibility of text frames comes at a small price. While you can set up your frames in advance without having the text ready to insert, that means you need to thread the text from one frame to another manually. On the plus side, it's much easier to redirect the flow of text through frames than it is through text blocks. If you decide to jump from one frame to a different frame from the one originally linked, you can do it easily. To thread text frames, you'll need to follow steps like these:

1. Select the first frame you want to thread. It can be a frame already containing text or an empty frame.

2. Click the bottom windowshade handle. Note that the cursor does not change to the loaded-text icon.

3. Click the top windowshade handle of the next frame in the sequence.

4. Repeat to link all the frames you want to link. Notice that plus signs appear in the windowshade handles of linked frames to indicate the text is continued in (or from) another frame.

5. If you wish to change the threading order at any time, just click in the bottom windowshade handle of the frame to be relinked, then select the top windowshade handle of the new frame to be linked to. The thread will follow from that new frame to the one the new one is linked to.

NOTE   Since text flowing from text frames can jump all around your document, PageMaker provides a facility for tracking down all the links. Simply click in a frame's windowshade handle, then use **Element>Frame>Go to Next** (to jump to the next frame in the sequence) or **Element>Frame>Go to Previous** (to locate the previous frame).

SELECTING TEXT

You may find selecting text confusing at first, because PageMaker allows you to select text with either the Pointer tool or the Text tool. In Chapter 2, you learned to select a word or paragraph by double-clicking or triple-clicking the **Text** tool and how to select a text block by clicking with the Pointer tool. Which is right?

Choose the tool based on what you want to accomplish. The Text tool is generally used to highlight parts of a text block. The Pointer tool is used to select the entire text block.

Selecting and Dragging Text

One of the unique features of PageMaker is its ability to allow you to select and drag text blocks and graphic elements anywhere on the page—even off the page onto the pasteboard. You have complete freedom to move text blocks. You can even place them on top of other text blocks, frames, or graphic elements, as shown in Figure 3.6.

Figure 3.6 *A drop shadow box with text, composed of two graphic elements and a text block stacked on top of one another.*

To drag a text block or frame:

1. Place the Pointer tool in the text block or frame you want to move.
2. Click the text block or frame to expose its boundaries. Then hold down the mouse button. The Pointer tool is replaced by a four-pointed arrow.
3. Continue holding down the mouse button and drag the text block or frame to its new position on the page. Or, drag it off the page onto the pasteboard, for later use.

NOTE

Although eventually you will want to position text blocks and frames accurately on the pages of your document, you don't have to do so immediately with PageMaker. You can drag a text block off the page, onto the pasteboard, and leave it there. Save and close the document, exit PageMaker, and when you return, you'll find the text block or frame where you left it, patiently waiting to be positioned.

EDITING TEXT

You can add, change, or delete words easily in the document layout window. You may wish to enlarge the view size to make the text easier to read; then:

1. Choose either the **Pointer** or **Text** tool in the toolbox (depending on the kind of editing you want to do, see the following "Deleting Text" section).

2. Then choose an editing option on the Edit menu from among the following: deleting, copying, cutting, and pasting.

Deleting Text

You can delete text one character at a time by positioning the Text tool insertion point to the right of the letter or word to delete and by pressing the **Backspace** key. Also, you can delete words, sentences, paragraphs, or entire text blocks. Here's how:

✦ To delete a word that will be replaced by another word, select the **Text** tool and highlight the word. Type the replacement word, and the word you type replaces the word you just highlighted.

✦ To delete words, sentences, or paragraphs within a larger text block, select the **Text** tool, place the insertion point before the beginning of the words you want to delete, and highlight the text. Then, press the **Delete** or **Backspace** key or choose the **Edit** pull-down menu and click the **Clear** command. The text is permanently deleted (although, if you immediately change your mind, you can reverse the deletion with the **Undo** command). Any text following the deleted text reflows into the space occupied by the text you just deleted.

✦ To delete an entire block of text, select the **Pointer** tool and click the text block or frame. Then press the **Delete** or **Backspace** key or click the **Clear** command on the Edit menu to delete the block. If you delete one text block among several on a page, deleting the text block or frame with the Pointer tool leaves the space that the text block or frame occupied. Text that follows does not reflow into the blank space.

Remember, the Text tool is used to highlight a portion of a text block or text frame. The Pointer tool is used to select an entire text block or frame.

NOTE

Cutting, Copying, and Pasting Text

Text is cut, rather than deleted, when you want to remove it from its present location and paste it somewhere else. To cut text:

1. Highlight the text you want to cut, using either the Pointer tool or the Text tool.

2. Choose the **Edit** pull-down menu and choose **Cut** (or press **Command/Ctrl+X**). The highlighted text will be deleted from its present position.

When text is cut it is actually copied to the Clipboard, where it remains until something else is cut or copied. Put the cut text anywhere else by positioning the insertion point where you'd like the text and choosing the **Edit** menu and the **Paste** command (or pressing **Command/Ctrl+V**). The text is pasted into position.

Text is copied when you'd like it to remain where it is but also want to use it somewhere else.

1. Highlight the text you'd like to copy, using either the Pointer tool or the Text tool.

2. Choose the **Edit** pull-down menu and select **Copy** (or press **Command/Ctrl+C**). The highlighted text is copied and remains highlighted. Click anywhere outside the highlighted text to unselect it.

When you copy text, it is actually copied to the Clipboard and replaces anything already in the Clipboard. Use the copied text anywhere else by positioning the insertion point where you'd like the text and choosing the **Edit** menu and the **Paste** command (or press **Command/Ctrl+V**). The text is pasted into position.

You can paste the same contents of the Clipboard as often as you like. For example, let's say you were developing a series of fact sheets for similar products. You could paste your company's name and address on each page of the fact sheet by positioning the insertion point where you'd like the text to appear and choosing **Paste** from the Edit menu. The Clipboard contents are copied onto your document each time you select the **Paste** command. Once you cut or copy something else (text or graphics), it replaces the contents of the Clipboard.

 If you want to cut text or graphics from your PageMaker document but not disturb what is already in the Clipboard, click the **Clear** command on the Edit menu or press the **Delete** key.

N O T E

Text pasted into a text block pushes the existing text to the right of the insertion point forward. The pasted text becomes an integral part of the text block into which it is pasted.

Text pasted into the document, but not in an existing text block, creates its own text block, with the default type and paragraph specifications in effect at the time of the pasting. Normally, the left and right borders of the text block are defined by the page margins. You can define a text block width equal to surrounding text blocks by pasting text with the drag-place method (described later).

Viewing the Contents of the Clipboard

The Clipboard is a feature built into your operating system, and is available to all applications. It does not need to be running to receive material copied to it; it works independently and in the background. On the Macintosh, you can view the current contents of the Clipboard at any time. To do so, click the **Window** pull-down menu, and choose the **Clipboard** command. The Clipboard window opens, displaying the most recent text or graphics you cut or copied from your PageMaker documents. When you have finished using the Clipboard, you can close it by clicking its **Close** box.

Drag-Placing Text

When pasting text from the Clipboard, you may want to define your own line length, rather than accept the line length that PageMaker provides. PageMaker normally uses the width of a column or the width of the page to determine the default line length. For a narrow measure of text, such as for a byline or photo credit, this makes an abnormally wide text block, as shown in Figure 3.7.

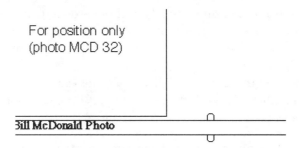

For position only
(photo MCD 32)

3ill McDonald Photo

Figure 3.7 *A small photo credit pasted under a photo has a default text*
block the width of the page.

To shorten the width of the text block, drag-paste the text instead of pasting it.
When you drag-paste, you define the width of the new text block. Here's how:

1. Choose the **Text** tool.
2. Position the insertion point in the upper-left corner of the area where
   you want to paste the text from the Clipboard.
3. Press and hold down the mouse button, and drag the pointer down
   and to the right to set the width you want for this text block. As you
   drag the pointer, a box opens, defining the size of the text block.
4. When you have established the boundaries for this text block, release
   the mouse button, click **Paste** or press **Command/Ctrl+V**, and the
   text flows into the text block. The text assumes the new line length
   and wraps at the right-hand boundary. Drag-placed text that has been
   copied from a wide text block to a narrower one needs more depth. If
   you see only the beginning of the drag-placed text, click it with the
   Pointer tool and pull down the bottom windowshade to reveal the
   remainder of your text.

N O T E

You needn't paste anything to drag out your own text block—you can do
steps 1 through 3 to create a new, empty text block to type new text in.
Simply position the Text tool where you want the text block to start and click-
drag the tool diagonally until the width (and depth) of the text block is
defined. Release the mouse button and start typing.

Power Pasting

Use the power-pasting feature when you need to repeatedly paste the same
graphic or text in columns or rows across or down the page. For example, let's

say you are laying out a form to track hours worked on different projects. Down the left margin are the days of the week. Across the top is Proj/Hours repeated in ten columns. Instead of typing the column heading ten times or pasting and aligning nine text blocks, use power pasting to do it automatically. Here's how:

1. Type the first column heading. Highlight it with the Pointer tool and copy it by choosing the **Edit** menu and clicking the **Copy** command (or press **Command/Ctrl+C**).

2. Hold down the **Command/Ctrl** and **Shift** keys and press **P**. A copy of the text is pasted on top of the text you copied. It will be selected, displaying the text block.

3. Leave the text block selected (don't click the mouse button), position the pointer on top of the text block, but not over the windowshade handles or sizing handles. Press and hold down the mouse button and drag the text block to the second column heading position. Remember to leave this second text block selected.

4. Power-paste the text block again, by pressing **Command/Ctrl+Shift+P**. A third copy of the text block is pasted and positioned the same distance from the second text block as you positioned the second one from the first.

5. Continue power-pasting across the page to create as many column headings as you need.

You can power-paste text or graphics across or down the page, as shown in Figure 3.8.

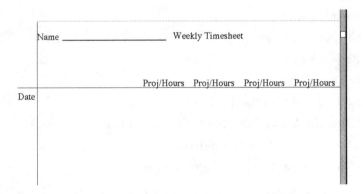

Figure 3.8 *Power-pasted text is added across the page of a form.*

Using Undo and Revert

"I shouldn't have done that!" If you don't utter words to that effect occasionally, you're probably not learning and using all of the capabilities of PageMaker. I encourage you to try different capabilities for two reasons: You will be surprised often by the result, and you can almost always back out of a command using either **Undo** or **Revert**.

To undo something you've just done:

1. Choose the **Edit** pull-down menu. Notice the **Undo** command in the Edit menu. If it is dimmed, you can't use it to undo your last action. If it is highlighted, it lists the action it would undo if you invoked it at this time. For example, if you've just cut some text and you pull down the Edit menu, the **Undo** command says **Undo cut**, meaning it can undo the deletion you just made.

2. Click **Undo** (or press **Command/Ctrl+Z**) to undo the action you just did.

Undo Command Conditions

You can use the Undo command after:

+ Moving or resizing a text block
+ Deleting text
+ Adding text
+ Deleting a graphic
+ Cropping a graphic
+ Removing pages
+ Inserting pages
+ Editing text with the Text tool
+ Using the **Undo**, **Edit**, **Copy**, **Paste**, and **Clear** commands
+ Changing the Page Setup dialog box
+ Moving column guides or guidelines

You cannot use the **Undo** command after:

+ Any commands from the File pull-down menu other than **Page Setup**

- ✦ Scrolling

- ✦ Changing the Page View size

- ✦ Selecting or canceling a selection

- ✦ Changing to line and fill specifications from the Element pull-down menu

- ✦ Any commands from the Type pull-down menu

- ✦ Pasting after cutting or copying with the Pointer tool

- ✦ Changes in style definition or selection

- ✦ Changes in color definition or selection

- ✦ Changes in text or paragraph attributes

In circumstances where **Undo** won't work, you can fall back on the **Revert** command (see also Chapter 1, the "Reverting to a Previously Saved Version" section). Remember that **Revert** undoes everything you've done since the last-saved version of the document. You can also close your current document without saving it, which does much the same thing as using the **Revert** command: Anything done since the last time you saved is lost.

Inserting and Removing Pages

PageMaker gives you complete freedom to add or remove pages. You specify where by moving to a page adjacent to where you want to add a page, or to the page you want to delete. Then select the command from the Page pull-down menu. The pages you add have the page setup parameters you specified for your existing pages, and use the master pages you set up in the same way your existing pages do.

Inserting a Page

Here's how to insert a page:

1. Using the **Go To** command (**Command/Ctrl+G**), select the page before or after the page you want to add. That is, if you want to add a page after page 27, go to either page 27 or to the current page 28.

2. Choose the **Layout** pull-down menu and select **Insert pages** to display the Insert Pages dialog box, shown in Figure 3.9.

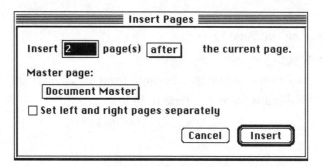

Figure 3.9 *The Insert Pages dialog box.*

3. The insertion point is positioned in the Insert Pages text box, which shows a default value of 2. Enter the number of pages to insert, or accept the default value.

4. Click one of the radio buttons:

   ✦ **Before current page**—Clicking this button inserts a new page before the page you are on. Your current page number increases by the number of inserted pages.

   ✦ **After current page**—Clicking this button adds a new page after the page you're on.

   ✦ **Between current pages**—If you have selected **Double-sided pages** in the Page Setup dialog box for this document, your pages are displayed as two-page spreads. Clicking this button allows you to add pages between the two pages currently displayed. Using this option changes the front and back orientation of the remaining two-page pairs in your document.

5. You can also choose which Master Page to base the inserted pages on—either the current Document Master or another Master Page you have designed (using the drop-down menu available from the Window:Master Pages palette.) Click on the list and select the Master Page you want. Turn off the **Set left and right pages separately** option, and you may specify a different Master Page format for facing pages.

6. Click **OK** to return to your document. You can undo the **Insert** command by immediately choosing **Undo** from the Edit pull-down menu.

Removing a Page

It is a good idea to move to the page you want to remove before actually removing it. This way you can confirm that it is indeed the page you want deleted. However, you can remove a specific page or pages from anywhere in the document.

To remove a page:

1. Choose the **Layout** pull-down menu and click **Remove pages**, to display the Remove dialog box, shown in Figure 3.10.

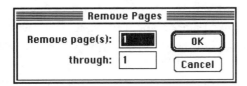

Figure 3.10 *The Remove dialog box.*

2. The insertion point is positioned in the Remove page(s) text box. The Remove and Through text boxes display the page number you are on. Accept the page number or enter the numbers of the pages to remove, and press **Tab** to position the insertion point in the Through text box.

3. If you are removing only one page, enter the same page number in both text boxes (for example, if you want to remove page 27, type **27** in both text boxes). If you want to remove more than one page, type the beginning and ending page numbers, inclusive, in the two text boxes (for example, if you want to remove pages 27 through 34, type those numbers in the two text boxes). Remember, when removing pages, you are entering the actual page numbers of the pages you want deleted. When adding pages, you're only dealing with the number of added pages.

4. Click **OK** or press **Return**. PageMaker displays a dialog box warning you that the contents of the pages will be deleted as well. Click **OK** to confirm the removal and return to your document. Click **Cancel** to cancel the deletion. You can undo the **Remove** command by immediately clicking **Undo** from the Edit pull-down menu.

ADJUSTING SPACING OF CHARACTERS, WORDS, AND LINES

Character, word, and line spacing provides the necessary white space around the words that tell your product's story, communicates your feelings, or creates emotion. Character spacing is necessary to separate individual letters in words. Some letters, such as *M*, *W*, *Q*, and *O*, are wider than others, such as *I*, *L*, *F*, and *J*. Letter spacing in PageMaker is proportional to which letters are being typed and helps to even up the spacing of lines of type in justified columns. Word spacing determines how many words fit on a given line. Too much spacing between words makes a line difficult to read and gives an unkempt appearance to a page of type. Line spacing, or leading (pronounced "ledding"), is the space between lines of type. Either too little or too much space, and the lines are difficult to read.

Unlike most word processors, PageMaker gives you absolute control over the spacing of characters, words, and lines. You can choose to allow PageMaker to judge the best spacing requirements automatically, or you can manually adjust spacing. The degree of accuracy varies, but in most cases, PageMaker allows you to make extremely fine adjustments. For example, you can set the amount of space text stands off from wrapping around a graphic in 1/1000-in. increments.

The 2880 Rule: Though screen resolutions vary greatly, PageMaker always prints pages more accurately than they're displayed. A typical screen resolution may be the equivalent of 96 dpi–100 dpi. The typical laser printer prints at 300 dpi, and high-resolution image setters, like the Linotronic L-330, can produce output as high as 2570 dpi. Just remember, regardless of how a page may look on the screen, it prints with an accuracy of 1/2880 in.

Adjusting Spacing

Nothing improves the professional quality of a publication more than establishing proper spacing between letters. Incorrect spacing (usually too much) is a shrieking sign of amateurish work. Overspacing letters is most obvious in large type sizes—as type increases in size, letter spacing should be proportionally reduced. Spacing in PageMaker is controlled through kerning, tracking, and leading.

Kerning

Change the kerning of a pair of letters, and you change the amount of space between the letters. Long ago, before the advent of computers, kerning letters involved trimming the vertical sides of lead type to make certain letter combinations fit closer together and look more natural. Now PageMaker does the trimming, but the principle is the same—some pairs of letters (called *kerned* pairs of letters) need closer spacing than other pairs. For example, in Figure 3.11, the letters *A* and *V* on the left should be kerned closer, while on the right the same letters look more natural and pleasing.

AVOID   AVOID

Figure 3.11 *The letters A and V are unkerned on the left and kerned on the right.*

Each font has a built-in table that determines which letter combinations will be kerned, as well as the optimal amount of kerning. PageMaker kerns these letter-pairs above a certain size, which you set in the Spacing Attributes dialog box.

In some cases, automatic kerning simply is not enough kerning to display type attractively, especially in larger type sizes—the larger the size of the letter, the more space, proportionally, is allowed on either side of the letter. PageMaker kerns away some of that space, but often not enough. In such situations PageMaker offers two additional ways of adjusting the spacing: *track* kerning and *manual* kerning. Let's look first at setting up automatic kerning for a specific type size:

1. To set a different kerning size threshold for selected text, highlight the text with the Text tool. To change the default size threshold for the entire document, do not highlight any text.

2. Choose the **Type** pull-down menu and select **Paragraph** to display the Paragraph Specifications dialog box.

3. Click the **Spacing** button to display the Paragraph Spacing Attributes dialog box, shown in Figure 3.12. Use this dialog box to turn kerning on and off, and to set a size threshold above which kerning will take place.

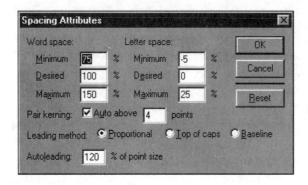

Figure 3.12 The Paragraph Spacing Attributes dialog box.

4. By default, kerning is on (the **Pair Kerning Auto Above** check box is marked with an X), meaning that all type above the default 12-point size shown in the Points text box will be automatically kerned. To turn kerning off, click the **Auto Above** box to remove the X.

N O T E

Just as the need to kern increases as the type size increases, so is the need to kern reduced as type gets smaller. In fact, in sizes below 10 points, kerning may actually make the type more difficult to read. The one unequivocal exception to this rule is when using the Times Roman font, which is more than likely resident in your laser printer. Times is not a particularly attractive font, and it has too much letter spacing. If you must use Times, I suggest setting the Pair Kerning Auto Above limit low enough to include all sizes of Times you will use in your document.

5. Enter a size value in the Auto Above text box to tell PageMaker the size type above which to kern. If you want all type, regardless of size, to be kerned, enter a value smaller than the smallest size type you use in your document. If you'd like only headlines kerned, enter a size just below the headline size (for example, if the heads will be 36 pt, enter **30** in the text box).

6. Click **OK** to return to the Paragraph Specifications dialog box, and click **OK** again to return to your document.

As I have already mentioned, only certain letter-pair combinations are automatically kerned. Those combinations are embedded in the PostScript font and can't be changed in PageMaker. You may find that you don't like the amount of kerning applied to a particular pair of letters kerned automatically by PageMaker. Or you might have a pair of letters not part of the font's kerning table that you'd like to kern anyway. You may also prefer to drastically kern two letters for visual effect as part of a logo or design. For whatever reason, you can also kern letters manually with PageMaker. Here's how:

1. Position the Text tool insertion point between the two letters you'd like to kern.

2. Press **Command/Ctrl+Right Arrow** to increase the space between the two letters in 1/25-em increments. To decrease the amount of space the same amount, press **Command/Ctrl+Left Arrow**.

3. For really fine work, you can adjust kerning in 1/100-em increments. Press **Command/Ctrl+Shift+Right Arrow** to increase space or **Command/Ctrl+Shift+Left Arrow** to decrease space between letters.

NOTE You may find it easier to work in such fine adjustments by first increasing the Page view size to 200% or 400%.

4. To remove manual kerning from letter pairs, select the text that contains the kerning and press **Command/Ctrl+Option/Alt+K**. If you manually change the kerning of a pair of letters, it only changes the kerning in that instance, not throughout your document.

To repeat the same kerning, copy the kerned letters to the Clipboard, then copy the letters wherever you need them in the current document (or create a new document and use the kerned letters in it). Alternatively, copy the letters to the Scrapbook, and you will always have them available for use—which is particularly handy if you are working with a repeating logo composed of kerned letter pairs.

Tracking

Adjusting the tracking of a word or group of words gives much more control over the spacing of letters and words. You can set tracking at values from very loose to very tight. Tracking is adjusted from the Expert Tracking submenu or in the Type Specifications dialog box.

PageMaker sets the default tracking to **None**, but it can be changed at any time for an entire story or for highlighted text. Here's how:

1. Choose the **Type** pull-down menu and select **Expert Tracking** to display the Tracking submenu, shown in Figure 3.13.

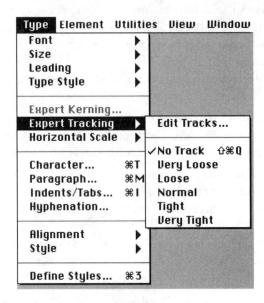

Figure 3.13 *The Tracking submenu.*

2. Select the amount of tracking you want by clicking the **Tracking** option. Normal tracking can improve the appearance of letter spacing by increasing it in small type and decreasing it in larger type. The other tracking options increase or decrease tracking by more drastic amounts, as in the following examples.

The top choice in the submenu, **Edit Tracking...**, lets you customize tracking for specific fonts at specific sizes. The changes you make will then be used by all PageMaker 6.5 publications. This is an advanced capability that comes in handy if none of the default tracking choices suits your needs.

Adjusting Leading

The leading measurement is the height of the line of type, measured from baseline to baseline. It includes the height of the type itself and the space above the type. The size of the line's leading must accommodate the height of the capital letters and such ascenders as the stem of a lowercase *d*, as well as the depth of such descenders as the leg of a lowercase *p*. The space that accommodates ascenders and descenders is called the *slug* of the line, as highlighted in Figure 3.14. The slug must be high enough that ascenders and descenders don't touch and must allow enough white space between the lines that type can be read comfortably. When you highlight a line of type with the Text tool, the type and the line's slug are highlighted, as shown in Figure 3.14.

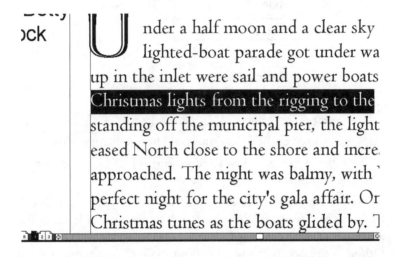

Figure 3.14 *Ascenders and descenders in the highlighted slug of a line of type.*

PageMaker can set leading automatically, or you can specify any leading value you wish for a specific purpose. Automatic leading is about 120% of the type size, although this can be adjusted. For example, if the type is 12 points high, automatic leading would give it about 14.5 points of white space, or 120% of 12. Manual and automatic leading are specified with the Leading submenu, shown in Figure 3.15, or in the Type Specifications dialog box.

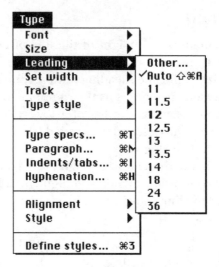

Figure 3.15 *The Leading submenu.*

To change the leading of a line of type:

1. Highlight the type whose leading you'd like to change with the Text tool.

2. Choose the **Type** pull-down menu and select **Leading** to display the Leading submenu.

3. Choose the amount of leading for the line of type by clicking the leading value you want. If you want to set an amount of leading that is not among the choices displayed on the Leading submenu, click on **Other** to display the Other Leading dialog box, or enter the amount in the Type Specifications dialog box, as described in Chapter 2.

Adjusting Hyphenation

When lines of text are justified, neither page margin is ragged—like the lines of text in this book, they are aligned evenly to both the left and right margins. Since words are different lengths, the spacing must be adjusted to make each line the same length. However, some lines would inevitably require more than normal space between one or more words to keep the right margin even. The multiple spaces between words makes for unsightly paragraphs, with what are called rivers of white space meandering through them.

To reduce the spacing between words in justified text, PageMaker can hyphenate words that would normally extend past the right margin. Hyphenation is controlled with the Hyphenation dialog box. To change the hyphenation:

1. Choose the **Type** pull-down menu and select **Hyphenation** to display the Hyphenation dialog box, shown in Figure 3.16.

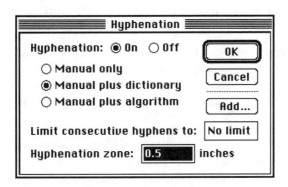

Figure 3.16 *The Hyphenation dialog box.*

2. Use the dialog box to set the parameters for hyphenating your text. Click a radio button to select the level of hyphenation you want:

✦ **Manual only**—Hyphenates only words you have marked to hyphenate by inserting a discretionary hyphen (hold down the **Command** key and press the **Minus** key) in the word where it would normally break. A discretionary hyphen means that PageMaker hyphenates the word where a discretionary hyphen is inserted, when needed, to justify a line of type that the word falls in. For example, to discretionary-hyphenate the word hyphenate, type **hy(Command/Ctrl+-)phen(Command/Ctrl+-)ate**. You do not see the discretionary hyphens, but if the word extends past the right margin of a justified line, PageMaker breaks the word at one of the two hyphens.

✦ **Manual plus dictionary**—Hyphenates the words to which you've added discretionary hyphens, as well as words hyphenated in the PageMaker dictionary. Any time PageMaker comes to a word that must be split between lines, it checks the dictionary and checks for discretionary hyphens to see how to break the word. If there is a conflict,

PageMaker always accepts the way your discretionary hyphen breaks the word.

✦ **Manual plus algorithm**—In addition to using the dictionary, PageMaker uses a mathematical algorithm (a set of arithmetic rules that theoretically define the way that many words are hyphenated) and your manually inserted hyphens to break words. Just as there are exceptions to every rule of English grammar, there are exceptions to the rules for hyphenating words. Because using the algorithm method may produce incorrect hyphenations, check PageMaker's work carefully.

3. The Limit Consecutive Hyphens To text box allows you to tell PageMaker not to stack more than x number of hyphenated lines. In typesetting jargon, two or more consecutive lines ending with hyphens is called a *ladder* and is usually unacceptable.

4. The Hyphenation zone applies only to unjustified lines of text. It is the width of the area in the right margin into which words that need to be hyphenated fall. For example, if you set the Hyphenation zone at 0.5 in., and a word at the end of the unjustified line crosses the zone (extends from 0.5 in. to the left of the right margin to any amount past the right margin), the word will be hyphenated. The wider the zone, the less often hyphenation will appear in a document. The narrower the margin, the more frequently words will be hyphenated.

Adding Words to the Hyphenation Dictionary

If you use a number of specialized words in your documents, you may want to add them to the hyphenation dictionary, rather than continually inserting discretionary hyphens. You can also change the hyphenation of words already in the dictionary. Follow these steps:

1. If you are in the Hyphenation dialog box, click the **Add** button. Otherwise, choose the **Type** menu and the **Hyphenation** command to display the Hyphenation dialog box first, then click the **Add** button to display the Add Word To User Dictionary dialog box, shown in Figure 3.17.

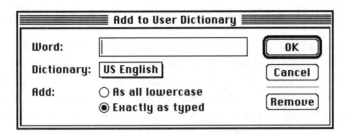

Figure 3.17 *The Add Word to User Dictionary dialog box.*

2. In the Word text box, type the word you want to hyphenate. To add words already in your document, highlight the word with the Text tool, then call up the Add Word To User Dictionary dialog box—the word is displayed in the text box.

3. Indicate where PageMaker should hyphenate the word by placing markers at each hyphenation point in the word. The marker is the tilde symbol (~), normally the key to the left of the number **1** key on the keyboard. You can rank the most favorable break in the word by entering one tilde, the second most favorable break with two tildes, and the third most favorable break with three tildes. PageMaker will try to honor the most favorable break, but if the word can't be broken there, it will try the second most favorable, and so on.

4. To change dictionaries, click the pop-up list and choose the dictionary you want to use. You must load the dictionary through the Adobe Installation program for it to be available.

5. To add the word in all lowercase letters, click the **As All Lowercase** radio button. To add the word exactly as typed in the Word text box, click the **Exactly As Typed** radio button.

6. To actually add the word, click **OK** or press **Return**.

7. To remove a word from the dictionary, type the word you want to remove in the Word text box, and click the **Remove** button.

Changing Word and Letter Spacing for Justified Text

Hyphenation helps to ease the burden of unmanageably large gaps between words in justified lines of text. But hyphenation is limited to breaking words at proper hyphen positions, which may still leave a lot of white space between words. To absorb that white space, PageMaker evens out the spacing of words and increases the spacing between letters in words. When it is done properly, the additional white space is spread out enough that it's not noticeable. You can adjust the amount of spacing given to words and letters in justified lines with the Spacing Attributes dialog box. Here's how:

1. Choose the **Type** pull-down menu and select **Paragraph** to display the Paragraph Specifications dialog box.

2. Click the **Spacing** button to bring up the Paragraph Spacing Attributes dialog box, shown in Figure 3.18. We will use this box to change the default values to minimum and maximum percentages of word and letter spacing.

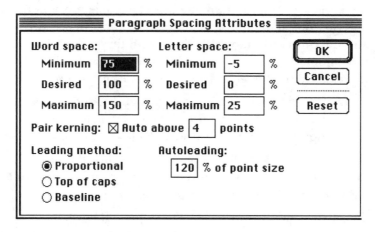

Figure 3.18 *The Spacing Attributes dialog box.*

3. Word space values set the amount of the space band between each word. The *space band* is the amount of space PageMaker moves the Text tool insertion point when you press the **Spacebar**. The space band is different for each font, based on what the font designer determined when the font was developed. To adjust word spacing, change the default values in the Word Space text boxes:

✦ **Minimum**. Enter a percentage of the desired value in the text box that sets the minimum amount of space between words. As PageMaker attempts to even out the word spacing in justified lines, it closes up words to this minimum amount.

✦ **Desired**. Usually a 100% setting, meaning the proper spacing for the font design's space band. Since the minimum and maximum spacing is based on the desired spacing, entering a different value here affects all spacing in the line. For example, if you want to tighten up the spacing of all words, simply enter a smaller value here, such as **90%** instead of 100%. To add spacing across the board, enter a value higher than 100% in this text box.

✦ **Maximum**. Enter a percentage of the desired value in the text box that establishes the maximum amount of space between words. The default values in the Word Space text boxes are very broad, allowing PageMaker to adjust spacing from half of the desired size all the way up to twice the desired size. To even out spacing on the page, consider increasing the minimum size to 80% and the maximum size to 120% of the desired spacing.

N O T E

While PageMaker makes every effort to honor your spacing requirements in the Paragraph Spacing Attributes dialog box, it will exceed the values you enter in order to justify the line correctly. PageMaker highlights the areas it exceeds, spacing values if you request it to do so by checking the **Loose/Tight Lines** check box in the Show Layout problems area of the Preferences dialog box (the **Preferences** command is on the File pull-down menu).

4. Letter-space values set the amount of *pen* advance for each letter. Pen advance is the amount of space bordering the letter, which the font designer determined when the font was developed. To adjust letter spacing, change the default values in the Letter Space text boxes:

✦ **Minimum**. Place in the text box a percentage of the desired value, which PageMaker will subtract to narrow the letter spacing.

✦ **Desired**. Zero means PageMaker will use the pen advance amount specified by the designer. To reduce or widen the overall spacing of all letters in the line, enter a negative or positive value, respectively.

✦ **Maximum**. Place in the text box a percentage of the desired value that PageMaker will add to widen letter spacing.

5. When you are finished changing the spacing values, press **OK** to return to your document.

Adjusting Indents and Tabs

In many word processors, tabs and indents are invoked with two different actions: *Tab* moves just the first line of a paragraph, and *Indent* moves all lines of the paragraph. In PageMaker, both tabs and indents are controlled by pressing the **Tab** key. You define what the **Tab** key does in the Indents/Tabs dialog box. The tool you use to select the Indents/Tabs dialog box determines what text is affected by the changes you make in the dialog box:

✦   Using the **Pointer** tool to select the dialog box means that the changes you make change the default Indent/Tab structure for the document, and affect the next paragraph you type.

✦   Positioning the Text tool insertion point in a paragraph means that changes made to the dialog box affect all text in the current paragraph. The Tab ruler in the dialog box is aligned to the text block's left edge.

✦   Highlighting text with the Text tool means that changes to the dialog box affect all of the highlighted text. The Tab ruler can be aligned to either the left margin of the page or to the left edge of the highlighted text block. If you want the ruler to be aligned to the text block's left edge, be sure the edge is visible when you invoke the dialog box.

Any of the following indent and tab steps, made without opening an existing document or creating a new document, will become the default indent/tab settings for PageMaker.

N O T E

Setting and Changing Tabs

To set or change tab stop positions:

1. Choose the **Type** pull-down menu and select **Indents/Tabs** to display the Indents/Tabs dialog box, shown in Figure 3.19.

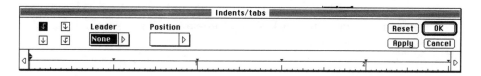

Figure 3.19 *The Indents/Tab dialog box.*

2. Click on one of the four tab-alignment icons. They define the alignment of text positioned at the tab stop:

    ✦ **Left alignment**. Text begins at the tab position and flows to the right side of the column.

    ✦ **Right alignment**. The last character of the text positioned to the right-alignment tab is aligned on the tab stop.

    ✦ **Center alignment**. Text is centered under the tab stop.

    ✦ **Decimal alignment**. Text—or, more usually, numbers—is centered by typing a period for the decimal aligned to this tab stop.

3. Once you have selected the alignment for the tab, position the arrow over the ruler where you want the tab, and click the mouse button.

4. Optionally, you can use the **Tab Action** button to do any of the following:

    ✦ **Add tab**. Enter an exact tab stop value in the Tab Action text box and choose **Add** to add a tab at that position. Or, you can add a tab by clicking with the Pointer tool at the position you want.

    ✦ **Delete tab**. Click on the **tab** to delete it, or enter the exact position in the Tab Action text box and then press **Delete** to delete the tab. Or, grab the tab by positioning the pointer over the tab icon, hold down the mouse button, and drag the tab icon off the ruler.

    ✦ **Move tab**. Enter the value for a new position for an existing tab stop. Highlight the **tab** and click **Move**. The tab moves to the new position. Or, you can grab the tab by positioning the pointer over the tab icon, holding down the mouse button, and dragging the tab icon to a new position.

    ✦ **Repeat tab**. Set a tab stop the distance from the zero point on the ruler you want for repeatedly positioning other tabs. Highlight the **tab** and click **Repeat**. The tab is then repeated the same distance from the highlighted tab. For example, if you want a tab every 2 in., highlight a tab stop at the 2-in. mark on the ruler and click **Repeat**. You'll see a new tab at the 4-in. mark. Click **Repeat** again and you'll see a tab at the 6-in. mark, and so on.

Setting and Changing Indents

To set or change indents:

1. Choose the **Type** pull-down menu and click **Indents/Tabs** to display the Indents/Tabs dialog box. The left indent icons are the top and bottom half of a right arrow on the left side of the ruler. The top half sets the first line paragraph indent. The bottom half indents all lines of the paragraph to the left.

2. To change the first line indent, click the top arrow and drag it to the right. The current position is displayed in the tab actions text box.

3. To indent the left edge of all lines in a paragraph, click and drag both halves of the arrow to the right.

4. To create a hanging indent, in which the second and subsequent lines of a paragraph are indented more than the first line, click and drag the bottom arrow more to the right than the top half.

5. To indent the right edge of a paragraph, click and drag the left arrow, on the right side of the ruler, to the left.

Setting the Leader Style

Leaders are special characters, often periods, that separate text from referencing numbers or other text on the same line. Leaders are handy in typing page numbers across from table of contents entries, or prices across the page from menu items. When you have selected a leader, tabbing across the page will produce a row of the characters you selected as the leader style. To choose the leader style:

1. Choose the **Type** pull-down menu and click on **Indents/Tabs** to display the Indents/Tabs dialog box.

2. Highlight the tab to which you want to assign a leader style.

3. Click the **Set Leader** button and choose the leader character, or click **Custom** and select your own character. The leader you select is displayed in the text box beside the list of leader styles. If you clicked **Custom**, the insertion point moves to the text box. Type the character you'd like for your leader.

Resetting the Tab Ruler

You can reset any changes you've made to the ruler tab positions by choosing the **Cancel** button or by clicking the **Reset** button. The tab stops in effect when you invoked the Indents/Tabs dialog box are reset.

To adjust the zero point of the Indents/Tabs ruler, click the **Left** or **Right Arrow** buttons to scroll the ruler's measurement numbers either lower or higher, respectively. Or, you can click one of the **tab stop** icons and drag it in the direction you'd like, off the ruler's left or right edge. The ruler scrolls in the direction you dragged the icon, once it's off the edge of the ruler.

TO SUM UP

In this chapter, you've seen how versatile PageMaker is in restructuring story text blocks and frames. You can thread or unthread text blocks or frames at will, giving you complete control of page layout. PageMaker's threading feature also allows you to roll up text blocks, temporarily removing them from the page without deleting them.

You've also seen how easy it is to drag and reposition text on the page, or drag it off the page onto the pasteboard. It's just as simple to add and delete pages in PageMaker. You can change the number of pages in your document at any time.

You've looked at how carefully PageMaker defines and adjusts the spacing of characters, words, and lines of text, giving you complete control over the look of your typography and the image you're creating.

In the next chapter, we'll cover the most important addition you can make to your documents: graphics.

CHAPTER 4

Adding Design Elements

- ✦ Adding graphics to your document
- ✦ Changing PageMaker options
- ✦ Creating graphics in PageMaker
- ✦ Importing graphics into PageMaker
- ✦ To sum up

The most important design element you can add to your page is visual relief from the printed word. Column after column of text may serve to communicate factual information, but it doesn't help the reader process the information and can look downright boring. Visual relief comes in many forms and can be as simple as one or two graphic lines to break up the text, or as complex as a four-color photograph. You may not think of white space as a design element, but it is perhaps the most important design element. A page with nice wide margins frames the text within the margins, drawing the eye to it, asking to be read. A text line with a shorter length, or measure, is more inviting and easier to read.

The careful placement and judicial use of graphic elements gives the page a professionally produced look. The elements help to emphasize and organize the page. PageMaker has a number of easy-to-use tools that can draw different types of circles, boxes, and lines. Boxes, polygons, and circles can be filled with any of a number of screens (shades of gray) or fill patterns. Lines can be any number of different weights (thicknesses), and several patterns of broken lines are available. Any text or graphic element can be rotated to any of 360°. Finally, PageMaker makes it easy to import graphics created in other graphics programs (such as Adobe Illustrator and Macromind Freehand) and scan photographs and drawings.

A word of caution: Keep your work simple. A little goes a long way in designing a sophisticated page, as shown in Figure 4.1. Boxes, circles, drop shadows, or reverse type cannot only add to but detract from the overall look of your document. The title page shown on the left side of Figure 4.1 uses too many drop-shadow boxes, thereby segmenting the title page and giving the impression that the proposal itself is confusing and disjointed. Furthermore, the text in the screened box on the page is difficult to read, and the page lacks consistency in the weight and style of lines. The page shown on the right side of Figure 4.1 uses a vertical rule to separate the report's title from its subtitle. The center text block is set in italics, giving it the look of an invitation. The dingbat (type ornament) following the italics is used to separate the two sales messages from the title. The vertical screened boxes continue the theme of the vertical rule above.

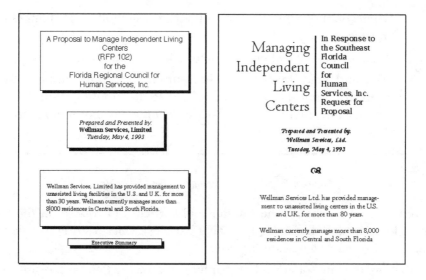

Figure 4.1 *Two examples of the same title page—one confusing and distracting with too many design gimmicks, and one simple and straightforward.*

ADDING GRAPHICS TO YOUR DOCUMENT

You can add graphics anywhere in your document by drawing a graphic with one or more of PageMaker's drawing tools, by importing a graphic that you developed in another program, or by importing a clip art image or a scanned photograph. As you learned in Chapter 2, PageMaker's tools can draw perpendicular and diagonal lines, boxes with either square or rounded corners, regular polygons, and circles and ovals. PageMaker's Rotating tool can rotate anything you draw, clockwise or counterclockwise, to any degree of rotation.

To use any of the drawing tools:

1. Click the tool you want to use. For this example, let's click the **Perpendicular Line** tool.

2. When you move the Pointer tool outside the toolbox, it changes to a crossbar icon.

3. Place the crossbar where you want to begin drawing the line.

4. Press and hold down the mouse button, and drag the crossbar to where you want the line to end. Release the mouse button. You will see your line, highlighted with sizing handles, as shown in Figure 4.2.

Figure 4.2 *A line with sizing handles highlighted.*

To resize the line, choose the **Pointer** tool and click anywhere on the line, highlighting it (and displaying the sizing handles). Click a sizing handle and drag it to shorten or lengthen the line.

To move the line (or any other graphic), choose the **Pointer** tool and click anywhere on the line (or graphic) to highlight it. When you click anywhere on the line except a sizing handle, a four-pointed arrow cursor is displayed. Use it to drag the line to a new position.

Adding Lines

Lines, or rules, are useful in breaking up large blocks of text. You can add lines as part of a paragraph specification, or as graphic elements. In Chapter 2, you learned that PageMaker can predefine paragraphs with lines above, below, or both. Now let's look at adding lines as graphic elements.

With lines, as with any graphic element, a little goes a long way. Lines can help to emphasize important information and direct the reader to information that should be remembered. However, if used in excess, lines can be distracting. You can also consider using lines to balance the "weight" of the page. By this I mean to contrast black and white—text and paper—on the page. To judge balance, choose a small view of the page that greeks the body text (or hold the printed page at arm's length and squint). You may find that you've got way too much text, and that this is throwing off the balance. If so, you might use a line to help offset the out-of-balance area. Finally, beware of intersections. By this, I mean be careful of crossing lines. They tend to attract the eyes like a magnet. If you must have vertical and horizontal lines on the same page, it's a good idea to keep invisible extensions of the lines from crossing each other. Lines added to master pages do, of course, display on all pages of the document (as long as you activate the **Display Master Items** command on the View menu). For some documents, adding recurring lines can be helpful in organizing the page. For example, let's say you give your text a narrow measure by creating a two-column format using columns of unequal width. In this case, a vertical line added to the narrow column's left margin adds balance to the lopsided column's width, as shown in Figure 4.3. Lines that set off page headers and footers can be useful, as shown in Figure 4.4. Adding lines to headers and footers is discussed later in this chapter.

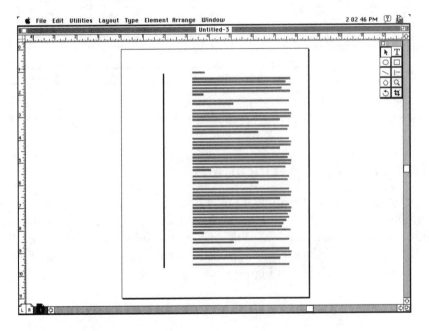

Figure 4.3 The vertical rule at the left balances the wider column on the right.

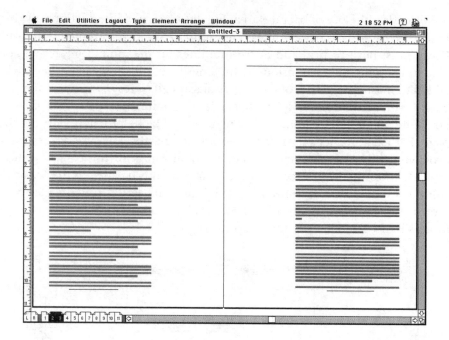

Figure 4.4 *Lines at top and bottom margins separate headers and footers from body copy.*

Changing Line Specifications

PageMaker offers a wide range of possibilities for lines. The weight can range from None (where the line is invisible) to 12 points. Styles include single lines, and combinations of weights, dashes, and other types of broken lines. All line specifications are chosen from the Stroke submenu (on the Element pull-down menu), shown in Figure 4.5.

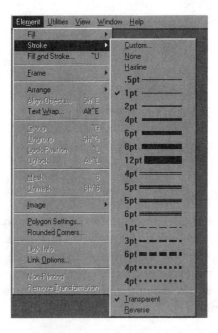

Figure 4.5 *The Stroke submenu.*

There are two ways to select a weight and style for a line. You can change the specification of a line's weight and style before selecting the line drawing tool (then the selection becomes the default specification for this and all other lines to be drawn, until the specification is changed). Or you can choose a line drawing tool, and then select a weight or style for the selected line only (the line will have the specification you have selected, but the default weight and style will remain the same.)

To change the weight or style of a line:

1. Choose the **Element** pull-down menu and choose **Stroke** to display the Stroke submenu.

2. Hold down the mouse button and move the pointer down the list to select the weight you want. Release the mouse button at the correct weight.

Use the same steps to select a different style for a line. Choose the **Stroke** submenu and move the mouse pointer down the list of styles to select the one you want.

You can change the weight or style of any line at any time. Simply choose the **Pointer** tool and click the line to select it. Choose the **Stroke** submenu and select a different weight or style.

N O T E

Adding Shapes

In PageMaker, you can draw square- and round-cornered boxes, circles, ovals, and polygons of any dimension. If you hold down the **Shift** key while you draw, PageMaker gives you perfect squares and circles. You can add shapes to a document's master pages to have a repeating graphic on every page, and, as with lines, you can draw shapes off the page and on the pasteboard, and either drag or paste them into your document later.

Changing Shape Specifications

PageMaker lets you modify both the weight and style of the border denoting the shape, as well as change the fill or color of the shape itself. To adjust the lined border of the shape, select the shape with the Pointer tool. Then open the Stroke submenu and select the appropriate line weight or style. Figure 4.6 shows some options.

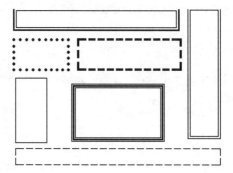

Figure 4.6 *Different weight and style borders for rectangles, using the Line submenu.*

To change the fill specifications of a shape:

1. Select the shape by clicking its border with the Pointer tool.

2. Choose the **Element** pull-down menu and use **Fill** to display the Fill submenu, shown in Figure 4.7.

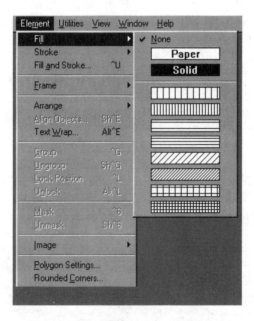

Figure 4.7 The Fill submenu.

3. Select the fill you want by moving the pointer down the Fill submenu. When you release the mouse button, PageMaker fills your shape with one of the following:

    ✦ **None**—Choosing **None** means that the shape will be transparent; that is, whatever is underneath it shows through.

    ✦ **Solid fill color**—Choose **Paper** if you want your shape to be the same color as the paper on which you are printing. Normally, the paper color is white, although you can define a specific color for the paper in the Define Colors dialog box (explained in Chapter 8, "Adding Color"). If you position text inside a shape and plan to add another shape underneath in a different color, you must choose **Paper**. Choose **Solid** if you want a solid black color for the shape.

✦ **Screened fill pattern**—The six choices are shades of black (actually screened percentages of black). If you are using a 300-dpi laser printer for your final printout, some of these screens will look coarser than others. You'll have to experiment to see which ones look better. If your printer will be a PostScript image setter capable of resolutions above 1000 dpi, all of these screens will look fine.

✦ **Lined fill pattern**—The eight lined choices offer different patterns to fill shapes.

Changing Line and Fill Specifications Together

Sometimes you may find it helpful to be able to make line and fill changes at the same time. The Fill and Stroke dialog box lets you do just that. Follow these steps:

1. Select the shape you want to change with the Pointer tool.

2. Open the Element pull-down menu and choose the **Fill and Stroke** command to display the Fill and Stroke dialog box, shown in Figure 4.8.

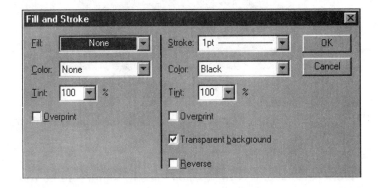

Figure 4.8 *The Fill and Stroke dialog box.*

3. Choose the fill pattern you want by clicking on the **Fill** pop-up list. You can assign a color to the fill by clicking the color you want in the Color pop-up list.

4. To change the line specification, click the **Stroke** pop-up list and choose the line you want. Again, you can change the color of the line by choosing a different color from the Color list. If you don't see the weight line you

want, choose **Custom** and enter any point value (up to 800 points) in the dialog box.

5. To force the fill or line to overprint on top of anything underneath the shape (instead of knocking out the object underneath), click the **Overprint** check box for the fill or the line. (Knockouts and overprinting are thoroughly explained in Chapter 8, "Adding Color.")

6. If you choose the **Transparent background** check box, the blank spaces between the dashes and dots in PageMaker's custom-line patterns will print as transparent rather than opaque.

A quick way to create a box around text is to use the Create Keyline addition. All you have to do is select the text you want to box, and the addition does the rest. Here's how:

SHORTCUT

1. Type the text you want to box and select the text block with the Pointer tool. You may want to adjust the size of the text block before activating the addition so that the text block is relatively the same size as the text.

2. Choose the **Utilities** pull-down menu and choose **Plug-ins...** to display the Plug-ins submenu. Then choose the **Keyline...** command to display the dialog box, shown below.

3. In the Extends text box, use the default values or enter your own values for the margin value between the text and the inside edges of the box.

4. To add the keyline (or box) in front of the text or graphic you're boxing, click the **Bring Keyline to Front of Object** radio button. To put the keyline behind the object, click the other radio button.

5. Click the **Knockout** check box and enter a trapping amount if you wish to trap the box to the object behind (which requires a knockout of the underlying object).

6. Click **OK** or press **Return** to create the box.

Trapping is the process of making one object that will be printed in one color slightly larger so that its edges overprint a surrounding object printed in another color, thus avoiding leaving a white gap if the two images are not precisely registered when printed. A *knockout* is the "hole" left in the surrounding object the component of the other color is printed into.

NOTE

Changing Round Corners

Depending on the needs of your design and layout, you may want to round the corners of square or rectangular boxes. To do so, first draw the box in the dimensions you want; then use the **Rounded Corners** command on the Element menu to change the corners. Here are the steps:

1. Select the box you wish to edit. If no object is selected, you will change the default corner radius for all boxes drawn in the future in the current document.

2. Choose the **Element** pull-down menu and choose **Rounded Corners** to display the Rounded Corners dialog box, shown in Figure 4.9.

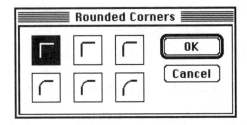

Figure 4.9 *The Rounded Corners dialog box.*

3. You can choose from six corner styles (square, and five radii of rounded corners). Click the corner style you'd like.

4. Click **OK** or press **Return** to return to your document.

To change a rounded-corner box back to a square-cornered box, you must select the box, open the dialog box once again, and choose the square-cornered icon.

Creating Drop-Shadow Boxes

Drop-shadow boxes or circles are actually two boxes or circles, one behind the other, slightly offset and colored black. Drop shadows add a nice graphic touch when used sparingly. To create a drop-shadow box:

1. Select the **Box** tool and draw a square or rectangle the size you'd like. When you finish drawing, leave the box selected (so that the sizing handles are visible).

2. Choose the **Copy** command from the Edit pull-down menu to copy the rectangle to the Clipboard.

3. Immediately paste the rectangle, by choosing **Paste** from the Edit menu. A copy of the rectangle is pasted over the original rectangle, shifted slightly to the right and down. The copied rectangle becomes the shadow for the rectangle you drew.

4. While the pasted rectangle is still selected, move it behind the original rectangle by choosing the **Send to Back** command from the Element>Arrange pull-down menu, or by pressing **Command/Ctrl+[**. The pasted rectangle is now behind the original rectangle.

5. Fill in the pasted rectangle with a solid color or with a shade of gray from the Fill submenu. Notice that you can see the pasted rectangle through the original rectangle.

6. To hide most of the pasted rectangle, color the original one. Use the Pointer tool to select the original rectangle. Choose the **Solid** paper color from the Fill submenu.

Now, let's add some text to the drop-shadow box:

1. Use the Text tool to define and open a new text block in the drop-shadow box: Position the insertion point in the upper-left corner of the box, press the mouse button and drag to the right and down, defining the text block as the size of the drop-shadow box.

2. Release the mouse button and type some text. Use the Type pull-down menu to change the type specifications and alignment to suit your needs. When you've finished, you'll have a drop-shadow text box.

SHORTCUT

You'll want to learn the shortcuts for changing the stacking order of objects in PageMaker:

✦ Bring to Front: **Command/Ctrl+]**

✦ Bring Forward: **Command/Ctrl+Shift+]**

✦ Send Backward: **Command/Ctrl+Shift+[**

✦ Send to Back: **Command/Ctrl+[**

Changing PageMaker Options

Out of the box, PageMaker is set for a number of default values, as we have seen in past chapters. Changing some of these settings can markedly improve your document. Let's take a look.

Adjusting Margins

The *measure* (or length of a line of text) is basically defined by the margins you set (and, of course, the overall size of the page and the point size of the type). An excessively long measure makes for difficult reading. A line set in 11-point type with PageMaker's default margin setting is much too long for an 8.5 x 11-in. page. Most 6 x 9-in. books use a 26- or 27-pica measure and 10-or 11-point type. Newsletters and magazines typically use a larger page, multiple columns, and a shorter measure—perhaps 18 picas—in a two-column format. PageMaker defaults to an 8.5 x 11-in. page with a 40-pica measure, which is much too long for most purposes. You will probably wish to change it, depending on your type size and the sort of document you are creating. You can shorten the measure in a number of ways, the easiest being to widen the left and right margins, squeezing the text between them. To change the default margin setting:

1. If PageMaker is up and running, save and close the document you're working on. With the program window visible, but with no document window open, changes made to PageMaker's margins become the new default settings.

2. Choose the **File** pull-down menu and choose **Document Setup** to display the Document Setup dialog box.

3. In the margins area of the dialog box, enter new, larger measurements for the left (inside) and right (outside) margins. Left and right margins of 2 in. each give you a line measure of 27 picas, which is easier to read than the default measure of 40.5 picas. If your document will have multiple pages printed on one side only and bound on the left edge, you can add a little more width to the left, or inside margin (the side that will be bound) because the pages will have to bend or fold open at the binding.

Setting and Adjusting Columns

When you are working with larger page sizes and still need a reasonable line measure, you can split the page into columns. Splitting the default 8.5 x 11-in. page size into two columns gives you a satisfactory measure of about 19 picas. A tabloid page size (11 x 17 in.), if divided into three columns, gives you a measure of almost 18 picas. Clearly, columns are a handy way to establish a readable line length. To set up more than one column on a page, do the following:

1. To set all pages with the same columns, open the master pages by clicking the **Master Page** icon in the lower-left corner of the document window. To set columns on one page only, move to that page.

2. Choose the **Layout** pull-down menu and select **Column Guides** to display the Column Guides dialog box, shown in Figure 4.10.

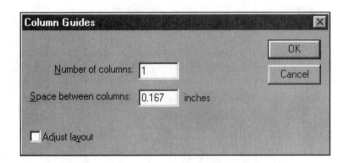

Figure 4.10 *The Column Guides dialog box.*

3. Enter the number of columns you'd like for this document (or page) in the Number of Columns text box. The default number of columns is 1 (PageMaker sees the default page as a one-column document).

4. Enter the width of the gutter (the area between the columns) in the Space Between Columns text box. The larger the value here, the wider the gutter and the more white space on your page. However, the wider the gutter, the narrower the columns will be. One pica is a normal gutter width. If you are working in inches instead of picas, 1 pica equals 0.167 in.

Setting Unequal Width Columns

On a smaller page, more than one column creates an unusually short line measure. One way to solve this problem is to create unequal width columns.

Here are the steps:

1. Display the Column Guides dialog box.
2. Enter **2** as the number of columns and leave the gutter setting as 1 pica, or 0.167 in.
3. Click **OK** to return to your document.
4. Select the **Pointer tool** from the toolbox.
5. Click and drag the column marker to either the right or left, creating a wide and narrow column, as shown in Figure 4.11. Even with smaller page sizes, the wider column wili be 18–24 picas, for a readable measure.

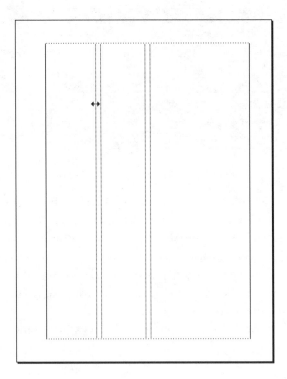

Figure 4.11 *Drag the column guide to either side to create columns of unequal widths.*

If you were to look at the Column guides dialog box again, you would see that the Number of columns text box now contains the word Custom. This signifies that you have customized the column guide position.

If you wish to set unequal width columns for all of the pages in your publication, add the columns to the master pages, as described earlier. For facing pages, the narrow column should go to the inside, close to the bound edge of the page.

An excellent use of the narrow column, in addition to giving text in the wider column a more readable line measure, is to hold margin notes. Use it to add small graphics, notes, warnings, or new text that relates to the text in the wider column across from it.

NOTE

You can modify margins and change columns for the master pages of a particular document using the fly-out menu on the Master Pages palette, which includes a Master Page Options dialog box.

NOTE

Creating Headers and Footers

Headers and footers are text or graphics located above and below the top and bottom margins, respectively. Generally speaking, headers and footers are used to display continuing information about a page, such as the chapter title and page number, the current date and time of publication, and the revision date of the document, for example. To add a header or footer to your document:

1. Click the **Master Page** icon to open the master pages for your document. If you have checked the **Facing Pages** check box in the Page Setup dialog box, you will see two master pages (as indicated by the dual-page Master Page icon, labeled L and R), representing a two-page spread. If you have not set up your document with facing pages, you'll see a single master page, as shown by the single-page Master Page icon. These icons are displayed both that the bottom of your page at the right and in the Master Pages palette, shown in Figure 4.12.

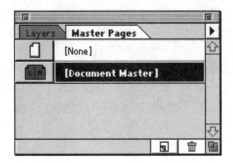

Figure 4.12 *The Master Pages palette has handy options you can use
to quickly edit the underlying pages of a document.*

2. To create a header, move to the top of the master page and drag a
    guideline out of the top ruler to position the header line.

3. Position the guideline above the top margin. Reset the ruler's zero
    points, if necessary, to precisely position the text for the header.

4. Format your text in the desired typeface, size, and style, using the
    Character Specifications dialog box. Enter the text and add lines,
    shading, color, or any graphic element you would like to have
    repeated on each page. Note that when the Text tool is active, the
    Text Control palette, shown in Figure 4.13 can be displayed on your
    screen (use the Window>Show Control palette to make it visible.)
    This palette makes it easy to change typestyle and size, specify leading
    and tracking, and enter all the other text parameters you'd normally
    select from the Type menu.

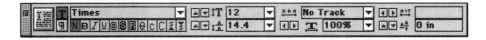

Figure 4.13 *The Text Control palette includes all the parameters
you'd normally select from the Type menu.*

5. To add a page number, position the Text tool insertion point where
    you want the page number to appear, and type **Command/Ctrl+Option/Alt+p**.
    A repeating page number marker is inserted. If you are working with
    facing pages, you must add a page number marker to both pages. The

marker you add to the left facing page displays *LM*, indicating Left Marker. The marker you add to the right page displays *RM*, or Right Marker. If you are not working with facing pages, the repeating page marker always displays *RM*.

N O T E   Automatic page numbering begins based on the starting page number you enter in the Page Setup dialog box. If you have facing master pages, you can create alternating left and right headers or footers. Whatever you enter on the left-hand master page is repeated on each left page of your document. Likewise, whatever is entered on the right-hand master page is repeated on each right page of your document.

If you find that you need a different header or footer on a page or two of your document or if you wish to change the header or footer on two facing pages, you can simply click **Display Master Items** in the View pull-down menu. This toggles off the Display Master Items command, and any header or footer you see will be hidden on both of the facing pages. You can then enter new text or graphics in the place of the master page items. If you wish to change the header or footer on a single page of a two-page spread, you must first cover the master page text or graphic with a solid paper-colored box, then add your own text or graphics over the box. Here's how:

1. Select the **Box** tool, and position the crossbar in the area of the page containing the master page item you want to hide.
2. Click the crossbar above and to the left of the master page item and drag diagonally, creating a box that borders the item. You can see the item underneath the box because the default fill color is None (meaning that you can see through the box).
3. Choose the **Element** pull-down menu and click **Fill** to display the Fill submenu.
4. Click **Paper** to give the box a solid color that is the same shade as the paper. The master page item is now covered by a white (paper-colored) box, and bordered in black. Let's remove the border:
5. Choose the **Element** pull-down menu and click **Stroke** to display the Stroke submenu.
6. Click **No Line** to delete the line around the box. Now the master page item is completely covered by the white-colored box, onto

which you can enter new text or graphics. To see an outline of the box, click along the edge with the Pointer tool. You will see the box's sizing handles.

N O T E   If you can't find the edge of the box because it is no longer visible, select the **Pointer** tool and click **Select All** from the Edit pull-down menu. All text blocks and graphic elements will then be selected, and you will be able to see the outline of the "invisible" box.

Creating Graphics in PageMaker

While PageMaker doesn't pretend to match the artistic capabilities of any number of drawing programs, like Macromind FreeHand, Adobe Illustrator, or CorelDraw, you can, with a little thought and imagination, produce some workable graphics with PageMaker. For example, you can rotate text and graphic elements in any of 360° of rotation, and in increments as small as 0.01° increments. You can also combine lines, boxes, and circles to create effective designs.

Combining Graphic Elements to Create Logos

While you will probably want to use a drawing program to finalize a design you sketch together, starting off in PageMaker can help you to visualize how a logo will look in your letterhead or business card. Let's put some elements together to create a rough logo for a high-rise construction firm called Advanced Construction, Inc.

1. Select the **Text** tool, and create a text block in a new document page, at the top-left corner.

2. Select an interesting typeface. Bold typefaces, like Latin Wide, are often used for logos, since they add weight to the name of a company and are very readable in a smaller type size. If you don't have Latin Wide, you can substitute Times Roman Bold. Type the company name in a reasonable size; try 18 points.

3. Now try the same name stacked, flush left, as shown in Figure 4.14.

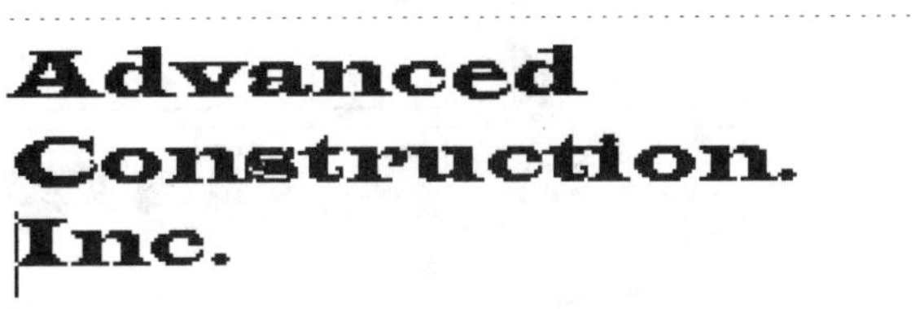

Advanced Construction. Inc.

Figure 4.14 The text is stacked and flush left.

4. Why don't we add some stacked lines, as shown in Figure 4.15, aligned to the left slant of the A in Advanced, to give the impression of a building. If you find that the A moves when you place the lines next to it, look at the Text Wrap command on the Element pull-down menu, and make sure it is turned off.

Figure 4.15 Stacked lines add a nice graphic touch to the logo.

5. Now slant the left ends of the lines by positioning a diagonal line over them, and aligning them evenly to the progressive slant of the lines. Choose the Stroke submenu and select a 6-point weight for this line. Click the line with the Pointer tool and adjust it so that it just covers the left ends of the horizontal stacked lines, as shown in Figure 4.16.

Figure 4.16 *The diagonal line creates a smooth transition.*

6. The only thing left to do is to color the diagonal line so that it cannot be seen. With the line still selected, choose the **Window** pull-down menu, and choose **Show Colors** to display the Color palette. Click **Paper** to hide the diagonal line by coloring it the same color as the paper. Your logo should look like the one shown in Figure 4.17.

◢Advanced Construction Inc.

Figure 4.17 *The finished logo.*

Rotating Text

Rotated text is a quick attention grabber. Vertically rotated text can be especially handy for section or chapter titles, because the titles can be positioned in left or right margins of the page and not use up the valuable space needed for text. Rotation can also be used in developing unique logo designs. To rotate text:

1. Use the Pointer tool to select the text block you wish to rotate. In this example, we'll rotate the letterhead for the Vertical Manufacturing Corporation.

2. Click the **Rotating** tool in the toolbox, position the crosshairs of the tool in the center of the text block and press and hold the mouse button. You will see a small starburst icon displayed over the center of the crosshairs.

3. Now drag the starburst icon out from the center of the text block (marked by the crosshairs). Still holding down the mouse button, you will see a line displayed in the direction that you're dragging the starburst icon. The line is called the *rotation lever*—an imaginary arm connected to the fixed point around which the text block rotates. See Figure 4.18.

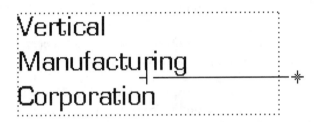

Figure 4.18 *The Rotating tool provides a fixed point around which the item rotates and a rotation lever to aid in exact rotation.*

4. Still holding down the mouse button, drag the starburst icon and the rotation lever in the direction that you'd like to rotate the text block. Let's drag the lever up in a counterclockwise direction until the text block is vertical. Now you can release the mouse button.

5. Add some thin vertical lines and you have a logo for a company that manufactures vertical blinds.

Getting Control with the Control Palette

Some designers working with PageMaker enjoy the free-form approach of the program, which gives you complete freedom in creating a design on the blank page. Others are more precise in detail, perhaps, and want the sort of minute placement control afforded by competing DTP packages (and traditional typesetting). It's left brain versus right brain, I suppose—I personally enjoy working with PageMaker in the traditional way, but many designers seek more control in the positioning and manipulation of text and graphics. If you fall into this latter category, you'll appreciate PageMaker's Control palette, which we've referred to several times so far. To display the palette, open the Window pull-down menu and choose the **Control palette** command. With an object selected, you'll see the palette shown in Figure 4.19.

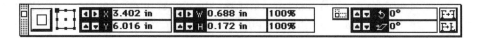

Figure 4.19 *Parts of the Control palette.*

The palette changes, depending on which tool you choose from the toolbox and what type of object you select with the tool. For example, if you choose the **Pointer** tool, the Apply button on the palette displays the Pointer icon (the button doesn't appear until you have created an object with the tool). Let's look specifically at the parts of the Control palette:

✦ **Apply button**—Use the Apply button to apply any alterations you make to values on the palette. For instance, if you change the X and Y coordinates of the object, to reposition it on the page, click the **Apply** button to have the new coordinates take affect. Alternatively, you can press the **Return** key to do the same thing.

✦ **Proxy**—The Proxy represents the selected object and gives you a reference to affect one specific area of the object, such as a corner dimension or a side sizing handle position. To make changes to a specific sizing handle, click the represented handle on the **Proxy** icon.

✦ **Page position**—This position represents the X, Y position of the object's upper left-hand corner relative to the document page. To move the object on the page, change one or both coordinate positions.

✦ **Size controls**—The size controls determine the size of the object.

✦ **Scaling percentages**—To make scaled changes to the dimensions of the object, enter percentage values in the two scaling percentage text boxes. For example, to reduce the size of the object by half, enter **50%** in each percentage text box.

✦ **Proportional scaling control**—To maintain the original proportion of the object, click the **Proportional Scaling** icon.

✦ **Rotation and skew**—These controls provide precise control over rotating and skewing objects. Click in the appropriate text boxes and enter the degree of rotation or skew you'd prefer.

✦ **Nudge buttons**—You can increment the current entry in a text box in minute amounts by repeatedly clicking the associated **Nudge** button. When you click the **Increase** or **Decrease Nudge** button, you change the value in the text box by 0.01 in. or 0.01°. If you hold down the **Command** key and click the button, you will make changes to the text box values in 0.01 in., or 1°.

✦ **Horizontal and vertical reflection controls**—Allow you to create either horizontal or vertical reflections of an object.

If you're not sure which value to enter in a text box on the palette, but you do know the math formula that will allow you to arrive at the correct value, you can enter the formula in the text box. For example, if you'd like to add 0.14 in. to the current value of a text box, click the insertion point in the text box immediately following the current value and type **+.14**. PageMaker then calculates the correct sum when you press the **Return** key or the **Apply** button. Then, you can add with the **Plus** key, subtract using the **Minus** key, multiply using the **Asterisk** key (*), or divide using the **Forward slash** key (/).

Skewing and Mirroring Objects with the Control Palette

Skewing and mirroring are two object orientations new to version 5 of PageMaker. Both orientations move the object in essentially a third dimension, forward or backward out of the vertical plane of the page. To skew an object (let's skew the letter A), follow these steps:

1. Select the letter text block and open the Control palette from the Window pull-down menu.

2. Enter the degree of skew in the Skew text box, or use the skew nudge buttons to scroll to the correct amount of skew you'd like. A positive amount of skew leans the letter backward. A negative amount of skew leans the letter forward.

3. Click the **Apply** button to apply the skew angle to the text box. The results might look like Figure 4.20, which shows the results of 75° of skew.

Figure 4.20 *A letter A text block with a positive skew of 75°.*

Mirroring is similar to skewing. It also rotates the object out of vertical or horizontal plane, depending on which mirror control you choose. As you do in skewing, select the object you want to mirror, and follow these steps:

1. Usually a mirrored object contains the object in the original plane as well, so that one can see the reflection of the original. To leave the original object where it is, first make a copy of the object and paste a copy directly over the original.

2. With the pasted copy still selected, open the Control palette and enter a mirror rotation value in either the horizontal or vertical mirror text boxes.

3. Press the **Apply** button to apply the value to the object.

Making Typographic Changes with the Control Palette

When you choose the **Text** tool and highlight text in a text block, the Control palette changes to reflect the many typographic options you have chosen through the Type pull-down menu, as shown in Figure 4.21.

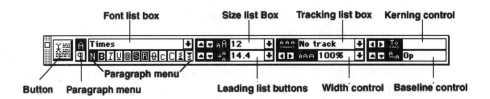

Figure 4.21 *Typographic features of the Control palette.*

The palette in Figure 4.21 shows the character view of the Control palette. If you click the **Paragraph view** button, you'll see a different palette with paragraph formatting controls, as shown in Figure 4.22.

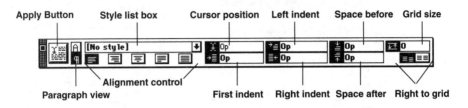

Figure 4.22 Paragraph formatting features of the Control palette.

IMPORTING GRAPHICS INTO PAGEMAKER

Based on the import filters you choose, you can import most standard graphic formats into PageMaker, including encapsulated PostScript files created in such programs as Adobe Illustrator or Adobe Freehand; tagged-image file format (TIF); files of captured screen images or scanned black-and-white or color photos; MacPaint files; PICT graphic files; Windows metafiles (ending in the DOS extension WMF);Windows Computer Graphics metafiles (CGM); Windows Paintbrush (PCX) files; and many others.

Placing Graphics

You import graphics with the Place command (in the File pull-down menu). To import a graphic:

1. Select the **Pointer** tool from the toolbox.
2. Choose the **File** pull-down menu and choose **Place** to display the Place Document dialog box, shown in Figure 4.23.

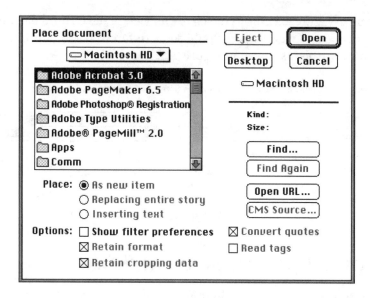

Figure 4.23 *The Place Document dialog box.*

3. Scroll through the list of file names to find the graphics file you want to place.

4. Click **OK** to return to your document. The Pointer tool changes to one of a number of place graphic icons, depending on the format of the graphic you're placing.

5. Position the upper-left corner of the icon to where you want the graphic placed, and click the mouse button.

Placing In-Line Graphics

PageMaker normally considers graphics to be independent objects on the page. If, however, the graphic relates directly to text in a specific line or paragraph, you should anchor the graphic to that text by placing an in-line graphic. When an in-line graphic is placed, it becomes an integral part of the text block. If text is inserted before the paragraph in which the in-line graphic is located, the paragraph and the graphic are pushed down the page together.

An in-line graphic is placed in the same way as an independent graphic is placed, except that you must select the **Text** tool first and click it in the text where you want the graphic to appear. Choose the **Place File** dialog box, and click the name of the graphics file to place. Then click **OK** or press **Return** to start the importing process.

Converting an Independent Graphic to an In-Line Graphic

If you've placed an independent graphic only to find that you'd rather have it anchored to the text as an in-line graphic, here's what to do:

1. Select the graphic with the Pointer tool. Choose **Cut** from the Edit pull-down menu to cut the graphic from its current position and copy it to the Clipboard.

2. Choose the **Text** tool and position the insertion point in the text block where you want the graphic to be placed.

3. Choose **Paste** from the Edit pull-down menu to paste the graphic from the Clipboard to the insertion point position. The graphic is pasted as an in-line graphic, an integral part of the text block.

Aligning In-Line Graphics

When you place an in-line graphic, it assumes the alignment characteristics of the surrounding text. That is, if the text is left-aligned, the graphic will be left-aligned. To change the alignment, highlight the in-line graphic with the Text tool and choose the **Type** pull-down menu, then the **Alignment** submenu to select a different alignment orientation for the graphic.

Sizing Graphics

Independent graphics are sized the same way shapes or lines are sized: Click the graphic with the Pointer tool, and grab one of the sizing handles to stretch or shrink the graphic in the direction of the arrow. Corner sizing handles effectively enlarge or reduce the overall size of the graphic. To enlarge or reduce the graphic proportionately (or resize the width and height by the same amount), press the **Shift** key, then click the corner handle and drag.

If you find that you have resized a graphic incorrectly, simply choose **Undo** from the Edit menu while the graphic is still selected. To resize an in-line graphic, select the graphic with the Pointer tool, click a sizing handle, and resize accordingly.

Cropping Graphics

Cropping trims away a portion of the graphic, rather than reducing the size of the graphic. In Figure 4.24, the Adobe practice TIFF file has been cropped.

Figure 4.24 *Before and after versions of a cropped TIFF using the Cropping tool.*

To crop a graphic:

1. Select the **Cropping** tool from the toolbox.
2. Click the graphic to select it and display the sizing handles.
3. Position the Cropping tool over the necessary side or corner sizing handle. For example, if you want to trim some of the bottom of the graphic, click the **bottom sizing** handle. If you want to trim both the bottom and the left side, click the **lower-left corner** handle. Hold down the mouse button; the Cropping tool changes to an arrow.
4. Drag the arrow side(s) you are cropping toward the center of the graphic.

You can uncrop any side you have already cropped, but only to the original size of the graphic before you cropped it.

OBJECT LINKING AND EMBEDDING

A step beyond cutting and pasting, and a more exact science than using PageMaker's import filters, *Object Linking and Embedding* is a powerful feature of both the Macintosh and Windows platforms that PageMaker 6.5 takes advantage of. It is called *OLE* (pronounced o-lay). Object Linking and Embedding lets you link or embed the actual data from other applications directly into your PageMaker documents. For example, instead of importing a WordPerfect document into PageMaker, you could either link or embed the document. Why bother when PageMaker can import most of the WordPerfect formatting? Because when you link or embed the document, you can make interactive changes to the document inside PageMaker by simply double-clicking on the **WordPerfect** text. At this point, the WordPerfect application automatically starts up, and you can instantly change your document.

There is one basic difference between OLE linking and OLE embedding: When you link the work of another application—it could be a spreadsheet from Excel, a WordPerfect or Word text document, an Illustrator image, or a Photoshop photo—you are actually pasting a copy of the original in your PageMaker document. When you change the work in the application that created it (called the *source*) the linked object in PageMaker is automatically changed. When you embed the source document in your PageMaker document, you're adding the original work, not a copy, and it contains everything needed for you to make changes to the work.

Setting Up an OLE Linked Object

The steps to add a linked object are simple: Create the object in the source application, save the object in the source application, then copy it to the Clipboard. In PageMaker, choose **Paste Special** from the Edit menu to paste the object just as you would paste anything else. Let's take a closer look.

1. Open an OLE server application like Excel. Server applications are OLE applications that create the object and serve it to the OLE client application (in this case PageMaker). Clients are those applications like PageMaker that receive objects, but do not serve them to other applications.

2. In Excel, create a spreadsheet and save it as an Excel file. Now copy the entire spreadsheet or just the range of cells you want to add to your PageMaker document using Excel's Copy command.

3. Now move back to your PageMaker document, and choose the **Paste Special** command on the Edit pull-down menu. Within seconds, the spreadsheet or portion of spreadsheet you just copied appears in your document.

4. Now the exciting part: double-click on the spreadsheet in your PageMaker document. You will immediately see Excel and the spread-

sheet you created a moment before. Make changes to the file, and the changes immediately become apparent in your PageMaker document.

Embedding an OLE Object

To embed an OLE object, follow these steps:

1. Open the Edit pull-down menu and choose the Insert Object command. You will see the Insert Object dialog box, shown in Figure 4.25. The dialog box displays all of the OLE server applications available on your system.

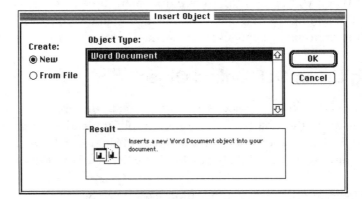

Figure 4.25 *The Insert Object dialog box.*

2. Scroll down the list of applications and double-click on the application you want to use to create the embedded object. For example, if you want to embed a scanned photograph in your document, you might double-click on **Adobe Photoshop**.

3. You will see the application you selected in the dialog box start up, and present a new, blank window. Create the object you want, or use the Open command to open the file.

4. When you are ready to embed the object, simply double-click on the application's **Close** box to close the application. The application presents a dialog box asking if you want to update the document. Click **Yes**.

5. You again will see the PageMaker document window, with the object you just created embedded in the PageMaker document. If you want to make changes to the object, double-click it and the server application immediately restarts.

To Sum Up

In Chapter 4, you've learned how easy it is to add graphics to your documents. You've seen the easy steps needed to import a wide variety of graphic formats. You've also learned that moving, sizing, cropping, and copying graphics are typically straightforward in PageMaker, as is linking or embedding OLE objects.

In the next chapter, you will practice setting up templates for a number of useful documents that will serve as master publications that you can use over and over.

CHAPTER 5

Setting Up Templates

- ✦ Setting up master page templates
- ✦ Creating a newsletter template
- ✦ Creating a fact sheet template
- ✦ Creating templates from existing documents
- ✦ To sum up

Templates save you time when doing the mundane tasks of desktop publishing. The more time you save doing the everyday chores of preparing a publication design, the more creative time you'll have to add the spark of brilliance that makes your publication unique. The real power PageMaker gives you is the ability to try before you buy: walk around in the publication for a little while, see how it fits, test the look, and feel. Take a tuck here, let a little out there, and suddenly it works. Or maybe it doesn't, in which case you've lost very little time; simply open a new file and start again.

As easy as PageMaker is in getting those initial design steps out of the way, a template makes design even easier. By making a template, you'll have to take those steps only once for each type of document. Templates are like master plans for your documents. They are created in exactly the same way as documents, using the same commands and options. Just as the Master Pages feature gives you uniformity of design, templates can offer a standardized set of designs: Large companies can use templates to ensure that forms, memos, procedural and technical manuals, and letterheads adhere to strict design standards. In a network environment, templates invite uniformity in creating departmental documents.

SETTING UP MASTER PAGE TEMPLATES

In Chapters 2 and 3, we touched on using master pages to anchor the format of all interior pages of a document. Now let's look at the Master Pages feature again, and find out exactly how it can help you to prepare a document. Master pages are an invisible formatting area that holds design elements and text to be displayed on all document pages.

For example, if you were developing a 12-page brochure, and you wanted the company name centered at the top of every page, you could:

✦ Move to the top of each page of your document; reset the rulers' zero points to measure from the top margin; pull down guidelines to set the baseline for the text; open a text block with the Text tool; specify the typeface, style, alignment, size, and leading; type the text; make some fine adjustments; add a line underneath the text for emphasis; and repeat all this 11 more times.

✦ Or you could do all of that once on each master page and then forget it.

NOTE

You can create new templates from scratch, or you can save as a template any document you have already created.

Clearly, adding repeating design elements or guidelines to the master pages can save an enormous amount of time in laying out the individual pages of a document. If you preformat the master pages and save the work as a template, you'll save even more time developing similar documents in the future. To set up a master page template:

1. Open a new document. In the Document Setup dialog box, decide whether the document will be printed on both sides and thus have facing pages, or whether it will be printed on one side only. Click the appropriate option boxes and click **OK**.

2. Move to the master pages by clicking the desired **master page** icon at the lower-left corner of the screen. In PageMaker 6.5 you may have several **master page** icons representing each of the master pages you incorporate in your publication. We'll use this feature later.

3. Open the View menu, and turn on Show Guides, Snap to Guides, and Show Rulers by clicking on the commands.

4. Choose the **File** menu and open the Preferences>General dialog box to select the measurement system you'd like for this document.

5. Choose a page view based on what you'd like to do: If you'd like to add guidelines, use the Fit in Window view (**Command/Ctrl+W**) to get a look at the overall layout of the page. If you want to add text, move up to a closer view of the page to align the type accurately.

6. Create whatever items you'd like on the master pages. If you want page numbers, add a page number marker by pressing **Command/Ctrl+Option/Alt+p** on each master page.

7. When you have finished with the master pages, you might want to lock the guidelines (**View>Lock Guides**). Click a page number to move back to the document, and check the position and look of the items you added to the master pages.

8. If all looks the way you want, save the file as a template (**File>Save**) by clicking the **Save as Template** radio button in the Save Publication dialog box. Give the template a unique file name.

You're not limited to two master pages per publication anymore. For example, you might want traditional left and right facing master pages, plus another right-facing page for a cover or first page of a chapter. Use the Master Pages palette's fly-out menu's New Master Page option to create a new page which you can modify as described above.

Creating Custom Page Sizes

There are several default Page Size options in the Document Setup dialog box. But there may be times when you need to work with an odd page size. For example:

+ If you work with magazines, you know that most are a standardized size, slightly smaller than the default 8.5 x 11 in. They generally measure 49 picas x 64 picas and 9 points.

+ If you want to bleed a graphic (a graphic bleeds when it is butted right against the edge of the page, covering the margin) printed on a laser printer, you'll need to set up a page size smaller than the standard 8.5 x 11 in. to account for the unprintable margins that almost all laser printers have.

+ If you are developing manuals that use a 5.5 x 8.5 in. format, or books (like this one) in a 6 x 9 in. format.

+ If you are producing visual aids—35 mm slides or 7 x 9 in. view foils—for a presentation.

In these examples, having a template already formatted with the correct page size and perhaps guidelines in position, can be a real time saver. To create custom page-size templates:

1. Use the Document Setup dialog box to enter the custom page specifications for each template.
2. Position basic design guidelines on the templates' master pages.
3. Save each template with a descriptive, unique file name.

Creating Custom Borders

If you have a continuing need to add jazzy borders around the pages of special documents—diplomas, forms, certificates, or invitations—adding the border to the master pages of a certificate template will save you from having to re-create the border time and again.

To create a custom border:

1. Since the border will be positioned outside the text margins, be sure to set wide-enough margins in the Document Setup dialog box.

2. Choose the master page for the document and select the **Fit in Window** view.

3. Choose the **Box** tool and draw a border, evenly spaced around the outside of the page margins.

4. With the border selected, choose a line weight or style from the Stroke submenu (**Element>Stroke**).

5. To make a fancier border, copy the border by selecting it with the Pointer tool and choosing the **Copy** command on the Edit menu. Then paste the copied border on top of the one you just drew by choosing **Paste** on the Edit menu.

6. Stretch the second border by clicking on the corner sizing handles and enlarging the border slightly more than the first. While it is still selected, give it a novel style using the Stroke submenu.

The result could look something like Figure 5.1, in which a frame was made using a dotted-line border with a double-line border on either side of it.

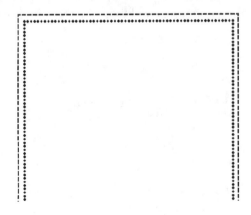

Figure 5.1 *A unique border created with boxes in different style line patterns.*

Creating Custom Forms

Although PageMaker was not developed specifically for designing forms, it's quite versatile. In fact, I know of at least one business, in Orlando, that does nothing but design and produce custom forms with PageMaker. The great thing about doing forms in PageMaker is that you're not limited in any way—you have complete freedom of design.

Guidelines are the key to professional looking forms. They help you to align the many lines and small text blocks that always seem to appear on forms. Use the master pages to hold guidelines and standardized text. With one form template, for instance, you can set up different forms for timesheets, invoices, and purchase orders. Here's how:

1. Position the company logo, name, and address in the upper-left corner of the master page.

2. Add guidelines in the top center of the page to designate an area for the form's title.

3. Pull down three guidelines to mark off an area in the upper-right corner for the date, name of department/client/buyer, name of supervisor/employee, and week ending date/account number.

4. Add enough horizontal and vertical guidelines to accommodate the employee timesheet, which has the most lines of the three forms. The same guidelines will allow you to lay out the invoice and purchase order. The top of the master page will look like the one shown in Figure 5.2.

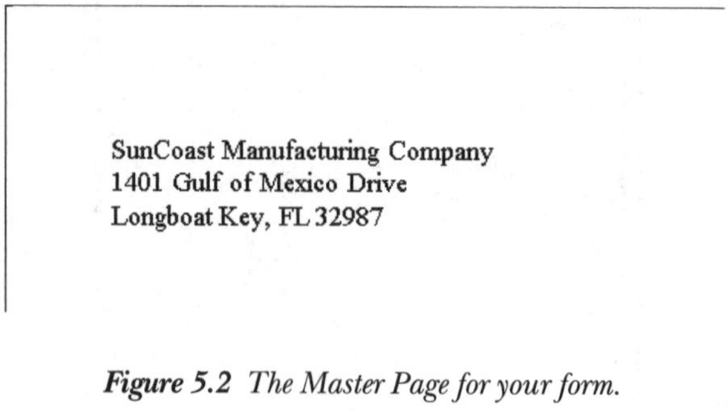

SunCoast Manufacturing Company
1401 Gulf of Mexico Drive
Longboat Key, FL 32987

Figure 5.2 *The Master Page for your form.*

5. In the bottom margin of the master page, designate an area with guidelines for the form number and add the text Form # in front of the area.

6. Save the template with a unique file name.

Now you're ready to create an employee timesheet on page 1, a company invoice on page 2, and a company purchase order on page 3. Open the template as a document and get started. The results could look like Figures 5.3, 5.4, and 5.5. Notice that all three forms share most of the same master page guidelines.

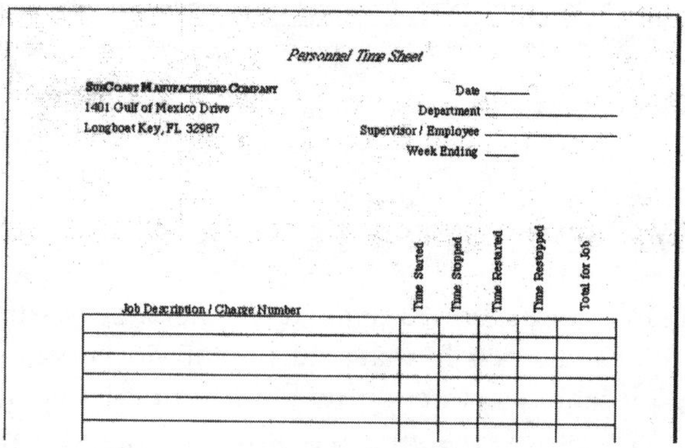

Figure 5.3 *First form: a personnel timesheet.*

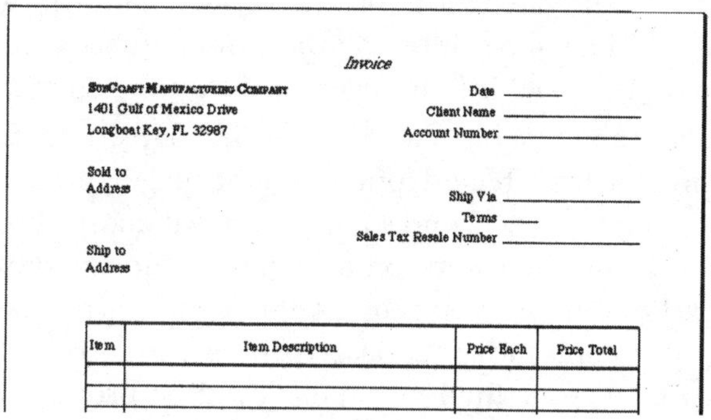

Figure 5.4 *Second form: A company invoice.*

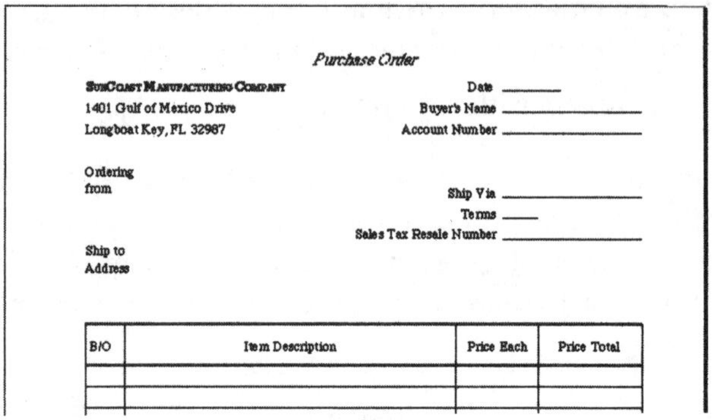

Purchase Order

SunCoast Manufacturing Company
1401 Gulf of Mexico Drive
Longboat Key, FL 32987

Date ______
Buyer's Name ______
Account Number ______

Ordering from

Ship Via ______
Terms ______
Sales Tax Resale Number ______

Ship to Address

B/O	Item Description	Price Each	Price Total

Figure 5.5 Third form: A company purchase order.

Creating a Newsletter Template

You can use the interior pages of a template in the same way that you use the master pages. You can literally format a document without entering a word of text by locating placeholders where you want text or graphics to go.

My experience indicates that there are two kinds of newsletters: those that need to be produced quickly because the material is timely, and those that are more sales-and market-driven, and you can spend a world of money and time producing them. We'll concentrate on the former. The typical newsletter is generally an 11 x 17 in. page printed on the front and back and folded to 8.5 x 11. This configuration yields four pages, as shown in Figure 5.6.

To add two more pages, print an 8.5 x 11 in. page on the front and back, and insert it inside the fold. To add four additional pages, print another 11 x 17 in. page on the front and back, and so on. If you will have a PostScript service bureau output your finished work on a high-resolution phototypesetter that can handle 11 x 17 in. paper, you can configure your PageMaker file for 11 x 17 and print proof copies on your laser printer reduced 77% (to give you about 8.5 x 11 in.). If your final mechanical will be produced by your laser printer (which probably can't handle paper as large as 11 x 17), then configure your page size as 8.5 x 11 in. in the Document Setup dialog box and check the **Double-Sided** and **Facing Pages** option boxes. You will have to do a little paste-up work to set up the pages to print on 11 x 17 in. paper, but you'll save money in doing the setup for your commercial printer.

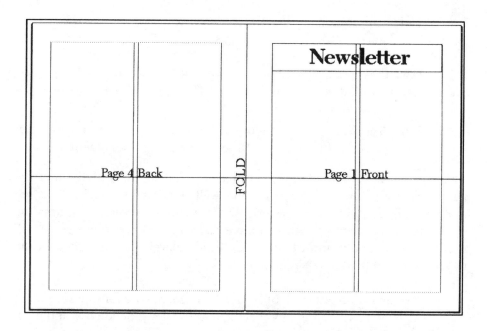

Figure 5.6 *Thumbnails of the front and back of a four-page, 8.5 x 11 in. newsletter.*

Setting Up an 11 x 17 in. Format

Setting up the newsletter template at the actual size of the page is handy because your commercial printer doesn't have to paste up any pages to shoot negatives; the work is camera ready. The only tricky part is adding an extra column that will simulate the fold between pages and the inside margins on either side of the fold. Here's how to do it:

1. Choose the **File** pull-down menu, and choose a **New** document to display the Document Setup dialog box.

2. Select **Tabloid** in the Page pop-up list (or enter the values **17** and **11** in the Page Dimensions text boxes) and click the **Wide** check box.

3. Enter a reasonable margin size, but make the left and right margin values the same. Click **OK** to move to your document.

4. Change the measurement system to picas by choosing the **File** pull-down menu and selecting **Preferences>General**.

Now let's add columns to the page. Remember, one of the columns will actually act as a margin area between the two pages.

1. Click the **master pages** icon to move to the master pages. Choose the **Layout** pull-down menu and click **Column Guides** to display the Column Guides dialog box.

2. Enter **5** as the number of columns. Leave the default spacing between columns set to **1** pica. Click **OK** to return to your document.

The page is now formatted with five equally spaced columns (defined by the left page margin, four column guides that we'll number 1 through 4 from left to right, and the right page margin). What we want to do next is to drag the four column guides to establish four equally spaced columns, which will squeeze the middle column to act as an inside margin for each page of the two-page spread that we're simulating.

1. Working from left to right across the page, first establish a zero point at the left page margin by clicking in the **Ruler Junction** box and dragging the vertical ruler's zero point to align with the left margin.

2. Drag the number 1 column guide to the right, aligning the left edge of the first column guide with the 18-pica mark on the ruler (the line measure for all columns will be 18 picas). Now, reposition the vertical ruler's zero mark to align on the right edge of the number 1 column guide (to give an accurate measurement of the number 2 column's width).

3. Move the pointer over to the number 2 column guide and drag the guide to align the left edge of the column guide with the 18-pica mark on the ruler. You now have two equal columns for one of the two pages.

4. Drag the vertical ruler's zero point all the way across the page to the right page margin.

5. Drag the number 4 column guide to the left to line up the right edge of the column guide with the 18-pica mark on the ruler. Reposition the vertical ruler's zero mark to align to the left edge of the number 4 column guide.

6. Drag the number 3 column guide to line up the right edge of the column guide with the 18-pica mark on the ruler.

Now you have four equally spaced columns on the two-page spread and a narrower column in the middle. All you have left to do is find the middle of the narrow column and mark the middle with a guideline. To do this:

1. Realign the vertical ruler's zero point with the right edge of the number 2 column guide (the left side of the narrow, middle column). The left edge of the number 3 column guide (the right side of the narrow column) will be resting on the 14-pica mark on the ruler. Just take half the measurement, which is 7 picas.

2. Drag a guideline out of the vertical ruler and align it on the 7 pica mark on the ruler. This guideline is the fold mark for your two-page spread, as shown in Figure 5.7.

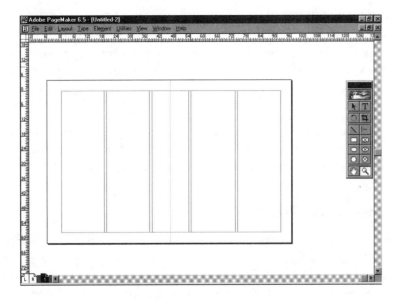

Figure 5.7 Column guides aligned for a two-column, 11 x 17 in. format newsletter.

Now that you've done it the hard way, here's an easier way to adjust the column guides. After you initially set up your five columns, position the vertical ruler's zero point on the left page margin. Then set the columns on your master pages to the following positions:

+ Set the left edge of the first column guide at **18** picas.
+ Set the left edge of the second column guide at **37** picas.
+ Set the center guideline at **45** picas.
+ Set the left edge of the third column guide at **52** picas.
+ Set the left edge of the fourth column guide at **71** picas.

I walked you through the longer process first to give you some practice realigning the ruler and measuring with the ruler.

Setting Up an 8.5 x 11 in. Format

To set up your newsletter template in an 8.5 x 11 in. format:

1. Choose **New** from the File pull-down menu to open the Document Setup dialog box.

2. In the Document Setup dialog box, create 8.5 x 11 in. facing pages, to be printed front and back, with equal width inside and outside margins.

3. To work in picas here as well, choose the **Preferences>General** dialog box (on the File menu) and choose **Picas** as the measurement system.

4. Click the **master pages** icon to move to the master pages of your document.

5. Format the document in two columns by choosing **Column Guides** (**Layout>Column Guides**). Enter **2** in the **Number of Columns** text box. Leave the default space between columns alone.

Setting Up the Front Page

The front page of your newsletter sets the tone for the publication. Is it serious or casual? Witty or strictly informative? Conservative or brassy? The impression made by the newsletter will also spill over to the company or organization it represents. Some of the design considerations for the front page include developing the masthead or nameplate, balancing the design, and setting the column width. Let's look at each of these separately.

Developing the Masthead

The most prominent element on the front page of any newsletter is the newsletter's title, sometimes called the masthead or nameplate. The masthead can be composed of a logotype, meaning the type characters making up the masthead name have the look of a logo—either through originally designed type or characters altered to give a proprietary look. Adobe Type Align, Adobe FreeHand, or Ares FontMonger are just some of the programs capable of altering the shape and baseline of type characters for a masthead logotype. You can also do a lot with PageMaker simply by adjusting the leading, tracking, and width of characters. The logotype for the masthead should be bold enough to support the size of any border that is around it. If not, the characters wind up looking anemic, as shown in the top example in Figure 5.8. In the bottom example, the same word is shown in a much better format.

Masthead
Masthead

Figure 5.8 *Helvetica 60 point type isn't strong enough to fill the border for this newsletter's masthead. In the bottom example, Gill Sans Ultra Bold is set in 72 points at 110% width, which nicely fills the space.*

To add a traditional masthead border and logotype to your front page:

1. Move to the first page of your document, not the master page. Choose a page view so that you can easily see its full width.

2. Select the **Box** tool from the toolbox. Position the crosshairs in the upper-left corner of the page margin, and drag out a box the width of the margins and several inches deep.

3. Select the **Text** tool from the toolbox. Position the insertion point in the upper-left corner of the box and drag open a text block almost as large as the border you just created.

4. Select an appropriate typeface for the masthead logotype, using the Type menu, or the Text Control palette.

5. Once the masthead name is typed in the box, center it by highlighting the name and pressing **Command/Ctrl+Shift+C**, and use the Text control palette to alter the type to your satisfaction.

Balancing the Design

Not only does the masthead logotype need to be large enough to fill the border around it, the border itself needs to be sized to balance the rest of the page. Figure 5.9 shows what a difference a properly sized masthead can make.

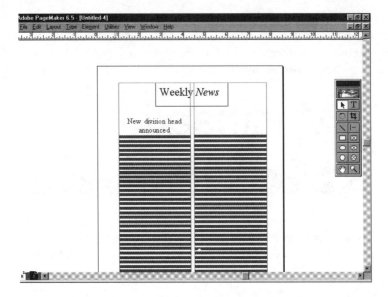

Figure 5.9 *The larger, bolder masthead and headline in the right-hand example demand attention and help to balance the columns of text.*

To quickly change the weight, style, leading, or other specifications of the logo-type or headlines:

1. Highlight the text with the Text tool.

2. Use the PageMaker shortcut **Command/Ctrl+T** to display the Character Specifications dialog box. Try a change to one of the specifications—for example, the type style—and choose **OK**.

3. The changes made in the dialog box are reflected in the type, which remains highlighted. To make an additional change, simply press **Command/Ctrl+T** to redisplay the Character Specifications dialog box and try another modification.

Setting the Column Width

A typical newsletter consists of two equally spaced columns. The easiest way to dress up this kind of page would be to move a column guide, giving the page uneven-width columns. Use the wide column to add prominence to the lead story. Use the narrow column to hold recurring items, like a table of contents, a meeting place box, a guest speaker box, a list of officers box, and so forth. To create unequal-width columns:

1. Move to the first page of your document.
2. Select the **Pointer** tool from the tool box and grab the column guide.
3. Drag the guide to the left 6 picas, giving you a left column 12 picas wide and a right column 24 picas wide.

In this kind of format, the left column is usually the narrow one. Your page should resemble Figure 5.10.

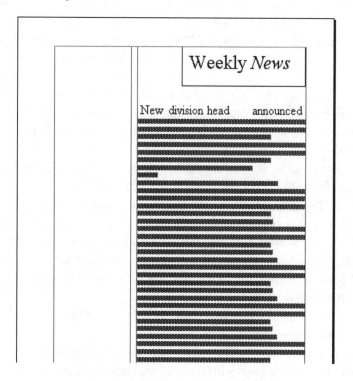

Figure 5.10 *The column guide moved to create a narrow and wide column.*

Adding a Recurring Initial Drop Cap

Any recurring item in your newsletter can be added to the newsletter template. In fact, the more you add to the template, the less work you'll have when you create each issue. For this reason, let's add an initial drop cap to the first character of the page-1 story. Here's how:

1. Place a column of text on the page to fill the right column (**File>Place**). You can use any text or nonsense text supplied by PageMaker in the lesson folders.

2. Use the Text tool to highlight the first letter of the story (it doesn't matter what the letter is, since you're going to change it in each issue).

3. Cut the letter from the text. Move to an area in the left column and drag-paste the letter—hold down the mouse button and drag open a text box. Release the mouse button and press **Command/Ctrl+V** to paste the letter.

4. Highlight the letter with the Text tool and increase its size to 48 points (press **Command/Ctrl+T** to display the Character Specifications dialog box).

5. Select the letter with the Pointer tool, and narrow the text block until it is only slightly wider than the letter (click the lower-right sizing handle and drag to the left until it is almost even with the right edge of the letter).

6. Drag the letter into position on top of the text in the right column, and align the top of the letter with the top of the text.

7. Press **Command/Ctrl+W** to choose the **Fit in Window** view. Click the column of text with the Pointer tool to select it. Click the bottom windowshade handle and drag it up to cover the top windowshade handle.

8. Click the **down arrow** key in the bottom windowshade handle and drag-place a new text block, butting up to the right edge of the initial cap and as deep as the cap.

9. Pull down a guideline from the top ruler, and align it to the bottom of the windowshade.

10. Click the bottom windowshade handle and drag-place the remaining text so that it is even with the left- and right-column margins.

When you're ready to open the template as a document and start your first issue, use the **Replace Entire Story** option in the Replace File dialog box (see the "Replacing Template Stories" section, later in this chapter).

Adding an Events Calendar

An events calendar doesn't have to be elaborate; it can simply consist of some events and dates set up in the narrow left column. To make one, do the following:

1. Select the **Box** tool.

2. Position the crosshairs in the upper-left corner of the narrow column. Click and drag the crosshairs to draw a box, margin to margin, several inches deep.

3. Select the **Text** tool, click the tool in the upper-left corner of the box, and drag open a text block.

4. Press **Command/Ctrl+T** to open the Character Specifications dialog box. Then choose a typeface and type style for the events calendar.

5. Set up a right-aligned tab at the right edge of the box by choosing the **Type** pull-down menu and selecting **Indents/Tabs** to display the Indents/Tabs dialog box. Click the **right-align tab** icon and click its position on the ruler. Click **OK** to move back to your document.

6. Give the box a title. Highlight the title with the Text tool and use the PageMaker shortcut **Command/Ctrl+Shift+C** to center the title on the line.

7. Press **Return** to move down a line, then type an event. Press **Tab** to move to the right-aligned tab stop, then type the date. Notice that the date fills to the left. Add as many events and dates as you need. When you open the template as a document to produce an issue of the newsletter, use the Text tool to highlight an event and date you'd like to change; then type the new event and date. The finished event calendar will look like the one shown in Figure 5.11.

Figure 5.11 Finished events calendar.

You can also add a date and an issue and volume number placeholder to your newsletter. The number of years a newsletter has been in publication is its volume number. That is, all issues in the first year of publication are part of Volume 1, those in the second year are Volume 2, and so forth. The issue is determined by the number of newsletters published in that year. For instance, if the newsletter is produced monthly, the January issue is number 1, the December issue is number 12. If the newsletter is biweekly, the last publication in December is number 26. To change the date, volume number, or issue number for each issue of your newsletter:

1. Use the Text tool to highlight the information you wish to replace.

2. Type the new information.

Setting Up Interior Pages

The inside pages are set up in the template in the same way as the front page. Add text or graphics as placeholders for real text or graphics. If you have recurring headings in each issue—different departments, perhaps—set up the heads in the template. If you regularly devote a page to employee photos, set up the borders for the photos in the template. Then when you place the pictures, you can size or crop them to fit the borders.

CREATING A FACT SHEET TEMPLATE

Simple two-color fact sheets, printed front and back, are the mainstay of many marketing efforts. Some fact sheets include photos, some don't, depending on the production budget. Whether they have photos or not, they generally share a common structure, which makes them good candidates for templates. Regardless of the specifics, most fact sheets will contain the following:

✦ Company name and address, product name, product model number

✦ Overall introduction to the product, that is, what does it do, how does it do it

✦ Sales rationale for buying the product

✦ Specific advantages of this product

✦ Technical details

✦ Specifications such as weight, size, and voltage

You may not know yet how much room each of these areas will require—or even if you'll include all of these areas—but we can still lay out a basic template.

Adding the Product Name

Let's start with the product name header.

1. First, define a new document with two facing pages, front and back.

2. Move to the right master page (the front page of the fact sheet). Open the Layout>Column Guides dialog box, and give the template a two-column format.

3. Move to the top of the page, pull down a guideline from the top ruler, and position it about a half inch under the top margin. This area will hold the product name.

4. To preformat the name, select the **Text** tool and drag open a text block in the upper-left corner, right above the guideline you just positioned.

5. Press **Command/Ctrl+T** to open the Character Specifications dialog box. Select a 36-point bold typeface for the product name (you'll probably change these specs when you open this template to create a real fact sheet).

6. Type **Product Name** in the text block.

7. Now open a similar text block on the same guideline near the right margin. Choose the same typeface and style, but select 18 points for the type size.

8. Type **Model No.** or **Version No.** on the guideline. The top of your fact sheet template should look like Figure 5.12.

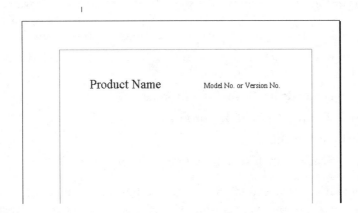

Figure 5.12 *The product name and model number added to the top of the fact sheet template.*

Before you do anything else, choose the **Select All** command from the Edit pull-down menu to select everything you've just done. Now copy it to the Clipboard, move the Text tool insertion point above the page onto the pasteboard, and click once. Choose **Paste** to paste a copy of the header above the page. You'll see why in a minute.

Adding the Introduction and Features Area

The next steps designate areas on page 1 (the front of the fact sheet) for a product introduction and a general discussion of the product's features.

1. Add a horizontal guideline about a third of the way down the page. The area between the line under the product name and this line will be for a product introduction. The area below the line will contain product features.

2. Choose the **Box** tool and position the crosshairs in the upper-left corner of the area above the guideline you just added. Draw a border around the area, as shown in Figure 5.13.

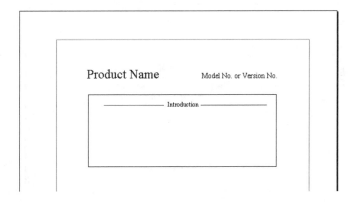

Product Name   Model No. or Version No.

—————————— Introduction ——————————

Figure 5.13 *An example of formatting for the introduction area of the fact sheet template.*

3. Choose the **Text** tool and drag open a text block at the top of the introduction area.

4. Press **Command/Ctrl+T** to display the Character Specifications dialog box, and format the type for the word Introduction. In the example, I selected an 18-point typeface with loose tracking.

5. Draw a box around the word. Choose **No Line** from the Element>Stroke submenu and **Paper** from the Element>Fill submenu. Move the box behind the word by pressing **Command/Ctrl+B**.

6. Add a 1-point line across the width of the box, and through the middle of the word Introduction. Move the line behind it and the box by selecting the line with the Pointer tool and pressing **Command/Ctrl+B**. Your page should look like the one shown in Figure 5.13.

7. Let's add a drop shadow to the box. Choose the **Pointer** tool and select the box by clicking on it. Fill in the box as **Paper** from the Element>Fill submenu.

8. The white-filled box has covered the word Introduction. While the box is still selected, move the filled box behind the type by pressing **Command/Ctrl+B**. Now the word is displayed.

9. Choose **Copy** to copy the box to the Clipboard, and **Paste** to paste the copy on top of the original (it will be offset a bit down and to the right). Move it behind the original box by pressing **Command/Ctrl+B** again.

10. Now fill the box by choosing **Solid** from the Element>Fill submenu. The introduction box should look like the one shown in Figure 5.14.

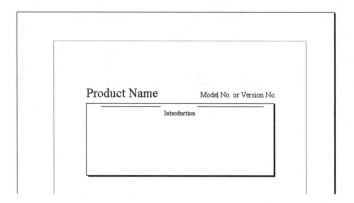

Figure 5.14 *A drop shadow added to the Introduction box.*

Follow the same steps to add a second box starting just below the introduction and ending just above the bottom margin. Add a drop shadow to the second box, and the headline Features in the same type specifications as the Introduction headline. Your page should be similar to the one shown in Figure 5.15.

Figure 5.15 *The completed front page of a fact sheet template.*

Adding the Specifications Area

Designating the back of the fact sheet as the area for detailed specifications is useful for two reasons. Those wanting only a cursory glance at the fact sheet needn't wade through a lot of technical jargon to understand what the product does; they can simply read the introduction or features material on the front. Giving the whole back page over to technical specifications allows all the room you will probably need to provide a detailed technical description.

To add a specifications area:

1. Click the left **master page** icon (the back of the fact sheet).

2. Choose **Select All** to select all of the header above the page on the pasteboard. Using the Pointer tool, click on the line outside the area of one of the sizing handles. The pointer will change to a four-pointed arrow. When everything is selected using the **Select All** command, dragging any one component moves all of the selected components. Drag the whole header down onto the page, aligning it to the left and right margins and the top page margin.

3. Choose the **Box** tool and draw a box the width and height of the margins.

4. Press **Command/Ctrl+T** to display the Character Specifications dialog box, and format the type for the word Specifications. In the example, I selected an 18-point typeface in small caps with loose tracking.

5. Add the word to the top center of the specifications box.

Adding the Company Name/Address Area

The company name and address can fit easily below the bottom margin. Remember to include the mailing address and a telephone number. You could also include a general disclaimer stating that specifications are subject to change without notice. Finally, you may want to include a copyright notice (the copyright symbol is Option/Alt+g).

CREATING TEMPLATES FROM EXISTING DOCUMENTS

As mentioned earlier in this chapter, you can create a template from an existing document by saving the document as a template (**File>Save As**). Simply choose the **Save As Template** radio button in the Save Publication As dialog box. PageMaker then saves a copy of your document as a new template. The template contains every element of the original document, including the same number of pages, the same font selections and type styles, and the same guidelines. Having saved the document as a template, you can now open the template as a new document and customize it for your needs. Say, for example, that you have completed the first issue of a 12-page newsletter (January Newsletter) and saved the file as a template. Next month, when you want to produce issue number two, simply open the template as a file and save it as February Newsletter.

Replacing Template Stories

Once they are saved as a template, it's very easy to swap the existing stories and graphics with new stories and graphics needed for the new publication. Here's how:

1. Using the Pointer tool, select the first story you want to replace.

2. Choose the **File** pull-down menu and choose **Place** to display the Place Document dialog box, shown in Figure 5.16.

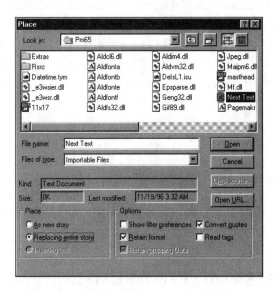

Figure 5.16 *The Place Document dialog box.*

3. Click the file name for the new story and click the **Replacing Entire Story** radio button.

4. Click the **Retain Format** check box if you want to retain the character and paragraph formatting and any style sheets assigned to the text in your word processor. If you do not check the Retain Format box, PageMaker imports the text and assigns the default type font and style to the text.

5. Choose **OK** to return to your document.

The entire story will be replaced by the new story you selected in the Page File dialog box. If the original story was longer than one page, even though it wasn't selected on additional pages, all of the pages of the story will be replaced.

Replacing Template Graphics

You can do the same thing when replacing a graphic:

1. Using the Pointer tool, select the graphic you want to replace.

2. Choose the **File** pull-down menu and choose **Place** to display the Place Document dialog box.

3. Click the file name for the graphic and click the **Replacing Entire Graphic** radio button. Choose **OK** to return to your document.

The original graphic will be replaced by the graphic file you selected in the Place File dialog box.

To replace the original headlines, bylines, photo credit lines, and other small text blocks, highlight the text block with the Text tool and type in the new text. When you begin typing, all of the highlighted text will be deleted, but the text you enter will retain all of the type specifications of the original type.

Multiple Masters

In this case, "multiple masters" doesn't refer to the Adobe PostScript font technology which allows the same basic typeface to serve as a "master" for many variant fonts. While we concentrated on a simple two-page spread with just left- and right-facing master pages, you'll also want to learn about PageMaker's ability to include an effectively unlimited number of different master pages in a publication. In truth, you're limited to about 256 master pages, but you'd obviously need a publication with more than 256 pages—each different—to exceed that limit.

As mentioned earlier in this chapter, you can use alternate master pages to give facing pages quite different formats, or to insert a page with a special format within a publication. This next section will show you how to work with PageMaker 6.5's extended master page capabilities.

Creating a New Master Page

You can create a new master page from scratch, or by saving a master page from an existing publication as a new template. To build a new master page, follow these steps:

1. Open a new document.

2. From the Window menu, choose **Master Pages**. The Master Page palette, shown in Figure 5.17, will appear. Select **New Master** from the drop-down menu on the palette.

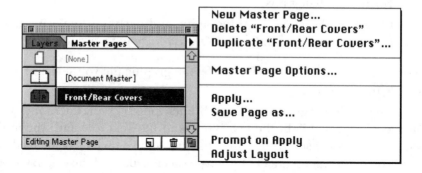

Figure 5.17   *Master Page palette.*

3. When the Create New Master Page dialog box (shown in Figure 5.18), appears, type in a name for the new page.

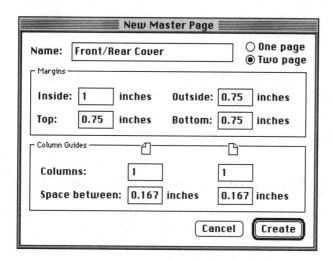

Figure 5.18 *Create New Master Page dialog box.*

4. Enter the margins, number of columns, and the intercolumn spacing you want for the new master. Click on the **One Page** or **Two Page** radio buttons (an option that appears only if your publication is double-sided).

5. When you're finished, click on the **Create** button to store your new master to disk.

Saving an Existing Page as a Master

You can select a page or master page in an existing publication and save it as a master for reuse. Because the procedures are almost identical, I'll use one set of instructions for both. Just follow these steps:

1. Load the publication containing the master page or page you wish to save.

2. If the Master Pages palette is not visible, go to the Window menu and select **Master Pages**.

3. To copy a current master page, select **Duplicate** from the drop-down menu on the Master Pages palette. To save a particular page layout as a new master page, select **Save Page As** from the palette menu instead.

4. Type in a name for the new master, then click on **Duplicate** or **Save**, respectively, to store the new master page to your disk.

Applying Pages from Your Master Page Library

Once you've developed a library of master pages, you can easily apply any of them to specific pages or a range of pages in your publication. Keep in mind that the new master may have different margins and columns from the specifications originally applied to the page you are changing, so you may have to reposition graphic objects and text on the revamped page.

Changing Pages

You can apply a new master to an existing page, or left- and right-facing spread, just by putting the page you want to change, and clicking on the name of the master page you want to apply (or its icon) in the Master Pages palette. You can also apply a new master to a range of pages in a publication. Just follow these steps.

1. If the Master Pages palette is not visible, open it by selecting **Master Pages** from the Windows palette.

2. Select **Apply** from the Master Pages palette's drop-down menu. The Apply Master dialog box (shown in Figure 5.19) will appear.

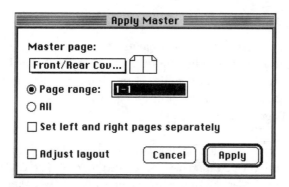

Figure 5.19 *Apply Master dialog box.*

3. Choose the master page you want to apply, and type in the range of pages. You can separate a range of pages with a hyphen (e.g., 8-15), or type commas between individual pages you want to include (e.g., 4,6,8,12,14). A hyphen following the last number in a series indicates that all following pages will be included: 4,5,9,12-, for example, would apply to pages 4, 5, 9, and from page 12 to the end of the publication.

4. You can click in the **Set left and right pages separately** check box to specify left- and right-facing pages separately. However, while you may use different master pages, the page range applies to both.

5. Click the **Adjust layout** box to apply any formatting changes from the new master page to the pages you are applying it to. By default, PageMaker won't move any existing objects on a page when you apply a new Master, unless you check this box.

6. Click on **Apply** to use the new masters.

Modifying Master Pages

To change or add text, guides, or objects on a master page, just display the page you want to modify by clicking on its icon in the lower left-hand corner of the document window, and make your changes. To modify margins or columns, or to change the name of the master page, use the **Setup** command on the Master Pages palette.

N O T E

Take advantage of the Guide Manager to create libraries of guides, which you can reuse when creating new Master Pages. You'll find Grid Manager, shown in Figure 5.20, in the Utilities menu, under PageMaker Plug-ins.

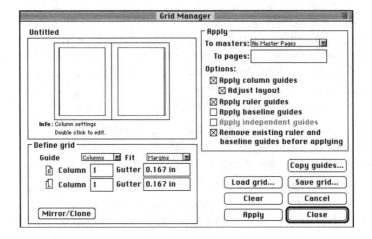

Figure 5.20 *The Guide Manager.*

TO SUM UP

In this chapter, you've learned how to use templates to save time and effort in developing recurring documents. You've seen how to set up multiple-form templates, and you've had a close-up look at developing a fact sheet template.

In the next chapter, you'll learn about another important PageMaker timesaver: styles.

CHAPTER 6

Setting Up Custom Styles

- ✦ Defining styles
- ✦ Applying styles to text
- ✦ To sum up

A *style* is simply a way to automate the formatting of text so that if you decide to change the formatting, you need only change the style, not each occurrence of the text that is in the style. Say, for example, you compose a multiple-page document in PageMaker and then decide you want to change the typeface of the body text. Without using a style, you would have to highlight each paragraph individually, invoke the Character Specifications dialog box, choose the new typeface, and click **OK** to return to the document. This could get tiresome after about the third paragraph. If you had used a style called Body Copy, you could simply change the typeface portion of the style specification—all the text marked with the Body Copy style would change automatically.

But styles don't apply only to body copy; they can be applied to any sort of characters on the page:

✦ **Headline or heading styles**. Set up each level of headline or each heading as an individual style so that you can make document-wide changes to the headings.

✦ **Logotype or special name styles**. Using a style for a product or company logotype means that you don't have to finalize the type before using it in the document. If you or your client decide on a different look for the logotype, all you have to do is change the style.

✦ **Header and footer styles**. Header and footer styles ensure consistency. You can set up other styles within a header or footer style (a page number style and a book title style, for example).

✦ **Bullet styles for lists**. Bullets are not simply round spots anymore. You can use a style to format square- or diamond-shaped bullets, in drop-shadow or outline, perhaps.

✦ **Text in bulleted or numbered lists**. Often the text in a list is formatted different from normal body copy. For example, body copy might be left-aligned to give a ragged right margin, but the text in lists might be justified. Applying a style to list text means there's one less thing you have to remember when formatting your document.

✦ **Drop cap or initial cap styles**. Setting up the drop cap as a style means you won't find yourself thinking, "Was that a 37-point cap or a 59-point cap the last time? I'd better go back and check." Again, one change to the style changes all drop caps in the document.

✦ **Byline styles**. Bylines may seem like a trivial matter, but in a large publication, finding them all and changing them to some other specification is not a trivial task.

✦ **Jump page callouts, photo credits, figure captions, footnotes, tables of contents, and index entries**. All of these should be formatted as styles rather than as individual text.

Styles are also used in the PageMaker 6.5's HTML publishing capabilities, discussed in more detail in Chapter 12, so you can quickly assign titles, subhead levels, and other text classifications to World Wide Web pages designed for use over the Internet.

N O T E

As you can see, there should be no characters in a lengthy document that are not assigned a style. The reason is threefold. First, it takes less time to format a style for a group of characters than to format the characters themselves. Second, when every group of characters is in a style, you won't miss anything when it comes time to change the character specifications. Third, when sending your completed document to a service bureau for high-resolution output, you will need to tell them all the fonts used in the publication. It's a lot easier to look through your styles to see the different fonts than to search through your document manually.

DEFINING STYLES

PageMaker styles are an integral part of the document for which they're created. When you copy a document, you automatically copy the styles. You can't see the styles without the accompanying document, but there is a way to copy the styles of one document to use as the basis for the styles of another.

PageMaker comes with six styles already defined. Any time you create a new document, these styles are available for your immediate use. You can alter the default styles and create new ones to customize certain publications, as we'll learn. To create a new style or alter an existing one, choose the **Type** pull-down menu and choose **Define Styles**. You will see the Define Styles dialog box, as shown in Figure 6.1.

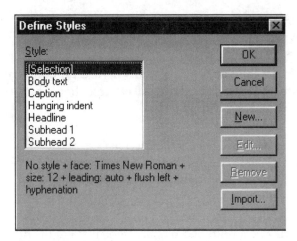

Figure 6.1 *The Define Styles dialog box.*

Use the Define Styles dialog box to create, change, and delete styles. Notice the six PageMaker default styles. The dialog box leads to the following functions:

✦ **New**. Choose this button to display the Edit Styles dialog box, allowing you to create a new style for this document.

✦ **Edit**. Click one of the existing styles and choose this button to display the Edit Styles dialog box. You'll be able to change the individual specifications tied to this style.

✦ **Remove**. Click on one of the existing styles and choose this button to remove it from this document. Removing a default style from the current document does not erase it from new documents you create in the future.

✦ **Import**. Click this button to display the Import Styles dialog box. Choose the document that contains the style(s) you want to add to the current document and click **OK** to copy the styles.

Creating New Styles

Let's set up a new style for a newsletter. We'll create a headline style using the Define Styles dialog box. Here's how:

1. Choose the **Type** pull-down menu and choose **Define Styles**.
2. In the Define Styles dialog box, click the **New** button to display the Edit Styles dialog box, shown in Figure 6.2.

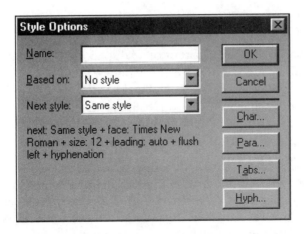

Figure 6.2 *The Edit Styles dialog box.*

3. Enter a descriptive name for the style—up to 17 characters—in the Name text box.

4. If you want to base the new style on an existing style in this document, click the **Based On** pop-up list and select the style name. The attributes of the style you select will be applied to the new style. You can then change any of the attributes to make the new style different. Otherwise, click the **Based On** pop-up list and choose **No Style**, indicating that the new style will not be based on any existing style.

5. For this example, let's base the style on the existing headline style. Click the pop-up list and choose **Headline**.

6. Click the **Next Style** pop-up list. You have three options with this list box:

    ✦ If you'd like the style you are creating to always be followed by a certain style, choose the name of that style from the list. For example, if you'd like the body text style to always follow the headline style, choose **Body Text**. Then whenever you format a headline in your document in the headline style and press **Return**, the text that follows will always appear in the body text style.

    ✦ If you don't want a style to always follow the current style, choose **No Style** from the list. After typing text formatted in this style and pressing **Return**, the text that follows will not be formatted in a style.

    ✦ If you want the paragraph that follows the current style to be formatted the same (as with body copy, for example), choose **Same Style** from the list.

7. Now decide what formatting specifications you want to add to this style. Choose:

✦ **Char**—Click the **Char** button to display the Character Specifications dialog box. Configure the typeface, size, leading, style, width, tracking, case, and so forth for the type in this style. Then open the Options dialog box, if you wish, to change type option values, such as the size and position of subscript or superscript type. Click **OK** or press **Return** to accept the specifications and return to the Edit Style dialog box.

✦ **Para**—Click this button to display the Paragraph Specifications dialog box. Set up the paragraph indents, spacing, alignment, and options for this style. You can also move to the Rules dialog box and the Spacing dialog box to further define how paragraphs in this style will be formatted. Click **OK** or press **Return** to accept the specifications and return to the Edit Style dialog box. If you are creating styles for a publication that will have a table of contents, click the **Include in Table of Contents** check box for all heading and subheading styles to automatically generate the table of contents entries.

✦ **Tabs**—Click the **Tabs** button to display the Indents/Tabs dialog box. Set up tab stops, choose tab alignments, and add leader tabs, if you wish. Click **OK** or press **Return** to accept the specifications and return to the Edit Style dialog box.

✦ **Hyph**—Click the **Hyphenation** button to display the Hyphenation dialog box. Set up hyphenation parameters for this style, if pertinent. Click **OK** or press **Return** to accept the parameters and return to the Edit Style dialog box.

8. For the style specifications to take effect, you must click **OK** or press **Return** to leave the Edit Styles dialog box. To leave the dialog box without saving the style, choose **Cancel**.

9. Now that you're back in the Edit Styles dialog box, click **OK** or press **Return** to return to your document.

Editing Styles

Editing styles is done in exactly the same manner as creating styles. Open the Define Styles dialog box, select the style you want to edit from the Style list box, and click the **Edit** button (it will be dimmed until you select a style). PageMaker displays the Edit Style dialog box. Choose from among the Type, Para, Tabs, and Hyph buttons to change whichever style specifications you'd like. Click **OK** or press **Return** when you're finished.

Removing Styles

The Remove button does just what it says. There's no additional dialog box and no warning that you're about to remove a style. To remove a style:

1. Choose the **Type** pull-down menu and select **Define Styles**.
2. In the Define Styles dialog box, select the style that you'd like to remove.
3. Click the **Remove** button. The style will be deleted from the Style list box and removed from your document. Any text that had already been formatted with the removed style will retain its formatting, but will be marked No Style. Any styles that were based on the style you removed will now be based on No Style. Also, any style that was set up so that the removed style followed it (defined as the *Next Style*) will now be followed by No Style.

Removing one of the default styles from a particular publication does not remove it from the PageMaker default style sheet in future documents.

N O T E

Copying Styles

You can use any style you've created in one document by copying that document's styles into the current document. Here's how:

1. Choose the **Type** pull-down menu and choose **Define Styles**.
2. Click the **Import** button to display the Import Styles dialog box, shown in Figure 6.3.

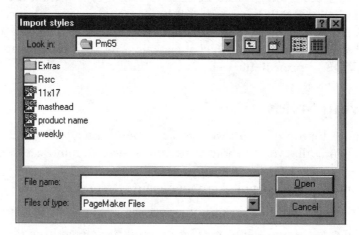

Figure 6.3 *The Import Styles dialog box.*

3. Choose the PageMaker document that contains the style(s) you want to copy into the current document.
4. Click **OK** or press **Return** to return to the Define Styles dialog box. The styles in the document you just selected will be added to the styles in the Style list box. Click **OK** or press **Return** to return to your document.

APPLYING STYLES TO TEXT

There are two ways to apply styles to your text: by using the Styles palette or by selecting the style from the Style submenu. To use the palette, choose the **Window** pull-down menu and choose **Styles palette**. The palette will be displayed under the toolbox on the right side of the document window. To display the Style submenu, open the **Type** pull-down menu and choose **Style** to display the submenu. Both the Styles submenu and the Styles palette are shown in Figure 6.4.

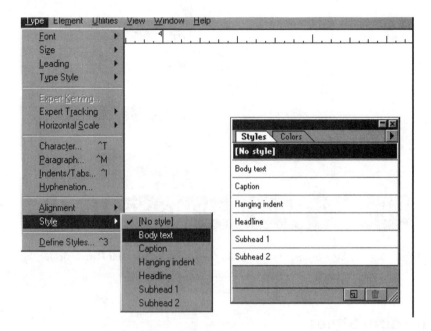

Figure 6.4 *The Style submenu and Styles palette displayed in a document page.*

To apply a style to a paragraph of text:

1. Select the **Text** tool and click the insertion point anywhere in the text you'd like to mark with a particular style.

2. Choose the style you want from the Styles palette or the Style submenu.

SHORTCUT

I find it a lot easier to use the Styles palette than the Style submenu. When the Styles palette is displayed in the document window, the style of the paragraph that your insertion point is in will always be highlighted in the palette, as shown in Figure 6.5.

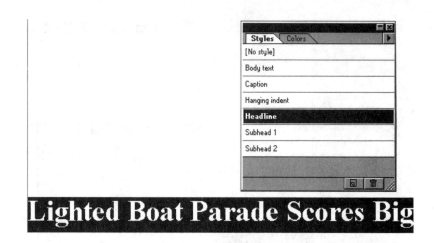

Figure 6.5 *Clicking the insertion point in the head "Lighted-Boat Parade Scores Big"*
highlights the modified Headline style in the Styles palette.

Changing Styles

You can change styles for a given paragraph at any time by simply selecting the text and choosing a different style. To do this, position the insertion point in the text that has the style you want to change and click another style in the Styles palette. The text will be changed to the style you selected.

Modifying Styled Text

Just because you have marked a paragraph with a given style doesn't mean you can't alter the specifications for that paragraph at any time. Just be aware that you are deviating from the style and that other text marked with the style won't contain the modifications. If the modifications are important, consider modifying the style or creating a new style for the text.

When text marked as a style has been modified, a plus sign (+) is displayed after the style name in the Styles palette. For example, let's say that in a paragraph marked with the default body text style, you selected a word and italicized it with the PageMaker shortcut **Command/Ctrl+Shift+I**. If you position the insertion point in the copy next to the italics, the Styles palette indicates Body Text. If you click the insertion point in the italicized word, the Styles palette says Body Text+.

TO SUM UP

A style is a set of formatting specifications for a paragraph, which is defined as anything preceding a carriage return. Styles standardize the formatting of similar paragraphs (for example, all paragraphs of body text are set in 12-point Helvetica, left-aligned, with 18 points of space between paragraphs, and so on). You can have as many styles as you need for a particular document. Styles allow you to make global changes to type, paragraph, and hyphenation specifications.

Styles are tied to the documents in which they are created; they stay with the document when it is copied. You can copy the styles of one document into another document. You can remove styles from a document. However, removing a default PageMaker style from one document does not affect future documents.

In the next chapter, you'll learn how to use PageMaker's new Layers capability.

CHAPTER 7

Using Layers

PageMaker's new *Layers* feature is one of the most significant additions to Version 6.5. It's potentially so useful and flexible that we're going to devote a chapter to explaining what layers can do for you. While the idea of using overlays in publishing isn't new, it's something of a novel feature in desktop publishing software and deserves a good, close look.

If you worked in publishing before the computer age, you'll remember the large *layout* boards from which PageMaker takes its pasteboard paradigm. Text and artwork were cut and pasted (or waxed) onto boards, which were then photographed to create an offset plate. Because the waxed pieces could be peeled off the board and repositioned, making changes in a layout was fast and easy. You could even stick items on the edges of the board temporarily and move them back onto the layout as required. PageMaker works in much this way, today, albeit the pieces are pasted, peeled up, and moved around electronically.

Another common feature of pre-DTP layouts were *overlays*. These were sheets of acetate, Mylar film, or even tracing paper placed on top of a layout board. Items to be printed in a second (or third) color could be marked on the overlays. Or, other instructions to the printer could be included. It was possible to read the instructions and the elements on the layout simultaneously, yet peel back the overlay when it came time to photograph the board.

In the 60s and 70s, overlays became an integral part of the drafting field, which is, in a way, a kind of highly technical and sophisticated form of publishing. One problem with technical drawings is that making changes or doing repetitive work (e.g., completing drawings for separate floors of a building in which most elements remained the same) was tedious. Pin-registered overlays allowed drafters to reuse some elements of a design, such as the basic layout of walls and windows, while creating new elements such as floorplans on separate layers.

That's the sort of flexibility layers give you in PageMaker. You can create a new layer as a sort of master page that can be applied only to specific pages of your document and turn those masters on or off as you desire. A layer can also be used to annotate a publication with comments that are viewed only when that layer is active. When the publication is printed, the layer with comments can be made invisible.

Layers also come in handy when you create a single publication for multiple audiences. Text in Spanish, French, and English, for example, can be placed on separate layers and used only as required. Or, you might develop a brochure that can be used for both customers and employees, with modifications made in customized layers. You can use layers to "store" elements temporarily out of sight, yet keep them available for instant access and copying to another layer when you need them. Place all your graphics on a single layer and turn off that layer when you want to print a copy of the publication quickly, sans images.

THE LAYERS PALETTE

The key to using layers in PageMaker is the new Layers palette, shown in Figure 7.1. Like other PageMaker palettes, it contains a fly-out menu, which I'll describe shortly, and other elements. If the Layers palette is not visible, you can display it by using the **Window>Show Layers** menu, or by pressing **Ctrl/Command+8**.

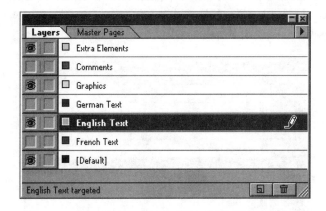

Figure 7.1 PageMaker's Layers palette.

The key elements of this palette are:

♦ **Show/Hide** Click on any of the boxes in this column to show or hide a particular layer. An eyeball icon appears in the box when that layer is visible. When a layer is not visible, none of the objects on it appear, and you can't select or move them. If you make a layer invisible, it doesn't print when the publication is output.

SHORTCUT

To quickly hide a group of layers, select the layers you want to remain visible by **Ctrl/Command**-clicking. Then, hold down the **Alt/Option** key and click in any box in the Show/Hide column. All the nonselected layers will become invisible. **Alt/Option**-click in the Show/Hide column again to make all the layers visible again. This is a fast technique if you have a publication with many layers and you want to make all but a few invisible.

✦ **Lock/Unlock** Click in the box in this column next to any layer to lock or unlock that layer. When the layer is locked, a pencil icon with a line through it appears. Locked layers are protected from changes: You can't add or subtract objects in a locked layer, nor move them or change their format. You can lock all the layers in a publication except for the selected layers using the technique outlined in the preceding Shortcut: hold down the **Alt/Option** key while clicking in the Lock/Unlock column to lock the nonselected layers. Unlock all the layers by **Alt/Option**-clicking a second time.

✦ **Active Layer** The currently active layer, or *target* layer, is highlighted in the Layers palette, and a pencil icon appears in that layer. If an object in the layer is selected, a box icon appears to the right of the pencil, as shown in Figure 7.2.

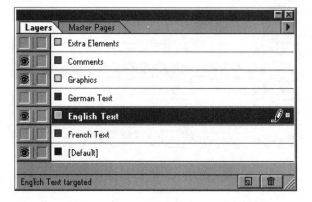

Figure 7.2 *A pencil icon appears in the highlighted active layer.*

✦ **Layer Name** When you create a layer, you can assign a descriptive name that helps you remember the purpose of that layer. In our example, we labeled layers with names like German Text, English Text, and French Text, along with others named Graphics, Extra Elements, and Comments. In this case, the purpose of each of these layers is obvious from their names.

✦ **Layer Color** A color can be assigned to a layer to make it easier to identify the layer's contents in your layout. You can select any object in any visible layer by clicking on it with the Pointer tool. The selection handles change to that layer's assigned color to tell you which layer it belongs with. To change either the name or color for a layer, double-click in the

Layer Name box, and the dialog box shown in Figure 7.3 appears. Enter the new name or select a color from the drop-down Color list.

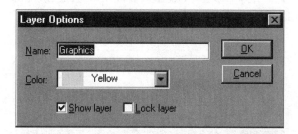

Figure 7.3 *Enter a new name or color for a layer in the Layer Options dialog box.*

✦ **New Layer Icon** The sheet with the upturned corner at the bottom right of the Layers palette is the new layer icon. Click on it to display the New Layer dialog box, shown in Figure 7.4. Enter a name for the layer and choose a color, or select the default values.

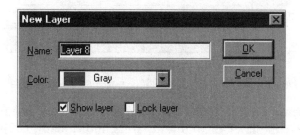

Figure 7.4 *The New Layer dialog box is used to create additional layers.*

✦ **Delete Layer Icon** Highlight a layer, then click this icon to remove the layer from your publication.

MOVING OBJECTS BETWEEN LAYERS

PageMaker makes it easy to move objects between layers. Just follow these steps:

1. Click on the first object you want to move. Selection handles will appear around the object in the color assigned to that layer. A colored box in the same color appears in the Layers palette in the far right column.

2. **Shift**-click to select the next object you wish to move. Selection handles and a colored box will appear, as in the preceding step. Figure 7.5 shows some text and a simple graphic placed on two different layers. Both have been selected.

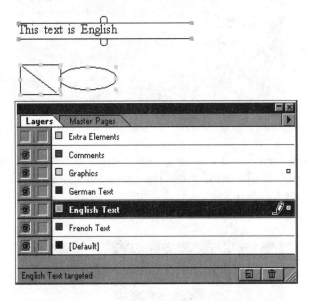

Figure 7.5 Both objects, on separate layers, have been selected.

3. Even though two objects have been selected, you can move them to the same layer or different layers, individually. Grab the colored box in the Layers palette for one of the objects, and drag it to a new layer. You may then grab the box representing the other layer's object(s) and drag it to the same layer or a different one. Note that if you select more than one object on a particular layer, they are all dragged to a single destination, but objects from different layers may be dragged to different destination layers.

CREATING DEFAULT LAYERS

If you'd like to have a certain set of layers available each time you create a new document (say, one for text, one for graphics, one for comments, and one for extra elements), just follow these steps:

1. Close all open publications in PageMaker.

2. Access the Layers palette.

3. Create and name any default layers you'd like to use.

From now on, whenever you create a new publication, it will already have the layers you've set up available.

ADDITIONAL OPTIONS

The Layer palette's fly-out menu has additional options, shown in Figure 7.6. I won't call them by the term *Layer Options*, as that is the nomenclature already used by Adobe for one of the menu's functions—changing the name and color assigned to a layer.

Figure 7.6 *The Layer palette's fly-out menu has additional options.*

These options include:

✦ **New Layer** Performs exactly the same function as clicking on the **new layer** icon in the Layers palette.

✦ **Delete Layer** Deletes any highlighted layers, the same as the delete layer icon in the Layers palette.

✦ **Merge Layers** Combines any highlighted layers into a single layer. The name of the layer that is on top in the Layers palette will be assigned to the merged layer.

✦ **Layer Options** Allows you to change the assigned name and color of a layer.

✦ **Show All/Hide Others** Displays all available layers/hides unselected layers.

✦ **Lock All/Lock Others** Locks all the layers/locks layers that are not selected.

✦ **Paste Remembers Layering** Select this option, and a check mark appears next to it. In that case, when you select multiple objects from different layers and copy them, they will be pasted down in the same order they were originally. You'd want to do this when copying objects from one publication to another, in order to preserve their layers and stacking order in the destination publication.

✦ **Select Target Layer** A quick way to select every object in the currently active target layer.

✦ **Delete Unused Layers** This option produces a dialog box, shown in Figure 7.7, which asks whether you want to delete each of the invisible layers in your publication. You can work through the layers one by one or delete all of them with one click.

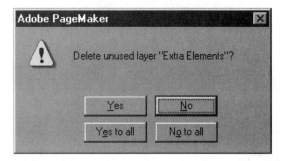

Figure 7.7 *Delete Unused Layers lets you eliminate extraneous layers quickly.*

CHANGING STACKING ORDER

You may want to change the order in which layers are displayed, because pieces that overlap can obscure one another. You might create text frames on one layer, for example, and drop shadow boxes on another layer. To properly display these sets of boxes, you'd need to make sure the text layer was located above the drop shadow layer on the Layers palette. To change the stacking order, just follow these steps:

1. Select the layers you want to move by clicking and **Shift**-clicking their layer names in the Layers palette.

2. Drag the layers to be moved up or down in the Layers palette. They will be moved to the new location you specify, while retaining their original relative order. Figure 7.8 may make this a little clearer.

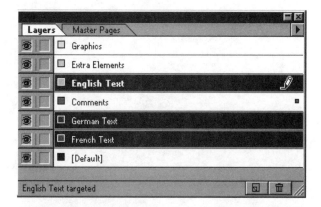

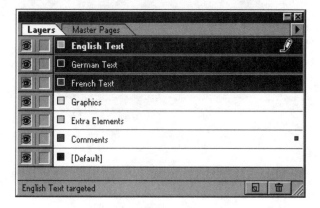

Figure 7.8 In the figure on top, three noncontiguous layers have been selected. Below, when dragged to the top of the Layers palette, they appear stacked in order.

To Sum Up

PageMaker 6.5's layers are a great way to organize your publication into groups of objects that are related in some way, and they let you control how those groups are displayed and printed. You gain a great deal of flexibility from layers, and you can streamline the way you create and work with standard components.

CHAPTER 8

Printing

- ✦ Targeting the right printer
- ✦ Printing your documents
- ✦ Working with service bureaus
- ✦ To sum up

Nowhere is the importance of desktop publishing more evident than in a sheet of paper emerging from a laser printer. Fonts in virtually any size are sharp and black, and pages contain boxes, circles, polygons, diagonal lines—elements that just a few years ago were practically impossible either to create or to print. It is the PostScript laser printer and the PostScript page description language that, in large part, account for PageMaker's magic. Before the development of PostScript by Adobe Systems, printing scalable fonts was limited to cumbersome typesetting systems that cost tens of thousands of dollars and used proprietary codes that only highly trained operators could understand. A mere dozen years ago the state of the art for producing text on the page was to have it typeset by a typesetting service or printed on an IBM SilentWriter impact printer (at the blinding speed of three pages a minute). Then, PageMaker and the venerable Apple LaserWriter came along and changed all that. Today, we drum our fingers on the desk because our laser printer churns out only 16 pages per minute! We have the far-reaching vision of folks at Adobe, Aldus (now part of Adobe), Apple, and Microsoft to thank for what is so easily taken for granted today.

Fonts are in many ways tied to the printers that use them. For example, a dot matrix printer cannot understand PostScript scalable fonts; it only knows to print lines of text in pica or elite, like a typewriter font (although a type manager, such as Adobe Type Manager or TrueType, which are used both on Macintoshes and Windows machines, can create bitmapped files that the dot matrix printer can print). If the dot matrix printer is a little more sophisticated, it may have a slot to hold font cartridges. These fonts emulate the look of typeset-quality fonts, and may offer an italic font, a roman or serif font, and a sans serif font. All PostScript printers come with at least 13 scalable fonts, comprising four font families. But you must print to the PostScript laser printer in order to use them.

Some laser printers print PostScript fonts, and some do not. The original Canon LBP-8A1 laser printer is an example of one that cannot print fonts; it basically emulates a dot matrix printer, printing pica or elite type. The early Hewlett-Packard LaserJet printer is about the same as the Canon—it prints pica or elite, period.

The Apple LaserWriter was the first laser printer to understand and print PostScript. Soon after the introduction of the LaserWriter, several companies began offering PostScript laser printers, including Texas Instruments. Today, there are many more brands of PostScript-compatible printers than there are non-PostScript printers.

While Macintosh owners need a PostScript printer for serious desktop publishing applications, those who work with Windows PCs have a choice. For example, the latest HP LaserJet 6P printer is built around HP's PCL-6 page description language, which works fine under Windows 95, as that operating system can translate PostScript and TrueType fonts into a format that PCL-6 can reproduce. The process is a little slower than direct PostScript printing, but for PC-oriented PageMaker users on a tight budget, a non-PostScript printer like the LaserJet 6P works fine.

If you later want to upgrade to PostScript, or need to use the same printer with both PCs and Macs, the 6P can be upgraded to the HP LaserJet 6MP model by adding a PostScript "personality" module, which contains 1 MB of RAM and fits in one of three SIMM slots inside the printer.

Printing PageMaker files is especially easy if you use your operating system's background printing feature. Under Windows 95, you can use the Printer Control Panel, right-click on your current printer and choose **Properties**, then click the **Spool Settings** button. Click the **Spool print jobs so program finishes printing faster** button to activate the most efficient background printing mode. On the Mac, you'll just use the Chooser window and click a button to turn background printing on or off for the printer you select. Click **On** to enable the feature.

Once background printing is activated, as you print in PageMaker, the pages are moved to temporary files on the hard disk, and your operating system's print spooler manages the chore of sending each page to the laser printer. Because the printer is still the slowest component in any desktop publishing system, a print spooler accepts the print-formatted file from the application (in this case PageMaker) and releases the application to go about its business. The print spooler then feeds the pages of the document to the printer at a rate the printer can accept.

SELECTING A PRINTER

You should select the printer you are going to use as a first step to printing from PageMaker. The process is slightly different on PCs and Macintoshes.

With a PC, use the **Start Menu>Settings>Control Panel** choice to pop up the Control Panel window. Click the **Printers** folder, right-click on the printer you want to use, and select **Set As Default**.

On the Macintosh, PageMaker requires using the LaserWriter version 8 (or later) PostScript printer driver, which is installed with your PageMaker programs. This driver replaces the previous version of the LaserWriter driver in your system. If you don't use the version 8 or later driver, you won't be able to choose a PostScript printer type in the Print Document dialog box, and the printed results will be less than expected. To choose the PostScript printer driver, click open the **Apple** menu and click the **Chooser** icon from the list. You will see the Chooser dialog box. Click the **PSPrinter** icon to select version 8 (or later) of the LaserWriter driver. If your laser printer is turned on and on-line, the AppleTalk cable connected, and the **AppleTalk Active** radio button clicked, you will see the name of your printer in the list box.

Targeting the Final Resolution

If you include black-and-white (or one-bit, monochrome) bitmap images in your PageMaker documents, you should establish the final resolution for the document when you begin developing it. The reason for this is that PageMaker will try to improve the resolution of the displayed image to match what you have set in the Target Output Resolution pop-up list in the Document Setup dialog box, which is shown in Figure 8.1.

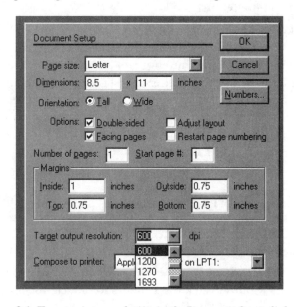

Figure 8.1 *Target printer resolution in the Document Setup dialog box.*

To change the printer resolution:

1. Choose the **File** pull-down menu and choose **Document Setup** to display the Document Setup dialog box, which is shown in Figure 8.1. Click the **Target Output Resolution** pop-up list.

2. Choose the resolution that will match the final printing device for your document. For example, if the document will be printed to a laser printer, you should select **300 dpi** as the final printer resolution (or **600 dpi** if your printer can support a higher resolution). If the final printing will be done at a service bureau on a high-resolution image setter, you should select a resolution compatible with the image setter.

3. Click **OK** to return to your document.

Choosing the Correct PostScript Printer Description File

The printer you target your document to should be the printer that will ultimately print the document. For example, if you will eventually use a PostScript service bureau to produce high-resolution negatives of your document pages, then you should select the *PPD* file (*PostScript printer description*) for the same model image setter. A PPD is a PostScript file that fine-tunes a number of PostScript features for the printer you will be using. For example, let's say that you will be printing to an HP LaserJet 5MP. To ensure accurate reproduction, you should select the LaserJet's PPD in the Print Document dialog box. Here are the steps:

1. Open the **File** pull-down menu and choose the **Print** command to display the Print Document dialog box, which is shown in Figure 8.2.

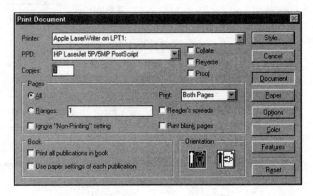

Figure 8.2 Print Document dialog box.

2. Notice that the printer is shown in the Printer area. The printer shown here reflects the default printer you specified earlier in the Windows 95 Printers Control Panel or your Macintosh's Chooser window. Now, click the **PPD** pop-up list to display the PPD files you've installed (like the example below). Scroll down the list and double-click the PPD for the type of printer or image setter that will be printing the document. Remember, the PPDs you see here are only those that you selected as part of PageMaker's installation; if you don't see the PPD you need, go back to the installation disk and reinstall the additional PPDs.

PRINTING YOUR DOCUMENT

It's a good idea to print proofs of your document as it is being developed. When you finish a page or two, print a proof copy to verify the alignment of all the text elements. As I stated earlier, PageMaker's accuracy is much higher in the printed version of the page than on the screen version (up to 1/2880-in.), so to be absolutely sure of very close alignments, print the page. It's easy. I'll list the steps first, then explain them in more detail. Here are the steps:

1. Choose the **File** pull-down menu and choose **Print** to display the Print Document dialog box, which is shown in Figure 8.3.

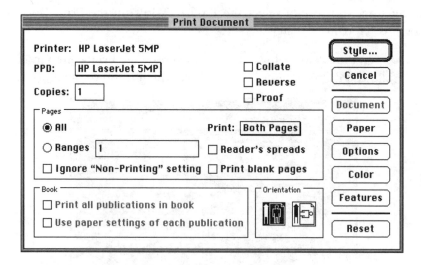

Figure 8.3 *The Print Document dialog box.*

2. Use this dialog box to set up the number of pages you want to print, the order that pages pass through the printer, and other conditions. Choose among the following options and features:

- ✦ **Copies**—Choose as many copies of the document as you need. The **Collate** and **Reverse Order** option boxes determine the order of printing.

- ✦ **Page Range**—Print the entire document or a range of pages.

- ✦ **Book**—Use special features to print the chapter or sections of a book that you've defined with the **Book** command.

- ✦ **Even/Odd Pages**—You can order even or odd pages to print separately, using the drop-down list next to the Print field. You can select **Odd**, **Even**, or **Both Pages**. Use this option if you are printing a document on the front and back. Odd pages are normally considered front pages, so print all odd-numbered pages first. Then insert the stack of printed pages back in the paper tray so that the back will be printed, and choose **Even Pages**.

- ✦ **Orientation**—Select the icon representing portrait or landscape orientation, as appropriate.

- ✦ **Other Check Boxes**—Other boxes in this dialog box allow you to tell PageMaker to go ahead and print "nonprinting" elements on your pages; print otherwise blank pages; and to print multipage spreads.

3. The Print Document dialog box is just the first of four dialog boxes that PageMaker uses to define exactly how you want your document printed. There is also a fifth button, **Features**, which contains options specific to your particular printer. To access the main dialog boxes, choose one of the following command buttons:

- ✦ **Paper**—Includes options for printing thumbnails, setting up tiling, and the paper size. For laser printers that can print duplex (print both sides during one pass of the paper through the printer), you can specify which edge will be bound.

- ✦ **Options**—Allows you to set the degree of graphic resolution to improve printing speed. You can also set up printer's markings and prepare the document to be printed to disk for use in sending to a service bureau.

- ✦ **Color**—Gives you infinite control in printing color pages to a color printer or color laser printer or printing color separations to either your laser printer or a high-resolution image setter.

4. Make the necessary changes to the dialog boxes and click **OK** or press
    Return to print the document.

PRINT DOCUMENT DIALOG BOX OPTIONS

As we've seen, the initial Print Document dialog box gives you a choice of
PPDs. It also lets you configure the order of printing, the page orientation, and
how documents that are members of a book grouping will be printed together.

Selecting the Printing Order

Two check boxes in the Print Document dialog box control the order in
which pages print with a laser printer. Normally, if more than one copy of a
multiple-page document is printed, PageMaker prints all page 1s first, then
page 2s, and so on. To print collated sets of the document, click the **Collate**
check box to put an X in it. Some laser printers print the pages of a document
beginning to end, others print end to beginning. To reverse the order of
printing, click the **Reverse Order** check box to put an X in it. To include
blank pages in the printed documents, click the **Print blank pages** check box
(the default setting is for PageMaker not to print blank pages).

Selecting a Range of Pages and the Number of Copies to Print

Normally, PageMaker prints all the pages of a document. If you want to print
only certain pages, click the **Range** radio button. In the text box, enter the
page number of the first page you want printed, then a hyphen and the last
page you want printed. To print all the pages of a document, just click the **All**
radio button. You specify the number of complete copies of your document by
entering the number in the Copies text box—you can print up to 32,000
copies at one time.

Printing Proof Copies

Sometimes it's nice to be able to knock out a quick copy of a page or document to check some small item yet not include placed graphics in detail.
Called *proof copies*, PageMaker can do just that. Click the **Proof** check box, and

you will see gray boxes instead of your graphics. Everything but the graphics will be as you have specified. Clicking the **Proof** check box drastically speeds up the printing of pages containing graphics or scanned photographs.

Changing the Printing Orientation

The standard orientation for printing in your laser printer is called the *portrait orientation*: The text is parallel to the short sides of the paper. To change the orientation to what is called *landscape* (in which the text is parallel to the wide sides of the page) click the **Wide** orientation icon. The orientation you select here should be the same as the **Tall/Wide** orientation you selected in the Page Setup dialog box when you first created your document.

Printing Files Associated with the Book Command

If the document you want to print is a member of a publication list created with the **Book** command, you can print it plus all other members of the publication list by clicking the **Print All Publications in Book** check box. For example, if you have designated PageMaker documents as the table of contents, the front matter, Chapters 1 through 22, the appendix, and the index as belonging to a publication list, clicking the check box prints all 26 documents—in the proper order and page-numbered correctly—at one time. If you want the page and printing setting you've made in the individual documents to have priority over any setting you make to the current document, click the **Use Paper Settings** of each publication check box.

Printing on Both Sides of the Page

Some laser printers can print *duplex* (that is, print on both sides of the page during one pass through the printer). This is a very handy feature if you need to print front and back originals. If you need to print front and back and aren't fortunate enough to own a duplex laser printer, here's how to do it:

1. In the Print Document dialog box, choose the **Odd** selection from the Print drop-down list to print all odd pages first.

2. If your laser printer prints multiple documents page by page (all page 1s first, then all page 2s, and so on), click the **Collate** option.

3. Print all odd-numbered pages.

4. To print the back side of the odd pages that have just printed, take the stack out of the discharge tray, still facing down, and put them back in the paper tray with the top of the page still toward the inside of the printer, printed-side facing down.

5. Select the **Even** option from the Print drop-down list to print all even-numbered pages. Again, choose **Collate** if necessary, and then print the pages. They will come out of the printer printed front and back.

PRINT PAPER DIALOG BOX OPTIONS

This dialog box, shown in Figure 8.4, controls the paper passing through the printer and sets how the image of the PageMaker document page will be produced on the paper. Under normal circumstances, you might only need to adjust the size and source of the paper, although the other options can be very useful. Let's look at them in more detail.

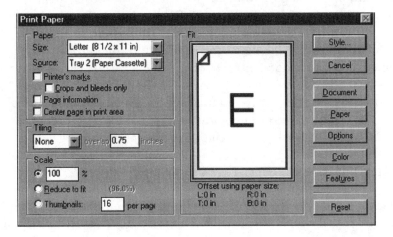

Figure 8.4 Print Paper dialog box.

Setting Paper Options

The paper types listed in the Size pop-up list are presented according to the printer you selected in the previous Print Document dialog box. The size for each paper type is shown to the right in the pop-up list. Where the printer allows for it, you can also select **Custom** as a paper type and define your own customized page size. (The type and size information is actually stored as part of the printer PPD.) The source of paper is also presented according to the printer type you have already selected. If you are printing to a printer that does not center the printing on the page, you can click the **Center page in the print area** check box to do so. However, if you are tiling the page, PageMaker ignores the checked option.

Printing Oversize Pages with Tiles

PageMaker can display and print type as large as 650 points. What may not be readily apparent is that since PageMaker can enlarge a page up to 1600%, you can actually print type large enough to fit on a billboard. Since no PostScript printer can take paper 8 ft wide, PageMaker has an option on the Print Paper dialog box called **Tile**. *Tiling* breaks up the ultimate size into smaller pieces (like tiles on the floor) that fit on the page size specified in the Page Setup dialog box. PageMaker sets an automatic overlap of the tiles that takes into account the unprintable margin around the edge of the page (you can manually set the overlap, if you wish). It also marks each page with alignment marks so that the pages can be arranged correctly. Finally, the tiles are numbered, so that you know what goes where. Use the Tiling drop-down list and the Overlap box to define the type of tiles and amount of overlap.

Printing Reductions and Enlargements

PageMaker can reduce or enlarge any document by the amount entered into the Print Paper dialog box's Scale text box. You can reduce documents as small as 5% of original size or enlarge them to 1600% of original size in increments as small as 0.1%. The option is useful when you want to print proofs of spot or process color separations when your page size is 8.5 x 11 in. Enter a reduction value of **85%**, and your spot color overlays print out with crop marks, registration marks, and color labels (or choose the **Reduce to Fit** radio button). If you scale your document to print larger than original size, you may have to invoke tiling to see the entire printed results.

Printing Thumbnails

Thumbnails are an easy way of looking at all the pages in a document, to see the overall design theme. You can print up to 100 pages of your document on one page. The thumbnails provide a storyboard look at a document. Text can't be read, but the placement of photos, graphics, columns, and headings is readily visible. A thumbnail is useful for showing your client progress on a project. To print thumbnails, click the **Thumbnail** option box in the Print Paper dialog box and enter the number of thumbnails you want per page in the Per Page text box. The more thumbnails you request on the page, the smaller each thumbnail will be. For greater page detail, print fewer thumbnails per page.

Setting Additional Print Options

Also in the Print Paper dialog box, you can add bullets and annotations to the page for your commercial printer to use and define print-to-disk files to send to your service bureau.

PRINT OPTIONS DIALOG BOX OPTIONS

The Print Options dialog box, shown in Figure 8.5, has several graphics and PostScript-oriented options. Normally, you will probably be anxious to print your graphic images at their normal resolution, if only to admire how they look. But the Print Options dialog box gives you several important choices to control the printed resolution of those graphics. For example, the **Optimized** choice in the Send Image Data drop-down list is a useful way to speed up the printing of scanned images that have a higher scanned resolution than your printer can reproduce. The higher the scanning resolution, the larger the graphic file, and the printer normally must read the entire file before it can compose the image, regardless of whether or not it can reproduce the image at the scanned resolution. If you click the **Optimized** choice, PageMaker only feeds the printer as much of the resolution as it can reproduce, thus significantly speeding up printing the image without any degradation in quality (although scanned line art may appear slightly blurred).

Another way to speed up printing is to check the **Low Resolution** option in the Send Image Data list, which sends the printer a low-resolution version of the TIFF (between 25 and 72 dpi). The TIFF will be recognizable but lack its original high resolution. If you click **Omit TIFF files**, the TIFFs won't print at all, which is handy if you just want a printout of the text portion of the document.

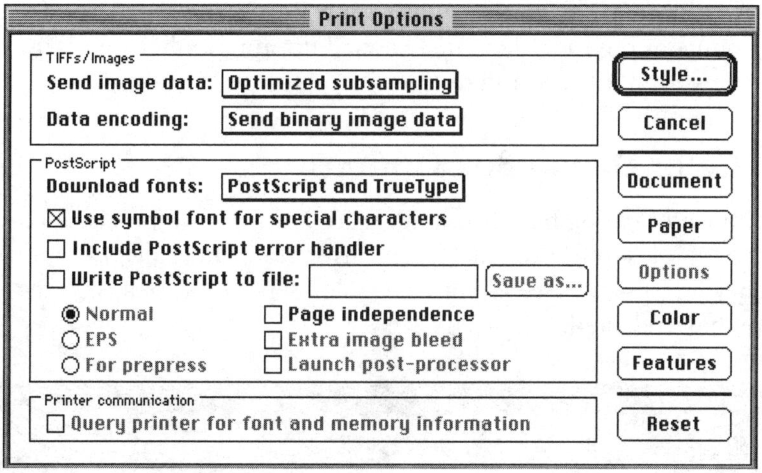

```
╔═══════════════════════════════════════════════════════════╗
║                     Print Options                          ║
╠═══════════════════════════════════════════════════════════╣
║  ┌ TIFFs / Images ─────────────────────────────┐          ║
║    Send image data: │Optimized subsampling │      ┌───────────┐
║                                                   │  Style... │
║    Data encoding:   │Send binary image data│      └───────────┘
║  └─────────────────────────────────────────────┘  ┌───────────┐
║  ┌ PostScript ─────────────────────────────────┐  │  Cancel   │
║    Download fonts:  │PostScript and TrueType│    └───────────┘
║    ☒ Use symbol font for special characters       ┌───────────┐
║    ☐ Include PostScript error handler             │ Document  │
║    ☐ Write PostScript to file:│        ││Save as...│
║       ● Normal       ☐ Page independence          │   Paper   │
║       ○ EPS          ☐ Extra image bleed          ┌───────────┐
║       ○ For prepress ☐ Launch post-processor      │  Options  │
║  └─────────────────────────────────────────────┘  ┌───────────┐
║  ┌ Printer communication ──────────────────────┐  │   Color   │
║    ☐ Query printer for font and memory information│ Features  │
║  └─────────────────────────────────────────────┘  ┌───────────┐
║                                                   │   Reset   │
╚═══════════════════════════════════════════════════════════╝
```

Figure 8.5 *The Print Options dialog box.*

Printing Documents to Disk

Generally speaking, PostScript service bureaus do not want you to send them PageMaker files. That's because they are probably not using PageMaker to print the files to a PostScript image setter. In most circumstances, they are printing PostScript files created by a variety of applications. Consequently, they probably want you to print your files to disk, creating a PostScript file rather than a PageMaker file. The service bureau then sends the PostScript file to the PostScript device using a file downloader (such as Adobe's Font Downloader).

To print a file to disk:

1. In the Print Options dialog box, click the **Write PostScript to file** check box.

2. Choose **PostScript** and **TrueType fonts** from the Download Fonts drop-down list. This means that any fonts in your system (not resident in your laser printer) that would download if you printed the document will be added to the print-to-disk file. This is an important option; without it you would see Courier substituted for the downloadable fonts unless the service bureau happened to have the same font on hand and took the time to download it to the printer before printing your file.

3. In the text box to the right of the PostScript check box, enter the name of the file. Click the **Browse** button to look through the folders on your hard disk and decide where to store this file.

Print Color Dialog Box Options

The Print Color dialog box shown in Figure 8.6 gives you precise control over handling color separations and printing color. You can also specify line frequency and line angles for process color separation plates, based on the PPD you have selected.

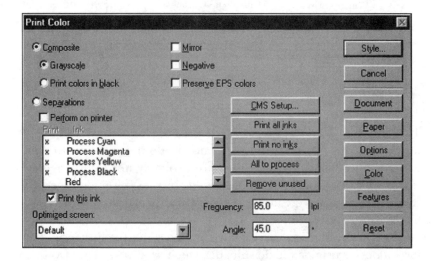

Figure 8.6 *The Print Color dialog box.*

Controlling Composite Printing

Printing a composite of a color document is the opposite of printing separations: Instead of the colors being separated, they are printed in place as either shades of gray (from a laser printer) or as close approximations of the colors (from a color printer). *Composites* are an important aspect of proofing your color job—it's difficult to visualize having all of the correct colors, especially spot colors, unless you run a proof through a color printer. The colors won't be exact, but you'll have a close idea of the finished work. To print colors on a color printer, click the **Composite** radio button. If you are printing to a laser printer, selecting this option shows the colors in shades of gray. If you click the

Print Colors in Black radio button, the colors all print in shades of black in the same screened percentages acquired with process and spot separations.

 PageMaker 6.5 includes some sophisticated color controls that are beyond the scope of this introductory/intermediate book. These include the Kodak Precision Color Management System (noted as CMS in the dialog boxes), which lets you match your equipment by selecting among the more than 60 monitor and printer profiles included. However, we'll take a quick look at these features within the in-depth discussion of color in Chapter 9.

Creating Mirror and Negative Images of Your Document

Both the **Mirror** and **Negative** check boxes are generally for use with an image setter. The **Mirror** option is normally used with the **Negative** option to control which side the emulsion is on for film negatives. If the negatives need to be right reading, and you want the emulsion-side up, click the **Mirror** check box to remove the X (the Mirror is turned off). Turn **Mirror** on by clicking the check box to add the X if you want the emulsion-side down. If the film needs to be wrong-reading, set **Mirror** to **On** if you want the emulsion-side up. Set it to **Off** if you want the emulsion-side down. Click the **Negative** check box to generate film or paper negatives. Leave the check box unchecked if you want to produce file or paper positives.

Controlling Separation Printing

To print separations, click the **Separations** radio button. The Separations pop-up list and command buttons will darken. Notice that the pop-up list contains the process colors cyan, magenta, and yellow, plus black, the registration color, and any spot colors you have defined for this document. Scroll down the pop-up list and click the colors whose separations you want to print and click in the **Print This Ink** check box to add an X in the Print column of the pop-up list—PageMaker only prints separations for the colors with X's in the Print column. To mark all colors with X's, click the **Print All Inks** command button. To remove all the X's, click the **Print No Ink** command button. If you want to convert all spot color separations temporarily to process separations, click the **All to Process** command button (the process equivalent of the spot color may not be the same tint).

WORKING WITH SERVICE BUREAUS

There are several things you can do to help process your job at a service bureau and reduce any misunderstandings. When you establish a relationship with a service bureau, give them a list of all your fonts (whether or not they are in a particular document) as well as a file with at least a couple of words set in each font. Ask the service bureau to print the file and look for any fonts that have been substituted with Courier. The substitution will indicate that your font and the service bureau's font are different even though they are named the same. Because there are so many fonts called by similar names, this kind of test is important.

If possible, give the service bureau a copy of the file you have printed on your own laser printer. If you request color separations from the service bureau, run a set of separations reduced to 85% so that the service bureau knows exactly what to expect with your job.

Ask to see an example of the service bureau's exposed film before requesting that your first job be printed on film. The negative film should be free of pin holes (hold the film up to the light to check).

If the service bureau gives you a choice of resolutions (for example, a Linotronic L330 can print at 1270- and 2540-dpi resolution), opt for the lower resolution for text, unless you are working with very fine serif type in very small sizes. The lower resolution costs less per page. If you request spot color or process color separations, be aware of the costs involved—film can cost twice as much as paper, and in creating separations you're producing several pages for each page of your document. The costs can mount rapidly.

Finally, don't expect the service bureau to proofread your work for you. The material should be correct before you give it to the service bureau, and, generally speaking, they are not responsible for your errors and do not proofread your documents.

A Word of Caution

Printing is not a science; it's an art. Adding PostScript and PageMaker, as accurate as they are, doesn't make printing foolproof. There are many variables, even with PostScript, including the following:

+ **Chemistry**. This includes the chemistry of the developer and fixer used in processing film and resin-coated paper in the image setter's processing unit, the speed of the material running through the processor, the temperature of the chemicals, and the temperature and humidity of the ambient air. All of these variables affect the exposure, developing, and fixing of the photographic paper or film.

✦ **Shelf life of materials**. The freshness of the chemicals, paper, and film plays a direct role in the developing process and the end quality of the printed page. Ideally, service bureau operators should buy supplies in small quantities and rapidly turn over their inventories of supplies.

✦ **Exposure**. The exposure settings in the image setter are different for film and paper and are affected by chemicals and air temperature.

✦ **Fonts**. As crisp as PostScript fonts are, different fonts reproduce differently. The thinner the letters or the more delicate the serifs, the more likely it is that characters will break up in small sizes. Italic type in small sizes can be particularly susceptible to breaking up. To keep the letters from breaking, the service bureau operator must expose the type longer so as to make the serifs stronger. The printer must compensate by exposing the printing plate longer and adding more ink. However, these longer exposures can create other problems. Achieving high quality is a delicate "balancing act" between the production of the PostScript originals on paper or film, and the printed results.

✦ **Paper, ink, dryers, folders, and die cutters**. All play a part in the appearance of the finished work. Different paper accepts and holds different quantities of ink; different inks have different properties; dryers make the ink dry faster but can change the quality of the finished print; and folders, die cutters, and other machinery, which aid in the production of the finished piece, can help or hinder a job.

✦ **Knowledge and experience of the operators**. All the computers in the world can't duplicate the knowledge of an experienced, capable service bureau operator and printer. Much of the success lies in their desire to do the job right and in their understanding of how to fine-tune and adjust very delicate machinery.

To Sum Up

Printing is the melody that gives life to the written word. PageMaker awards the designer boundless freedom in developing the printed page, with accuracy as sharp as tacks. You've learned how easily PageMaker handles all of the chores of producing a camera-ready printing mechanical.

In the next chapter, you'll see how easy it is to add color to your document.

CHAPTER 9

Adding Color

✦ Using PageMaker's default colors

✦ Working with color graphics

✦ Defining custom colors

✦ Editing, copying, and removing colors

✦ Screening text and graphics

✦ To sum up

225

Sometimes even the best choice of words arranged in the best possible lay-out can't approximate the effect of a touch of color on the page. Color is like a flashing arrow drawing the eye to your words, magnifying their meaning, clarifying the results. Color invokes emotions—think about Christmas without red and green, or the Fourth of July without red, white, and blue. Color imbues a document with sharp or subtle moods. It gives the message subconscious appeal—recall the blue of IBM's logotype, for instance, or the broad red stripe of the Coast Guard emblem.

You work with color all of the time and probably don't even think about it. Putting black text on a white page still adds color to the page. Black is created by combining all of the primary colors (proved to me every time I watched my three-year-old son Michael mix too many fingerpaints together; he got black every time). Normally, one-color printing is black—in part because the toner for laser printers and high-speed photocopiers is black. Unless you can add a toner of another color, your printed output will be black.

Even a one-color, black-on-white document can be dressed up by a commercial printer using colored ink and/or paper. For example, you could print medium blue ink on a buff or beige stock, dark gray ink on a light gray stock, or maroon ink on a light gray stock. Suddenly your plain document is starting to look pretty jazzy.

Adding a second-color ink can make a tremendous improvement for very little increased cost. Or, you can create the appearance of a second color using a screen of the single-color ink. For instance, a 20% screen of black yields light gray; 20% of a dark green makes a very nice shade of light green, and so on. In this case, the second color is free!

PageMaker's color capabilities support all of the examples I have just given you. PageMaker can provide your commercial printer with screens of solid colors, color overlays for each color you add to a design, knockouts for printing one color on top of another, and much more.

USING PAGEMAKER'S DEFAULT COLORS

PageMaker's colors are displayed and activated with the Colors palette. Similar in use to the Styles palette, the Colors palette is a small window containing the default colors and any custom colors you define.

Opening the Colors Palette

To open the Colors palette:

1. Choose the **Window** pull-down menu.

2. Choose **Show Colors** if it isn't already active to reveal the Colors palette. The palette will be displayed on the right side of the document window, under the toolbox, as shown in Figure 9.1.

Figure 9.1 *The Colors palette.*

3. Or, as an alternative, you can use the PageMaker shortcut **Command/ Ctrl+J** to open the Colors palette window.

PageMaker 6.5 comes configured with six default colors (as opposed to just three in PageMaker 5.0) shown in the Colors palette: blue, green, red, cyan, magenta, and yellow. "Defining Custom Colors," later in this chapter, covers the different color models and the Pantone Matching System (PMS).

To see colors on your computer, you must have a color monitor. To print color, you must use a color printer.

N O T E

Default colors are similar to default styles, in that they are always present when new documents are created. And, like styles, changing or removing a default color from a particular document doesn't alter the default colors in future documents.

You can color text that is created in or imported into PageMaker. You can also color any element drawn with one of the drawing tools, or any imported graphic. Some graphics, like TIFF and EPS files, print in the color you specify, although they will not be displayed in that color.

The Colors palette has several useful tools for coloring items on the page (see Figure 9.2). Let's take a look:

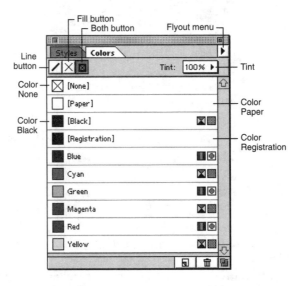

Figure 9.2 *Parts of the Colors palette.*

+ **Fill button**—Click this button to color the fill of a shape.

+ **Line button**—Click this button to color a line or the lined border of a shape.

+ **Both button**—Click this button to apply a color to both the line and fill.

+ **Tint menu**—Use this drop-down menu to select a percentage of tint to use for a line, a fill, or both.

✦ **Color None**—Removes colors applied within PageMaker to an object, such as a line, an object's Fill color, or colors added to an EPS graphic. This is a good tool for creating transparent lines and fills.

✦ **Color Paper**—Applies the color of the paper on which the document is printed. As opposed to the color None (which makes the colored object transparent), coloring something with the paper color means whatever is behind it is hidden. The best example of the paper color is used in creating a drop shadow behind a box (see "Adding Additional Colors to Shapes," later in this chapter). You cannot modify the color Paper.

✦ **Color Black**—This is the standard process black color used in your publications. You cannot modify this color; however, you can apply screens of black to create shades of gray.

✦ **Color Registration**—Registration is really not a color, but an attribute you can apply, similarly to a color, to anything you want to print on all separation overlays. For example, if you wanted to create your own crop marks, you would mark them with the Color Registration so that the crop marks would appear on all separation plates.

Adding Color to Text

There are a number of reasons you might want to color text. For example, in technical manuals and proposals, coloring headings helps refine the look of the page and breaks up large blocks of text. Adding colored callouts to an illustration helps to show a distinct separation between the figure and its annotation. In brochures and marketing literature, color can add class and emphasis.

There are two methods of coloring text in PageMaker: (1) selecting the color as part of the text specification, and (2) marking the text using the Colors palette.

Using the Character Specification Dialog Box

To color text as part of the text specification:

1. If you're about to type new text, choose the **Text** tool and place the insertion point where you want to start the text. If you want to color text that is already on the page, highlight the text with the Text tool.

2. Choose the **Type** pull-down menu and choose **Character** (or press **Command/Crl+T**) to display the Character Specifications dialog box, shown in Figure 9.3.

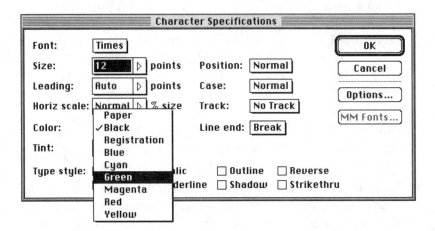

Figure 9.3 *The Character Specifications dialog box.*

3. Click the **Color** pop-up list to open the list box and click one of the choices:

    ✦ **Paper**—Just as in the Fill submenu, Paper indicates the color of the paper for this document.

    ✦ **Black**—This color can't be changed in the Define Colors dialog box. All text is initially set to this color.

    ✦ **Registration**—This refers to crop marks and registration marks that PageMaker prints when the Printer's Marks option box is checked in the Print dialog box. Text marked as Registration prints on every page with color overlay registration marks or page crop marks.

    ✦ **Blue**, **Green**, **Red**, **Cyan**, **Magenta**, **Yellow**—Text marked with any of these colors will be displayed in that color on your color monitor. If printed on a color laser or inkjet printer, the marked items will be printed in a color similar to what is displayed on your monitor (an exact match depends on the number of colors your monitor is capable of displaying, the resolution of your monitor, and the color resolution of the color printer). If you select **Spot Color Overlays** in the Print dialog box, PageMaker will print a color overlay for each of these colors used in the document.

4. Click **OK** or press **Return** to return to your document. If you highlighted text to color, it will now be displayed in the color you selected. If you position the insertion point back in the text, the Color list box in the Character Specifications dialog box will display the color you selected.

Using the Colors Palette

To mark text in a color using the Colors palette, select the **Text** tool and highlight the text you want to color. In the Colors palette, click the color you want for the highlighted text.

The text is displayed in the color you select on a color monitor. If you position the insertion point back in the text, the Colors palette displays the color you selected. To change the color to another color or back to black, simply highlight the text again and choose the new color.

Using the Style Palette

In longer documents, you may find it easier to assign a color to certain text you've already defined as a style. Then, whenever you choose the style, you automatically assign the color:

1. Choose the **Type** pull-down menu and choose **Define Styles**.
2. In the Define Styles dialog box, select the style to which you want to add a color assignment. Click the **Edit** button.
3. In the Edit Style dialog box, press the **Char** button to move to the Character Specifications dialog box.
4. Choose a color for the type by clicking the **Color** pop-up list and choosing a color from the list.
5. Click **OK** or press **Return** in all of the nested dialog boxes to return to your document.

Now, whenever you choose the style with the color assignment, you will also color the text in that style.

WORKING WITH COLOR GRAPHICS

Any graphic created with or imported into PageMaker, with the exception of scanned color TIFF files, can be colored. Some graphic formats (including encapsulated PostScript files) can be marked with a color, but will not be displayed in the color (they will, however, print in the specified color). To fill a graphic with a color other than black, simply create the graphic shape, choose the color you'd like from the Colors palette, and choose **Solid** from the Fill submenu. The graphic shape will be filled with the color you selected. Graphics created in PageMaker can also be shaded using the shade percentages in the Fill submenu (see "Screening Text and Graphics," later in this chapter).

Adding Color to a Graphic Shape

You can easily add color to the squares, rectangles, ovals, and circles you create in PageMaker. To color a PageMaker graphic shape:

1. Choose the **Box** tool and draw a rectangle on the page.

2. While the border of the rectangle is still selected, choose a color in the Colors palette and click the color. The border of the rectangle will change to that color. As an alternative, you can click the **Line** button and click the color you want to add to the line.

3. If you want the border color to be some percentage tint other than 100%, select the percentage you'd like from the drop-down Tint list.

4. Click the **Fill** button on the Colors palette, and choose a color from the list, and a percentage (if other than 100%) from the Tint list.

Changing the Viewing Resolution of Scanned Images

Even very fast computers will tend to choke on TIFF files displayed at high resolution in PageMaker, especially in the 200% or 400% page views. The images are just so big that it takes a few moments for the screen to redraw as you scroll up or down the page. Full gray-scale TIFFs can easily be 500 or more kilobytes, and just a small scanned color photo can exceed several megabytes. To speed up the redraw (or *screen refresh rate*, as it's called), you can change the display of the TIFF file to a lower resolution. The Preferences dialog box is used to set the display resolution of graphics. Follow these steps:

1. Choose the **File** pull-down menu and choose **Preferences** to display the Preferences>General dialog box, shown in Figure 9.4.

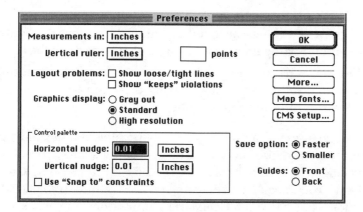

Figure 9.4 *The Preferences dialog box.*

2. In the Graphics area of the dialog box, choose the appropriate display resolution:

    ✦ **Gray out**—Graphics at this display resolution are represented as a gray box. Gray out provides the fastest refresh rate at high page magnifications.

    ✦ **Standard**—This is a good compromise between details and speed. You'll see a pretty good representation of your graphic.

    ✦ **High resolution**—This gives the highest resolution possible, but it also gives the slowest redraw.

    Click the radio button for the display resolution you want.

Another way to see an individual graphic in high resolution (if Standard or Gray Out is in effect) is to press **Option/Alt+Shift** while the graphic is being refreshed (when you move up or down the area of the page that the graphic is in using the scroll bar, or when you move to another page containing a graphic).

DEFINING CUSTOM COLORS

If the default colors provided in the Colors palette don't fit the bill for a particular document, you can create a custom color. PageMaker provides three color models (or schemes of color blending) to use in customizing a color. The models are:

    ✦ RGB treats color in much the same way that your color monitor does: It blends percentages of red, green, and blue.

✦ HLS (hue, lightness, and saturation model) treats color hues as degrees in a color wheel, increasing or decreasing the lightness and saturation of the hue as percentages of 100 to create the color.

✦ CMYK stands for the primary colors of four-color printing: cyan, magenta, yellow, and black. Mixing them in varying percentages of 100 yields different color combinations.

PageMaker also gives you a number of color-matching libraries and a provision for adding more customized libraries as they become available. The most popular color matching system is surely PMS. It has become the de facto standard as a standardized way of defining and mixing ink. It is used by most commercial printers to reproduce colors. However, PageMaker also provides matching systems from Colorcurve Systems, DaiNippon, Focoltone, Toyo, and TruMatch.

To define a custom color:

1. Click the **New Color** icon at the bottom of the Colors palette (it looks like a page with an upturned left bottom corner), or select **New Color** from the Colors palette's fly-out menu. Choose the **Element** pull-down menu and choose **Define Colors** to display the Color Options dialog box, shown in Figure 9.5.

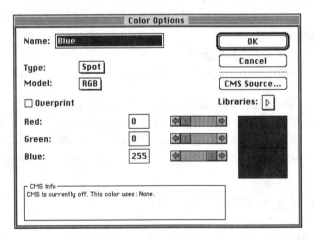

Figure 9.5 *The Color options dialog box.*

2. Choose the color model you'd like from the Model drop-down list or open the Libraries list and choose among the color-matching libraries.

3. For each color model, choose the kind of color by selecting **Spot**, **Process**, or **Tint** from the Type drop-down list.

4. Choose a color from the library with the color picker that will pop up, and click **OK**.

5. Accept the default name of the color supplied by the library or enter your own name for the color in the Name text box. The name will be displayed on the Colors palette and will print outside the margin on spot color and process color separations (so your commercial printer will know which color overlay is which).

You can call your new color whatever you'd like, but the name should be descriptive of the color. For example, you could call a light green Light Green, since there is already a default green on the Colors palette. Or you could call it Logo Green if your client uses a particular shade of green for a company logo.

You don't have to actually select a color to create a special name for a color. For example, if you want to print this document on a special brand of paper, or print selected pages on different colors of paper, you can itemize the colors of the paper as custom colors. Then, before placing anything on the page, draw a square-cornered box the same size as the overall page size (using the Fit in Window view), mark the box as the special paper type or paper color, choose **Fill Paper** (**Element>Fill**), and choose a color for the paper. Then when you print out your spot color overlays, the specific paper types or paper colors will be automatically specified for the commercial printer. To create a custom paper type, simply enter the name in the Name text box (like Classic Laid Bone) and click **OK** or press **Return**. The name is added to the Colors palette.

Similarly, you can name a custom color Varnish if you want your commercial printer to varnish the printed page. Varnish is a clear coating applied over the ink to keep the ink from smearing, and to add gloss to the page. Varnish is treated like a spot color by your commercial printer and needs its own spot separation. For a jazzy effect, varnish only certain areas of the page, such as graphics or photos. By making the varnish a color, it's a simple matter to fill with the varnish color the graphic boxes that will hold photos. To add Varnish to the Colors palette, enter **Varnish** in the Name text box and click **OK** or press **Return**.

Defining RGB Colors

To create an RGB color:

1. In the Color Options dialog box, select **RGB** from the Model drop-down list to select the **RGB color model**, as shown in Figure 9.6.

You will see three color text boxes and slide bars to enter values for red, green, and blue.

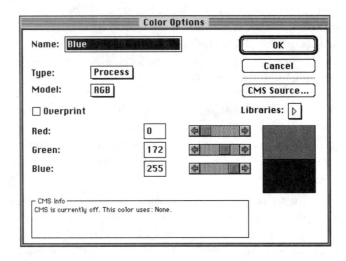

Figure 9.6 *The Color Options dialog box with the RGB color-mixing model selected.*

2. Position the insertion point in the appropriate text box and type a percentage of 100 for each of the colors, or adjust the slide on the slide bar to the value you want. The resulting color mix is displayed in the preview box to the right. (The top half of the box shows the latest color adjustment, the bottom half shows the original color setting). Entering a higher value results in a higher proportional mix of the color.

3. When you have defined the color you'd like, click **OK** or press **Return** to save the color. The name of the color you created is displayed in the Colors palette.

Defining HLS Colors

To create an HLS color:

1. In the Color Options dialog box, select **HLS** from the Model drop-down list to select the **HLS model**, as shown in Figure 9.7. You will see three color text boxes and slide bars to enter specific color values for hue, lightness (sometimes called *luminance* or *brightness*), and saturation.

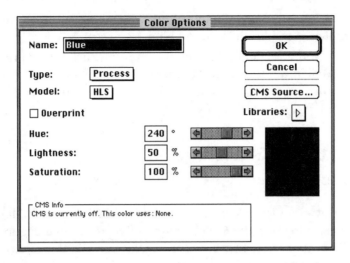

Figure 9.7 *The Color options dialog box with the HLS color-mixing model selected.*

2. Position the insertion point in the appropriate text box and type a value, or adjust the slide on the slide bar to the value you'd like:

    ✦ Hue is adjusted from 0° to 360° on an imaginary color wheel containing the full color spectrum. Entering a specific degree in the hue scale provides an exact position in the color spectrum.

    ✦ Add saturation to intensify the color. Zero percent saturation would be a complete lack of the color, or white. One hundred percent saturation of the hue would be the pure color.

    ✦ Lightness adds a specific level of light intensity to the hue, like increasing the brightness of a light bulb. Zero percent lightness is black, no matter what the level of saturation is for the hue, and 100% lightness is white.

    When all three variables are combined, you create a color. For example, if you select 205° of hue you will be in the blue color spectrum. But without saturation and lightness, you'll see only black in the preview box. Now increase the lightness by moving the slide on the slide bar toward the right. As you increase the value, the preview box changes from black to lightening shades of gray to white. Now set the level of lightness at 50%. We still have no color because saturation is set at zero. Now begin to add saturation and the preview box changes from a dull gray to a bright medium blue.

3. When you have defined the color you want, click **OK** or press **Return** to save it and return to the Define Colors dialog box. Click **OK** again to return to your document. The name of the color you created is displayed in the Colors palette.

Defining CMYK Colors

To create a CMYK color:

1. In the Color Options dialog box, choose **CMYK** from the Model dropdown list to select the **CMYK color model**, as shown in Figure 9.8. You will see four color text boxes and slide bars to enter values for cyan, magenta, yellow, and black.

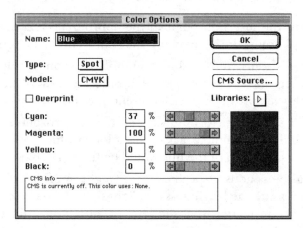

Figure 9.8 *The Color options dialog box with the CMYK color-mixing model selected.*

2. Position the insertion point in the appropriate text box and type a value, or adjust the slide on the slide bar to the value you want.

    The CMYK model of specifying color is the system used most often for printing process color [also called four-color printing, because the four colors (cyan, magenta, yellow, and black) are used to produce all printed colors]. Because this color model is used most often in printing process color, the four colors are also known as process blue (cyan), process red (magenta), process yellow, and process black.

    As you adjust the percentages to fine-tune the color you want, keep in mind that the more color you add, the darker and duller the color becomes. So try to keep the total percentage of the cyan, magenta, yellow, and black values below 240%. For example, a dark, royal blue that is 100% cyan, 100% magenta, and 40% yellow is a vibrant color. Increasing the yellow to 100% makes the blue almost black. Likewise, be judicious with your use of black: A little goes a long way.

3. When you have defined the color you want, click **OK** or press **Return** to save the color.

The name of the color you created is displayed in the Colors palette.

Defining Pantone Colors

To create a Pantone color:

1. In the Color Options dialog box, click the **Libraries** list box (shown below) and choose one of the **Pantone color libraries** to display a Pantone Color dialog box, shown in Figure 9.9.

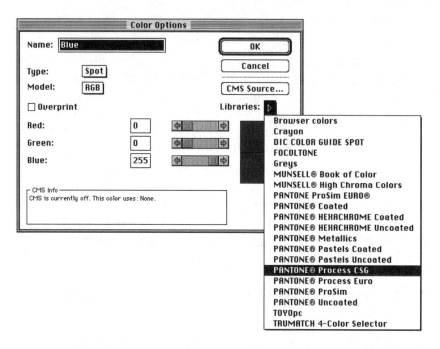

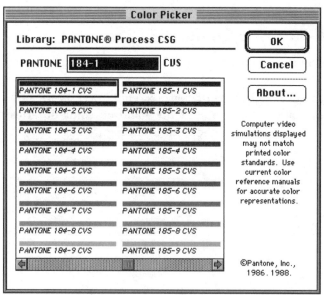

Figure 9.9 *The Pantone Color dialog box.*

2. If you know the Pantone color number, enter it in the text box. Otherwise, scroll down the list of sample colors and select the one you'd like. The color numbers shown match the Pantone Matching System Color Formula Guide, which is used by printers around the country as a standardized way to mix custom colors of ink (much the way custom house paint colors are mixed).

3. When you have selected the color you want, click **OK** or press **Return** to save the color and return to the Color Options dialog box. Click **OK** twice more to move through the nested dialog boxes and return to your document.

The name of the color you created is displayed in the Colors palette. You can choose one of three other color-matching libraries, including a Pantone library of matching process (instead of spot) colors.

N O T E
PageMaker 6.5 supports advanced color-matching libraries, such as Pantone's Hexachrome libraries, which use more than four process inks, to produce remarkably accurate colors. There are two versions of the Hexachrome colors: one for coated and one for uncoated stocks. You can also create your own custom libraries that include colors that consist of your choice of two to eight ink hues.

Defining Color Tints

A tint of a solid color is essentially a screen of the color. You can create screens of solid colors you have already defined by choosing one of the standard screen percentages on the Tint drop-down list.

However, if you want a percentage other than those provided on the submenu, you must first define the tint in the Color Options dialog box. Here are the steps:

1. Activate the Color Options dialog box.

2. Choose **Tint** from the Type drop-down list to display the tint color controls, shown in Figure 9.10.

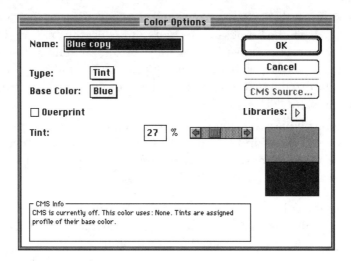

Figure 9.10 *Tint color definition controls.*

3. Click the **Base Color** pop-up list to open the list box and choose the color you'd like to create a tint with. It can be any of PageMaker's predefined colors, or a color that you've added to the list.

4. Click and drag the **Tint** scroll box to the amount of tint you want, or enter an exact percentage in the Tint text box.

5. Give the tint a descriptive name, and click **OK** or press **Return**.

EDITING, COPYING, REMOVING, AND REPLACING COLORS

PageMaker allows you to change the values of colors once they're defined. But remember that when a value is changed, all text and graphics marked with that color are also changed.

Also, when you change the name of a specified color, the name is changed automatically in the Colors palette and on spot color overlays. PageMaker gives you an easy way to change color models: A color defined in one model is defined automatically in every other model. For example, if you customize a particular shade of blue in the RGB model, clicking each of the other color model option buttons (or the **Pantone** button) gives you the settings for the same color in the other models. For example, as shown in the following table, if you define an RGB color, PageMaker defines the same color in the other color models.

It is equally easy to copy custom colors from other PageMaker documents into the current document, or to remove a color you no longer want.

Editing Colors

To edit a color:

1. Select the Colors palette.
2. Double-click the color you want to edit to display the Color Options dialog box (this is the same dialog box you used to create the colors).
3. Change the values for the color.
4. If this color is a Pantone color or a color from one of the other color matching libraries, click the **Libraries** list box and choose the **Pantone** library or the other matching system you'd like. Click **OK** or press **Return** when finished.

Copying Colors

It's not necessary to create the same custom color for more than one document. Instead, simply copy the colors you created in the first document. Follow these steps:

1. Activate the Colors palette.

2. Click the fly-out palette's **Import Colors** choice to display the Import Colors dialog box, which is shown in Figure 9.11.

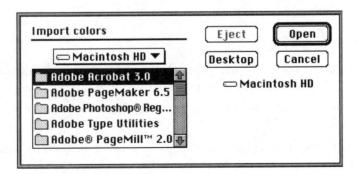

Figure 9.11 *The Import Colors dialog box.*

3. Locate the folder and document that contains the colors you'd like to copy into your current document.

4. Click **OK** or press **Return** to go back to the Color Options dialog box. The colors in the document you specified are copied to the current document and are added to the list of colors in the dialog box. If colors in both documents have the same name, PageMaker warns you and asks whether you want to replace the existing color with the color of the same name. If you choose **Yes**, the current color name is copied over. If you choose **Cancel**, the color is skipped and not copied.

Removing and Replacing Colors

Custom colors that you define, as well as the PageMaker default colors, can be removed from a document at any time. Simply follow these steps to remove a color from a publication:

1. Activate the Colors palette.

2. Choose the color you want to delete, and choose **Delete** from the fly-out menu. PageMaker warns you that you are removing the color, and that it will change all items marked in the color to black. You cannot remove the colors [None], [Paper], [Black], or [Registration] or any color associated with an EPS graphic that is still placed in your publication.

3. Click **OK** or press **Return**. The item you have selected will be changed to black or the replacement color. If you removed a color, the color will be deleted from the color list and any items marked in the color will be changed to black.

To replace one color with another, follow these steps.

1. Activate the Colors palette.

2. Select the color you want to replace with another in the scrolling list, and choose **Color Options** from the flyout menu.

3. Change the name of the color to the exact name of the color you wish to replace it with.

4. Click **OK** once to exit the dialog box, a second time to confirm the change.

To remove a color from a selected object only:

1. Select the object, then click on either the **Line** or **Fill** buttons in the Colors palette to specify whether you want to replace the colors of the outline or fill.

2. Click **None** on the Colors palette

To remove unused colors from a publication:

1. Activate the Colors palette.

2. Click the **Remove Unused Colors** in the flyout menu.

PageMaker will delete any color in the Colors palette that is not currently being used in your publication.

SCREENING TEXT AND GRAPHICS

There are two ways for a commercial printer to print a colored ink on paper: (1) using a custom-mixed spot color ink (as discussed earlier), which coats a printing plate and makes an impression on paper, or (2) by screening one or more process colors to get the correct printing color. Why don't we talk about *screens* (*halftone* and *printer's*) for a minute?

Photographs that we snap with our cameras and have developed at the drug store are known as continuous-tone photos and can be developed as prints or as slides (*transparencies*). If you look at one with a magnifying glass you will see that the colors gradually blend into one another—they are all solid, continuous tones, whether they are light or dark. With one obscure exception, it is impossible to print these continuous tones onto ordinary paper; they must be converted to *halftones*.

Halftones are made by photographing the continuous-tone photo through a very fine screen. The screen breaks up the continuous tones into dot patterns—the darker the color, the larger and closer together the dots. The lighter the color, the smaller and fewer the dots. When the photo is printed, a dot of ink appears for each dot created by the screen, and the image is transferred to paper. Take a moment to look at any printed photo with a magnifying glass. Compare it with a photo you've taken. You will immediately see the difference between photographic processing and printing.

Halftone screens are measured in lines per inch—the more lines, the finer the detail and the higher the resolution of the printed photo. Typical screens are 55, 65, 85, 110, 120, and 133 lines per inch. The screen to be used is determined by the type of printing and the type of paper. For example, newspapers typically use 85-line screens for their photos because newsprint is so coarse and the ink is so watery that dots from a finer screen simply run together and blur. High-quality magazines generally use 133-line screens, and may use 150- or even 200-line screens, again depending on the printing press and the type of paper.

The screen for a continuous-tone photo, scanned into a TIFF file and placed in PageMaker, can be specified by the Image Control dialog box. In this dialog box, you can adjust the brightness and contrast of the photo, indicate the number of lines per inch for the line screen, and specify the angle of the screen (more about this in "Adjusting Scanned Image Screens," later in this chapter).

Printer's screens are measured in percentages of solid colors. The dot-patterned shades on the Fill submenu are percentage screens of black or any color on the Colors palette. Specifying a line or box as a 75% screen in the Fill submenu means that when the screen is turned into a printing plate, only 75% of the color prints through the screen. Therefore, if you color the screen black, you get a second color in the screened area that looks dark gray. If you specify a dark red ink, the color in the screen prints medium red and so on. If you're already using a solid color on the page, the screen is a way of getting a free second color on the same page.

There are two important considerations concerning screens:

✦   If you are preparing a document for commercial printing, and you've included screens to produce screened colors, you must have film negatives for final output from the PostScript imagesetter. The negatives are necessary to make the printing plate. Normally, the printer gets positive paper from customers, which must first be reshot as a negative, and the negative used to generate the plate (the plate needs to be a negative so that when it's inked against paper, the resulting impression will again be a positive). If you give the printer a positive mechanical, the screens will not survive the photographic transition to negative. The printer will have to cut out the PageMaker screens and strip new screens into the negative.

✦ The 10% screen on the Fill submenu acts differently based on the resolution of the final output device. It will look fine when proofed on a 300-dpi laser printer. However, when the output is from a PostScript imagesetter at less than about 2500 dpi, the 10% screen loses most of the screen dots (too much white space appears between each dot for the dots to provide a screen of the ink color). When the screen is output at 2500 dpi or higher, it is again filled in properly to provide 10% of the solid color. Be careful when using 10% screens.

Creating Text Screens

Officially, PageMaker cannot produce screens of text, only of graphic shapes. However, depending on how you print the final document, you can indeed produce very effective screens of type. For example, while you cannot specify a certain percentage screen for text, by coloring text different colors, PageMaker screens the solid type and produces a very effective screen, as shown in Figure 9.12.

Figure 9.12 *A sample of a text screen produced by specifying the screened text in different colors. Boxes filled with screens in increasing percentages from the Fill submenu are shown for comparison at right.*

If you then note the color in the Color Options dialog box as a screen of the color, PageMaker produces a separate spot color overlay for the screen, and your commercial printer can print it. Here are the steps:

1. Open the Color Options dialog box from the Colors palette's flyout menu, and set up a new color-named text screen. Choose a color that produces a nice screen when printed on your laser printer (you'll have to experiment to find the right colors. I used different Pantone grays in the 400 range). If you set up more than one color as a screen,

give a distinct name to each one: very light screen, light screen, medium screen, and so on.

2. Type the text you want to screen. Give the text whatever specifications you want using the Character Specifications dialog box (**Command/Ctrl+T**).

3. Highlight the text with the Text tool and choose a screen from the Colors palette.

Creating Graphic Screens

As I have mentioned, any graphic shape created in PageMaker can be screened by using the Fill submenu. Follow these steps:

1. Draw a shape using one of the drawing tools.

2. While the shape is still selected (displaying its sizing handles), click the **Fill** button, and choose a screen percentage from the Tint drop-down list.

3. To color the screen in a color other than black, while the shape is still selected, click the color you want in the Colors palette.

That's fine for shapes, you say, but what if you'd like to screen a heavy line? That's easy. Just do the following:

1. Select the **Line** tool and draw the line.

2. Select the weight of the line from the Line submenu.

3. Choose the **Box** tool and draw a box on top of the line, exactly the same size. You may prefer to increase the page view in order to draw more accurately.

4. From the Stroke submenu, choose **None** to eliminate the border around the box.

5. From the Tint drop-down list, choose the screen you want for the box.

6. Now select the line under the box, and delete it. You'll have a screened line in its place.

Adjusting Scanned-Image Screens

Any scanned photo, placed as a TIFF file in a document, can be refined using PageMaker's Image Control feature. Follow these steps:

1. Select the image with the Pointer tool.

2. Choose the **Element** pull-down menu and choose **Image>Image Control** to display the Image Control dialog box, shown in Figure 9.13.

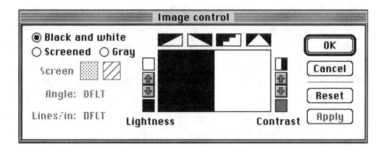

Figure 9.13 *The Image Control dialog box.*

3. Use this dialog box to adjust and control the final printed image. You have the following options:

   ✦ **Lightness**—Use the slide control, or enter a percentage value to adjust the lightness of the image. Add more lightness (a higher value) to make the image lighter. Reduce the lightness value to make the image darker.

   ✦ **Contrast**—Use the slide control or enter a percentage value to adjust the contrast of the image to the surrounding background. Entering a higher value increases the contrast. A lower value reduces the contrast.

   ✦ **Screen patterns**—This may seem a little confusing, but bear with me. PageMaker provides two patterns of screens for photographs: (1) screens made up of varying sizes of dots, and (2) screens made up of varying thicknesses of lines. The dot screen box (the left box) produces normal photographic screens (based on the number of lines per inch in the Screen Frequency text box). The dot pattern is normally selected when you are working with photos. The right box represents a special effects lined-screen pattern (the head in the Adobe logo is screened with this lined-screen pattern). The pattern uses lines of various thicknesses to provide the details of the photo.

+ **Screen angle**—The default angle (indicated by DFLT) is 45_ for most PostScript printers. You can specify your own angle by entering a value here, from 0° to 360° .

+ **Screen frequency**—This choice determines the number of lines per inch for the screen. The default setting (indicated by DFLT) means that PageMaker assigns the number of lines per inch based on the PostScript device to which you are printing. For example, if you are printing to a 300-dpi laser printer, the maximum lines per inch the printer can handle is 53. PageMaker automatically assigns that frequency to the image. If you print to a higher resolution device, PageMaker automatically increases the lines per inch accordingly. You can enter any value in the text box from 10 to 300.

4. Click the **Default** button to reset the default values you changed in the appropriate text boxes.

5. Click the **Apply** button to see the results of the values you entered on the selected image. You can click on the title bar of the Image Control dialog box and drag it out of the way if it is blocking the image.

6. Click **OK** or press **Return** to save the values you changed, and then return to your document.

Creating a Color Library

You can create a custom library consisting of just the colors you want to use in a particular publication. Just follow these steps:

1. Open the Colors palette and add custom colors you define, or colors drawn from one of PageMaker's color libraries, using any of the techniques described earlier in this chapter.

2. From the Utilities menu, choose **PageMaker Plug-ins Create Color Library**. The dialog box shown in Figure 9.14 will appear.

3. Type a descriptive name and a file name for the new library in the boxes provided.

4. Define a layout for your library, using up to 10 rows and 10 columns.

5. Add notes about the library, such as which publications you use it with, in the Notes box.

6. Click **Save** to store your new color library.

```
┌─────────────────────────────────────────────────────────┐
│ ══════════════════ Create Color Library ═══════════════  │
│                                                           │
│  Library name: │                    │    ╭──────────╮    │
│                └────────────────────┘    │   Save   │    │
│  File name:    │ Custom.bcf          │    ╰──────────╯    │
│                └─────────────────────┘   ┌──────────┐    │
│  Preferences                              │  Cancel  │    │
│      Colors per column:  │ 5 │            └──────────┘    │
│                                           ┌──────────┐    │
│      Colors per row:     │ 3 │            │ Save as… │    │
│                                           └──────────┘    │
│  Notes:   ┌───────────────────────────┐                  │
│           │                           │                  │
│           │                           │                  │
│           │                           │                  │
│           └───────────────────────────┘                  │
└─────────────────────────────────────────────────────────┘
```

Figure 9.14 *Create Color Library dialog box.*

NOTE PageMaker also features an advanced capability that allows you to create your own color library with colors that you define using up to eight different inks, and values from one of the supported color models. This is a highly technical manual method (rather than the pick-and-choose way of assembling existing colors described above) that is chiefly of use to graphics professionals.

TO SUM UP

In this chapter, you have learned how easy it is to add color to your document. You've also learned that color really depends on the way the document will be printed: If printed to a color laser printer, virtually any color you create will be replicated when printed. However, if you plan to take the document to a commercial printer, you must specify colors the printer can create. You've learned that, except for separating the colors of color photographs, PageMaker offers sophisticated color tools that make it as easy to add, create, and print spot colors as it is to compose the page.

In the next chapter, you see how easily PageMaker deals with long documents such as books and proposals.

CHAPTER 10

Developing Long Documents

- ◆ Using the Story Editor
- ◆ Checking your spelling
- ◆ Using the Find feature
- ◆ Using the Change feature
- ◆ Linking text and graphics
- ◆ Compiling chapters into a book
- ◆ Creating an index
- ◆ Creating a table of contents
- ◆ To sum up

Long documents are multiple-page publications with stories or chapters, possibly containing black-and-white or color photographs or graphic illustrations. Long documents can be magazines and trade publications, professional journals and technical reports, sales presentations and proposals, books (like this one), and catalogs. Long documents are different things to different people. If you are comfortable producing one-page fact sheets, then a 12-page brochure may seem like a very long document. If you normally work with technical manuals or proposals, then a 200- or 300-page document may not be especially intimidating.

A long document magnifies the multitude of decisions necessary to write, edit, design, lay out, and produce information in the form of a book or manual—your decisions seem to increase exponentially with the number of pages in the document. Consider the problem of changing a proper name. Let's say you are producing a proposal for the Parker Active Waste Recycler, and the chairman of the board wants to rename the company after his newborn granddaughter. So now you face changing 342 product name references to Cindilou's Urban Recycling Center. How do you find all those references; how can you be sure you won't miss one or two?

Long documents often involve many writers, editors, designers, graphic artists, managers, reviewers, proofreaders, test readers, and others just wanting to help stir the pot. How can you be sure which is the latest level of revisions to the work? When was the text for Chapter 2 last edited? How can a new chapter be inserted between two chapters? Isn't there a way of adding a spreadsheet to the text? Is the spreadsheet updated? For computer software manuals and proposals, there's always a new revision needed just around the corner. How do you change the text files without disturbing the layout and pagination of the existing book? Can you edit existing graphics, or must they be created from scratch?

It is obvious that long documents require special attention, whether highly stylized color magazines or commercially produced volumes. Whether you are experienced in book-length publishing or not, PageMaker's long-document capabilities make the task a lot easier.

Using the Story Editor

Up to this point, I've suggested you enter text on the page in the document window (what PageMaker calls the *Layout Editor*), because it's a good way to learn the software, and typing in the Layout Editor gives you complete WYSI-

WYG control over the page. However, PageMaker also contains a word processor called the *Story Editor*. Use the Story Editor when writing or editing longer passages of text.

The Story Editor can be a welcome relief from the distractions of working in the Layout Editor. Sometimes the text needs the full attention of a writer or editor, who doesn't want to bother with formatting type, aligning graphics, and other layout activities. Using the Story Editor is faster than writing the text in a word processor and then placing the text in PageMaker.

Opening the Story Editor

The Story Editor is not only easy to use, but also easy to access. You'll find yourself switching frequently to the Story Editor, to make text changes or type new text. Stories that were started on a word processor and placed in PageMaker can be finished or edited in the Story Editor. To open the Story Editor:

1. Choose the **Edit** pull-down menu.
2. Choose **Edit Story** to display the story view, shown in Figure 10.1.

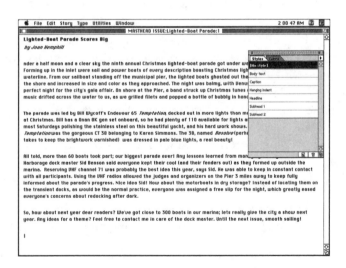

Figure 10.1 *The Story Editor window.*

When you're working in the Story Editor, you're seeing the story view. When you're in the Layout Editor, you're seeing the layout view. To keep from confusing you with these views and the page view size (which is applicable only in the layout view), I refer to the views as their respective editors.

The Story Editor provides a blank typing area, like a white sheet of paper, to type on. The insertion point is similar to the Text tool insertion point. It marks the position at which characters will be typed or deleted. While you can't use the Toolbox tools, if the Style or Color palettes are visible in the Layout Editor, they will also be available in the Style Editor, as shown in Figure 10.1 (or, you can open the palettes using the Window pull-down menu). You can mark text in styles and colors the same way you do in the Layout Editor. The colors will not be visible until you switch back to the Layout Editor. Some style changes—namely bold and italics—are shown in the Story Editor. Type size changes are not displayed in the Story Editor, nor are paragraph specification changes (other than indents). The typeface and size displayed in the Story Editor is that which is specified in the story view area of the Preferences dialog box. You may have noticed that some of the commands in the menu bar are different when you are working in the Story Editor. I'll explain the differences in a moment.

How the Story Editor Names Stories

Stories displayed in the Story Editor are named with the first 19 characters of the first sentence of the story. For example, a story beginning "Computers can be grouped according to the type of central processing unit (CPU)" is named Computers can be gr:1. The colon and the number 1 indicate that this is the first story with this name (a second story starting with the same first few words would be named with a :2, a third story starting with the same words would be named with a :3, and so on). Since the Story Editor considers any text block a story, a headline that is in a separate text block would be named by the same convention. If the headline is less than 19 characters long, you will see the whole headline, a colon, and the number 1 as its story name.

Switching between the Story and Layout Editors

There are several ways of moving between the Layout Editor and the Story Editor, depending on what you are doing at the moment. For example:

✦ After you access the Story Editor the first time, you can switch between the Story Editor and the Layout Editor using the Window pull-down menu.

The Window pull-down menu, shown in Figure 10.2, was opened while the Story Editor was active. It shows the document Masthead and two stories used in the document.

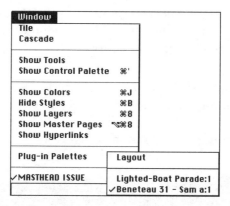

Figure 10.2 *The Window pull-down menu shows the story submenu with the stories opened in the current document.*

✦ To move to a different story in the Story Editor, choose the **Window** pull-down menu and click the story you want. If you want to move back to the document, click the document file name.

✦ Once you are in the Story Editor, you can move back to the Layout Editor by clicking anywhere in the Layout Editor window. You can move back to the same story in the Story Editor by choosing it from the Window menu (see Figure 10.3).

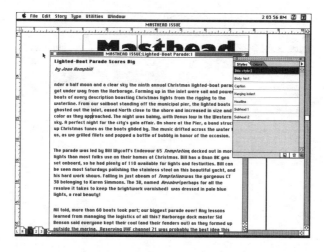

Figure 10.3 *Click the document window to move from the Story Editor (in the foreground) to the Layout Editor (in the background).*

✦ Use the PageMaker shortcut **Command/Ctrl+E** to toggle between the Layout Editor and Story Editor. The position of the insertion point is maintained between the two editors.

✦ Once you are in the Story Editor, click the **Size** box and shrink the story window to reveal the document window (and the Layout Editor) underneath. You can reduce the size of all stories and your document, as shown in Figure 10.4, or click on the document or one of the stories to continue work, as shown in Figure 10.5.

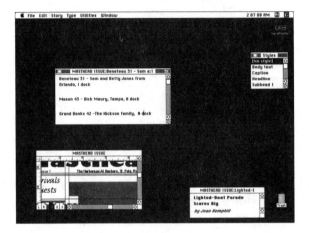

Figure 10.4 The laid-out document and stories reduced on the desktop.

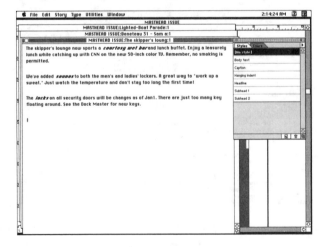

Figure 10.5 The laid-out document and stories opened in cascaded fashion.

Closing the Story Editor and Placing the Story

If you create a new story in the Story Editor, you will want to place the story in the Layout Editor. PageMaker gives you several ways to do this:

✦ Open the File pull-down menu and choose **Place** to place the story. The Story Editor closes, and the insertion point changes to a loaded-text icon, indicating that the story is ready to be placed on the page in the Layout Editor.

✦ Close the Story Editor window by clicking the **Close** box in the upper-left corner (or, upper-right corner in Windows 95). PageMaker displays an Alert dialog box, shown in Figure 10.6, indicating that the story has not been placed.

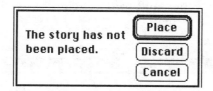

Figure 10.6 An Alert box warns you that the story you are closing has not yet been placed.

To place the story, click the **Place** button. The insertion point changes to a loaded-text icon, indicating that the story is ready to be placed on the page in the Layout Editor. Click the **Discard** button if you want to throw away the story you just finished. Choose **Cancel** to return to the Story Editor.

Differences between the Story and Layout Editors

The most visible difference between the Layout Editor and Story Editor is that in the Story Editor some of the items on the menu bar change, as shown below. For example, the Story Editor replaces the Layout pull-down menu with the Story menu (shown below) and hides the Element menu (since the Story Editor works only with text, none of the element commands are applicable).

Also, some commands on some of the pull-down menus are not available in the Story Editor. For example:

✦ **File menu**—The **Document Setup** and **Print** commands are dimmed, because you're not working with pages in the Story Editor, just stories. To print what you have done in the Story Editor, first move back to the Layout Editor.

✦ **Utilities menu**—The **Find**, **Find Next**, **Change**, and **Spelling** commands are available in the Story Editor. The first three commands are for searching and replacing text (see "Finding and Changing"), and the **Spelling** command checks spelling (see "Checking Your Spelling"). The menu includes commands for marking words and phrases for an index, and creating an index and a table of contents (see "Creating an Index" and "Creating a Table of Contents").

In the Story Editor, PageMaker defines a story as any single text block. For this reason, in a newsletter like the one shown in Figure 10.7, each block of text, including headlines, bylines, and so on, is considered an individual story in the Story Editor.

Figure 10.7 *Text blocks selected with the **Select All** commands show individual stories in the Story Editor.*

Text blocks that are threaded together in the Layout Editor comprise the same story in the Story Editor. While a text block may be split among several pages in the Layout Editor, you will see it as a continuous story in the Story Editor.

Although graphics are not displayed in the Story Editor, in-line graphics (those that are part of a text block) are shown with the in-line graphic symbol.

Closing the Story Editor

There are several ways to close the Story Editor, including:

+ Open the Story pull-down menu and choose **Close Story** to move back to the Layout Editor. Choose **New Story** to open an additional story window to begin typing a new story.

+ If you have several stories open, hold down the **Option/Alt** key as you access the Story menu to make the **Close All Stories...** choice appear.

+ Click the **Close** box in the upper-left corner (upper-right in Windows 95) of the Story Editor window to close the window and return to the Layout Editor.

Displaying Special Characters

While working in the Story Editor, you may find it helpful to see the hidden marks for spaces, tabs, and paragraphs. When the hidden marks are displayed, you can use the **Find** and **Change** commands to search for the marks and delete them or change them to something else. For example, you could search through the story for tabs and then delete the tabs (see "Using the Find Feature" and "Using the Change Feature").

To display the hidden marks:

1. Choose the **Story** pull-down menu and choose **Display ¶**.
2. PageMaker redisplays your story showing the following symbols:

    + **Space markers**—A dot is shown each time the **Spacebar** is pressed.

    + **Tab markers**—A tab marker is shown every time the **Tab** key is pressed.

    + **Paragraph markers**—A paragraph marker is shown each time the **Return** key is pressed.

In addition to the hidden marks, the following symbols are displayed whenever they occur in the text block, regardless of whether or not you are displaying the hidden marks:

✦ **In-line graphic marker**—Displayed wherever you have placed an in-line graphic in the text. The graphic itself will not be displayed in the Story Editor.

✦ **Page number marker**—Any time you insert a page number marker (**Command/Ctrl+Opt/Alt+p**) in the text, a marker symbol, rather than the actual number, is shown in the Story Editor. In the Layout Editor, the actual number is displayed.

✦ **Index entry marker**—Shown whenever you have marked a word for inclusion in the publication's index.

Displaying Style Names

Style names for each paragraph marked as a style can be displayed in the Story Editor. To display the names, choose the **Display Style Names** command from the Story pull-down menu. PageMaker adds a left margin to the story window, called a *sidebar* and displays any style names assigned to paragraphs, as shown in Figure 10.8.

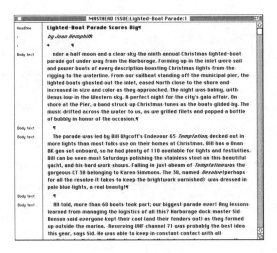

Figure 10.8 *The Story Editor showing the sidebar with style names.*

You will notice some small dots in the sidebar. The dots correspond to each paragraph in the story. Click the dot to highlight the associated paragraph. You can also highlight an entire paragraph by clicking its sidebar style name.

CHECKING YOUR SPELLING

A speller can be a help or a hindrance, depending on how you use it. A *speller* compares each word in a document with a list of words and calls your attention to any discrepancy. A speller can give you a false sense of confidence that a document is spelled correctly, when in fact it can contain wrong, but correctly spelled words. For example, the words principle and principal are both spelled correctly, but the speller does not care which word you use. Nor does a speller help you with the words it's and its, bear and bare, or ware, where, and wear (it's up to you to use the correct word). A speller does not understand the correct order of words in a sentence. If, by chance, you transpose two words, the speller will not notice. Similarly, if you type if where you should have typed is, the speller does not detect the error.

If you have used earlier versions of PageMaker, or if you've used a word processor without spelling capabilities, you know what it's like to dream about having a spell checker. Fortunately, PageMaker now has a full-featured speller that adds a number of related capabilities to its strength in managing long documents. The speller can be used only in the Story Editor.

Starting the Speller

The speller can check any single story in a publication, or all of the stories. To start the speller:

1. Open the Utilities pull-down menu.
2. Choose **Spelling** to display the Spelling dialog box, shown in Figure 10.9.

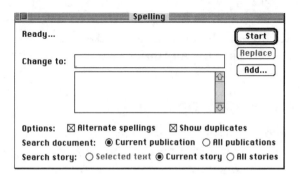

Figure 10.9 The Spelling dialog box.

The Spelling dialog box offers the following commands and options:

✦ **Start button**—Click to begin spell checking a story.

✦ **Replace button**—When the speller finds a discrepancy, it highlights the word in the story and displays it in the Change to Text box. Edit the word or choose from a list of possible words and press **Replace**. The speller replaces the incorrect word with the one in the text box, or with the word you selected from the list.

✦ **Add button**—If the speller comes to a word that isn't in its dictionary, it pauses and highlights the word. If the word is spelled correctly, you may want to add it to the dictionary by clicking the **Add** button.

✦ **Alternate spellings**—The default setting is to have PageMaker suggest alternative spellings to words it does not understand. However, to speed up the spelling program, you can click the box to remove the X and disable the option.

✦ **Show duplications**—The normal setting for the spelling program is to search for and report duplicate words. Click the box to remove the X if you wish to disable the option.

✦ **Current publication**—You can specify whether you want the speller to check the spelling of the currently displayed publication by clicking the **Current Publication** radio button, or all open documents by clicking the **All Publications** radio button.

✦ **Selected text option**—If you have highlighted text with the insertion point and start the speller, the **Selected Text** radio button will be marked, indicating only the selected text that is checked for spelling.

✦ **Current story option**—If you want to check the spelling of the currently displayed story only, click the **Current Story** radio button.

✦ **All stories option**—If you want to check the spelling of all stories in the document, click the **All Stories** radio button.

Positioning the Spelling Dialog Box

If the Spelling dialog box is blocking some text you want to read, click the title bar and drag it to another area of the Story window. If you click anywhere in the story text while the Spelling dialog box is active, you will move the Story window to the foreground, and the Spelling dialog box will move behind it.

To activate the speller again, you can either restart it from the Edit pull-down menu or reduce the size of the Story window so that you can see and activate it. Simply click on the upper border of the story window and drag it down a bit, or click the **Size** box to reduce the Story window and reveal the Spelling dialog box, as shown in Figure 10.10. Then choose **Start** to begin spell checking. When a misspelled word is located, the story window will maximize automatically, and the word will be highlighted.

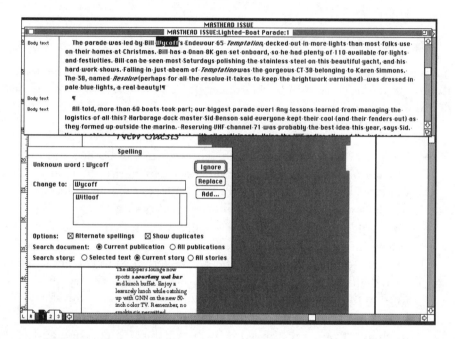

Figure 10.10 *Story reduced in size to reveal the Spelling dialog box underneath it.*

Correcting Misspelled Words

To begin the spell checking, click the **Start** button. The speller starts comparing each word in the story with its dictionary from the insertion point position forward to the end of the story. If the speller is started in the middle of a story, when it reaches the end it asks if you want it to go back to the beginning and check the part of the story before the insertion point's location.

At the first spelling discrepancy, the speller pauses to let you know the word doesn't match any of the words in its dictionary, as shown in Figure 10.11.

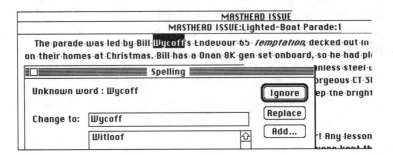

Figure 10.11 *The speller stops and highlights a word it doesn't find in its dictionary.*

The misspelled word is displayed in the Change To pop-up list. The speller attempts to identify words in its dictionary that come closest to what the misspelled word should be. These words are displayed in a list under the Change To pop-up list. Do one of the following:

✦ If the word is misspelled and the correct word is displayed in the list of possibilities, click the correct word to highlight it and click **Replace**. The correctly spelled word replaces the misspelled word in the story, and the speller continues spell checking.

✦ Alternatively, if the word is misspelled and the correct word is displayed in the list of possibilities, position the insertion point in the Change To text box and edit the misspelled word to correct it. Then click **Replace** to replace the misspelled word with the correctly spelled word in the story. The speller continues spell checking the story.

✦ If the word is misspelled and the speller offers no possible alternatives to choose from, edit the word in the Change To text box and click **Replace** to replace the misspelled word with the corrected word in the story. The speller continues spell checking the story.

✦ If the word is not misspelled, but you don't wish to add it to the spelling dictionary, click **Ignore**. The speller ignores the word and continues spell checking.

✦ If the word is not misspelled, and you want to add it to the spelling dictionary, click **Add**. The word is added, and from that point on the speller knows how to spell the word. The speller continues spell checking the story. See "Adding Words to Different Dictionaries."

Correcting Duplicate Words

When PageMaker's speller encounters a pair of duplicate words, it stops on the second word, highlights it, and displays "Duplicate word:(name)" in the dialog box, as shown in Figure 10.12.

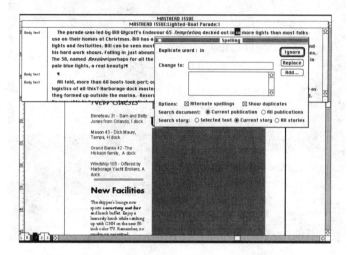

Figure 10.12 *The speller notifies you of duplicate words.*

If the duplicate words are a typing error, click the **Replace** button to delete the second occurrence of the word and continue spell checking. If the duplicate words are correct, click **Ignore** to continue.

Adding Words to the Different Dictionaries

The English language contains many words, more than any other language. There are about 450,000 words defined in Webster's New International Dictionary. If you add all of the English technical vocabularies (for disciplines including computer science, medicine, engineering, and physics) you will add hundreds of thousands, if not millions of words. While PageMaker's dictionary is large, you may want to add many technical terms it doesn't contain. Here's how:

1. Start the speller by choosing **Spelling** from the Utilities menu.

2. When the speller encounters a word not currently in its dictionary, and you wish to add it, choose the **Add** button. The speller displays the Add Word To User Dictionary dialog box, shown in Figure 10.13.

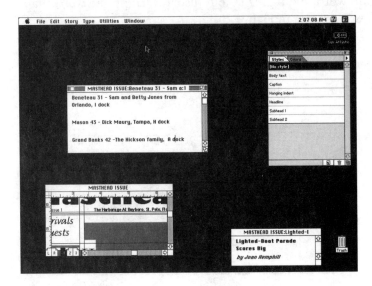

Figure 10.13 The Add Word to User Dictionary dialog box.

Use this dialog box to add the highlighted word to the spelling dictionary. This is the same dialog box used to add a hyphenated word to the hyphenation dictionary (see "Adding Words to the Hyphenation Dictionary," in Chapter 3).

3. In the Word text box, change the spelling of the word to the way you want it to be recorded in the dictionary. Enter tilde marks to indicate the most favorable hyphenation breaks, as explained in Chapter 3.

4. If you have purchased additional dictionaries from Adobe Corporation, click the **Dictionary** pop-up list to open the list of available dictionaries. Choose a different dictionary, if you want.

5. The word will normally be saved in the dictionary in all lowercase letters. If you want the word to be saved as shown in the Word text box, click the **Exactly as Typed** radio button.

6. To save the word in the dictionary, click **OK** or press **Return**. To cancel the word, click **Cancel**. You will return to the Spelling dialog box. Click the **Continue** button to continue spell checking the story.

Removing Words from the Dictionaries

You can remove any word from the spelling and hyphenation dictionaries. To remove a word, type the word in the Word text box and click the **Remove** button. The word is removed. Click **OK** or press **Return** to return to the Spelling dialog box.

Closing the Speller

When the speller finishes checking the document, it reports "No spelling errors detected" in the dialog box. Close the dialog box by clicking the **Close** box. Likewise, you can close the speller at any time while you are spell checking a document by using the Close box.

USING THE FIND FEATURE

In long documents, corrections are often multiplied by the number of pages involved. For example, if a model number changes, there may be many references to the old model number in the document. Each reference must be ferreted out and changed; there can be no old model numbers remaining. PageMaker's Find feature is capable of finding all instances of the old model number, and, when used with the Change feature, can change the old number to the new one automatically.

Like the speller, the Find feature has some limitations. It's very literal and finds exactly what you request. For example, if you ask PageMaker to find all occurrences of the word *men*, it finds the word, but it also finds any words with *men* in the word, such as *women, elements, cumbersomeness, gentlemen,* and *immense.* The reason for this is simple: You didn't tell PageMaker to look for complete words. If you had added a space before and after the word, PageMaker would have located only the exact matches you were looking for. The lesson here is to be careful and literal when you want to either find or change something.

Searching for Words

There are any number of reasons why you might want to search for a word in a document, from outright changing the word, to altering the type specifications, to simply moving to an area of the story where you know the word is located. To access the Find feature and search for a word:

1. Position the insertion point where you want to begin the search.

2. Open the Utilities pull-down menu and choose **Find** to display the Find dialog box, shown in Figure 10.14.

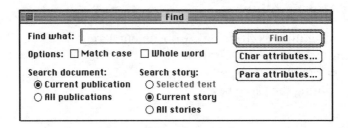

Figure 10.14 *The Find dialog box.*

3. Type the word you wish to search for in the Find What text box. Enter the word exactly as you want PageMaker to search for it. For example, if you were searching for figure references in this chapter to check the sequence of figure numbering, you might enter the word **figure**. PageMaker would not only find the figure references, but any in-text references to the figures as well. By entering **Figure 10**, Find takes you only to Chapter 10 numbered figure references, in order. By entering **Figure 10.9**, PageMaker takes you to that exact figure reference.

4. Choose **Find** to find the first instance of the word you entered. PageMaker searches from the insertion point forward to locate the first occurrence of the word. The word is highlighted when found, as shown in Figure 10.15.

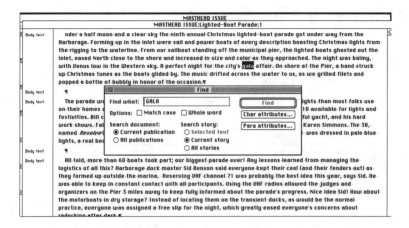

Figure 10.15 *Find highlights first use of an entered word.*

5. To search for the next occurrence of the word, click the **Find Next** button (after finding the first occurrence of the word or phrase, the **Find** button changes to the **Find Next** button).

   If you began your search in the middle of the story, when PageMaker reaches the end of the story you'll be asked if the search should continue from the beginning.

6. To close the Find dialog box, click the **Close** box.

Using Find Next

Once you have located your first occurrence of the word or phrase with the Find dialog box and closed the box, you can use the **Find Next** command to search for the same word or phrase. There is no dialog box. **Find Next** simply highlights the word or phrase when found, or reports that there are no more occurrences of the word or phrase.

Positioning the Find Dialog Box

If the Find dialog box is in the way of some text you want to read, click the title bar and drag it out of the way. You can place the dialog box anywhere on the page, even tuck some of it under the bottom border of the Story Editor's window, as shown in Figure 10.16 (just leave enough showing so that you can still click the **Find** button).

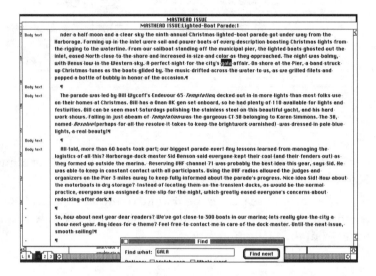

Figure 10.16 *Most of the Find dialog box is tucked below the story border to maximize the view of the text.*

If you click anywhere in the story text while the Find dialog box is active, you will move the Story window to the foreground and the Find dialog box behind it. To activate the Find dialog box again you can restart it from the Edit pull-down menu, or, by reducing the size of the Story window, you can see and activate it. Simply click on the upper border of the Story window and drag it down a bit. Or, use the Size box to reduce the size of the story to reveal the Find dialog box underneath, as shown in Figure 10.17. Then choose **Find** to search for the word entered in the Find What text box, or type in a different word. When the word is located, the Story window automatically maximizes, and the word is highlighted.

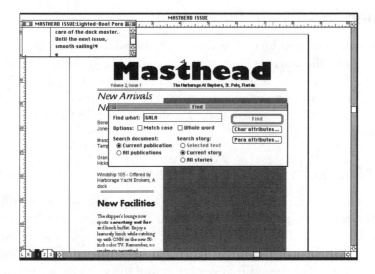

Figure 10.17 *The Story window is reduced in size to reveal the active Find dialog box underneath.*

Matching the Case of Words

Normally, the Find feature looks for both lowercase and uppercase versions of the word you are searching for. If you want PageMaker to match the uppercase and lowercase letters exactly as typed in the Find What text box, click the **Match** option box to add an X in the box. Then, if you enter a proper name, or a word with an unusual case structure (like **LaserWriter**), PageMaker will find it and not find lowercase versions of the word.

Matching Only Whole Words

If you are looking, for example, for all references of the word *ion* and don't wish to find every word ending in *tion*, click the **Whole Word** option box to add an X in the box. Then PageMaker will find only the whole word you entered in the Find What text box.

Defining the Search Pattern

If you have highlighted text to search, the **Selected Text** radio button will be checked. If not, the **Current Story** radio button will be checked. If you want to search all of the stories in the current document, click the **All Stories** radio button. To look through the current story only, leave the **Current Publication** radio button checked. To look through all open publications, click the **All Publications** radio button.

Searching with Wildcard Characters

Wildcard is a software term that has come to mean a special character or characters that represent any other character. In PageMaker, the wildcard is the caret symbol (**Shift+6** [^]) together with the question mark. A wildcard is useful when you are searching for a word and are not entirely sure how you spelled the word. For example, you want to find the word *rendezvous* but can't remember if you spelled it correctly or if you changed the *ez* to *is*. To ensure that PageMaker finds the word regardless of the two letters in question, you could replace the two letters with wildcards. In the Find What text box, you would type **rend^?^?vous**. PageMaker would search for the word, ignoring the two letters between *d* and *v*, and find each occurrence of the word.

Searching for Phrases

You can enter a phrase in the Find What dialog box, as well as individual words. Just be sure of the order and spelling of the words, or use wildcards where you are not sure. To enter a phrase, simply type the words you want in the text box (you can enter as long a string of words as you want). Use the **Right** and **Left Arrow** keys to move through the phrase. Use the **Del** or **Backspace** key to delete words. Or highlight the word with the insertion point and type the correction. When you are finished entering the phrase, click the **Find** button to search for the string of words.

Searching for Special Attributes

PageMaker can find not only words, but words with specific type attributes. For example, PageMaker can find instances of the words *Apple Macintosh* in the Caption style and when specified in 9 point Helvetica Narrow italic. Or, it could identify all uses of the word *PageMaker* in second-order headlines, when specified in 24 point Palatino bold. To identify the special attributes you want to search for:

1. Click the **Char Attributes** button in the Find dialog box to display the Find Character Attributes dialog box, shown in Figure 10.18.

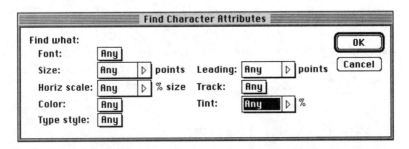

Figure 10.18 *The Find Character Attributes dialog box.*

2. Use this dialog box to set up specific attributes for the word or phrase you'd like to find. Choose among several options. These include font, type size, type style, width, color, leading, tracking, and tint.

3. When you've set your options, click **OK** or press **Return** to search.

If you click in the **Para Attributes** box, you can search for specific styles from your style list, left, centered, or justified text, as well as top of caps, baseline, or proportional leading attributes.

Searching for Bookmarks

No, PageMaker doesn't have a Bookmark feature. However, bookmarks are very useful in marking your place in a long document, and it's easy enough to make a bookmark. The key to a bookmark is using the **Find** command to take you back to the bookmark. Here's how:

1. Place a bookmark in the text where you are currently working. The bookmark can be any letter or symbol, but it's a good idea to make it unique to the document (using the dollar sign, for example, isn't a good idea because you might use it in the text as well). I use two question marks as a bookmark, but anything not ordinarily used in text will do nicely.

2. To find the bookmark, simply choose **Find** from the Utilities menu, enter the bookmark in the Find What text box, and click the **Find** button. PageMaker takes you to your bookmark. Remember to delete the bookmark in your text before continuing.

It's easy to set up multiple bookmarks in the same document by numbering them. For example, the first bookmark is ??1, the second bookmark is ??2, and so forth.

It's a good idea, before printing, to check your stories for bookmarks you may have failed to delete. You'll see how in the next section, "Using the Change Feature."

USING THE CHANGE FEATURE

The Change feature is often the next step after finding something—you want to change it to something else. That's why Change incorporates the **Find** command with the **Change** command in one dialog box. An easy example of using the **Change** command is to replace the two hard returns with one hard return that are often added between paragraphs in text. Simply invoke the **Change** command, search for double hard returns (by using **^p^p**), and replace with one **^p**. In a long document, you will save a great deal of time and manual editing.

Replacing Text

The **Change** command can also be used to replace multiple occurrences of one word with another word. For example, it would be an easy matter to replace all occurrences of the word *PageMaker* in this book with Adobe PageMaker 6.5 by using the **Change** command. Just enter **PageMaker** as the word to search for and **Adobe PageMaker 6.5** as the text with which to replace the word. The **Change** command is very similar in use to the **Find** command. Follow these steps:

1. Since you will be making changes to your story, save the document first by choosing **Save** from the File menu. Then, if you change something incorrectly, use the **Revert** command to revert back to the version of the document before you started these steps.

2. Open the Utilities pull-down menu and choose **Change** to display the Change dialog box, shown in Figure 10.19.

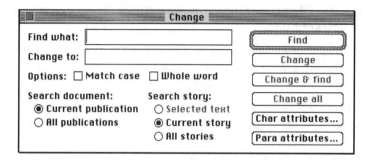

Figure 10.19 *The Change dialog box.*

3. Enter the word or words you want to search for in the Find What text box.

4. Enter the replacement word or words in the Change To text box.

5. Now define how the word or phrase matches will take place:

✦ To match the exact uppercase or lowercase letters in a word or phrase, click the **Match Case** option box to add an X to it.

✦ If the search will not be case-sensitive, leave the option box unchecked.

✦ If you want the text in the Find What text box to match the whole word, click the **Whole Word** option box to add an X to it.

✦ If you want partial matches of the text in the Find What text box (so that searching, for example, for *add* would also find *addition*), leave the option box unchecked.

6. If you have selected text in the story to be searched, the **Selected Text** radio button will be checked. If not, the **Current Story** radio button will be checked. If you want to search all stories in the current document, click the **All Stories** radio button.

Once you have defined what you are searching for and with what you are replacing the text, you have the following choices:

✦ Click the **Find** button to find the first occurrence of the text you entered in the Find What text box. PageMaker begins searching from the insertion point forward and highlights the first instance of the searched-for word or phrase. If you want to change this occurrence, click the **Change** button. If not, continue searching by clicking the **Find Next** button.

✦   Click the **Change** button to change only this occurrence of the searched-for word or phrase. Click the **Find Next** button to find the next occurrence.

✦   Clicking the **Change & Find** button is the same as clicking the **Change** button and the **Find Next** button, separately. Change & Find changes the currently found occurrence of the word or phrase and searches for the next occurrence.

✦   Click the **Change All** button to find and change all occurrences of the searched-for word or phrase. Take care in using this option, as it can result in strange, unexpected combinations of words.

Replacing Special Attributes

Attributes can be assigned to both the searched-for text and the replacement text. The steps are easy:

1.   Click the **Para Attributes** button in the Change dialog box to display the Change Paragraph Attributes dialog box, shown in Figure 10.20.

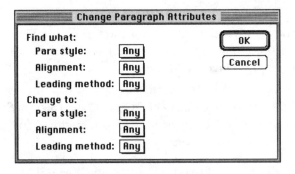

Figure 10.20 *The Change Paragraph Attributes dialog box.*

2.   Use the Change Paragraph Attributes dialog box to set up specific attributes for the searched-for word or phrase. Then select the attributes you want to assign to the replacement word or phrase. Choose among the following options:

✦ **Paragraph style**—Click the pop-up list to display the currently defined styles for this document. The Para style list box defaults to Any, meaning that all styles are eligible to be included in the search and replacement. You may select a style as part of the attribute search or replacement criteria.

✦ **Alignment**—Click the pop-up list to display the options (Any, flush right, etc.).

✦ **Leading Method**—Click the pop-up list to display the options, such as Any or Proportional.

3. Click **OK** to return to the Change dialog box.

4. Click the **Char Attributes** button to select character attributes to search and change. Choose among the following options:

✦ **Font**—Click the pop-up list to display PageMaker's list of fonts. The list box defaults to Any, meaning that all fonts currently used in the document are eligible for search and replacement. You may select a font to be included in the search or replacement criteria.

✦ **Size**—Click the pop-up list arrows to display a list of type sizes. The list box defaults to Any, meaning that all sizes of type are eligible for search and replacement. You may select a specific size to be included in the search and replacement criteria.

✦ **Horizontal scale**—Click the pop-up list to select a percentage.

✦ **Leading**—Click the pop-up list to choose the amount of leading to search or change to.

✦ **Track**—Click the pop-up list to specify the kind of tracking to search or change to.

✦ **Tint**—Click the pop-up list to select a percentage tint to search for or change to.

✦ **Type style**—All of the type styles are available to select as part of the search and replacement criteria. Notice that the list box has **Any** checked, meaning that all type styles are eligible for search and replacement. Choose specific type styles, if you wish, by checking the appropriate option on the list.

5. Click **OK** to return to the Change dialog box.

6. When you have selected the attributes you want for the search and replacement criteria, click **OK** to apply the changes.

Linking Text and Graphics

Whenever text and graphics are imported or placed into a document, PageMaker links the file automatically. The link is an invisible connection between the application that created the file (called the *external application*) and the copy of the application's file used in the PageMaker document (called the *linked text element* or the *linked graphic element*). The link is fluid. As the external application makes changes to the file, the linked element is changed whenever the PageMaker document is opened or whenever you manually update the link.

With text and graphics linked to a PageMaker document, many people can continue refining their parts of a document, while the document itself is designed, formatted, and composed in PageMaker. For example, in developing a large proposal in PageMaker, the engineering department can continue editing and amending the technical sections written in WordPerfect files that are linked to the PageMaker proposal. The art department can continue altering graphics files of drawings made in Adobe Illustrator that are also linked to the PageMaker document. And the financial wizards can continue recalculating material costs and milestone payments in Microsoft Excel spreadsheets linked to the same PageMaker document. While the changes are being made, the internal linked text and graphic elements are updated so that when the proposal is printed for reviews, it is current.

Any application's files that can be imported or placed in PageMaker are linked (PageMaker will even link other PageMaker documents). However, the application's files must be accessible to PageMaker, either on a floppy or hard disk of the computer or on the file server in a recognized search drive of a network. It is important to keep in mind that the link is a one-way street; updates go from the external file to the linked element, but changes you make in PageMaker to the linked element don't update the external application's file.

Checking the Status of Links

The status of all links in a document are available at any time through the Links dialog box, shown in Figure 10.21. Open the dialog box by choosing the **Links Manager** command from the File pull-down menu. Currently linked files are displayed in this dialog box, indicating the file name, the kind of file, and the page of the document. Choose a file by clicking it, and the status of the file is described in the Status line.

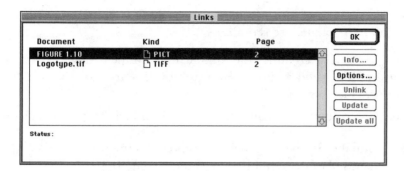

Figure 10.21 The Links dialog box.

Link Status Codes

Status marks that are next to the file name show the current status of the linked file. You will see one of the following codes:

✦ A question mark (?) means the internal element's external file cannot be found. To locate the external file, click the file displaying the question mark and choose the **Link Info** button to display the Link Info dialog box.

✦ NA means the item in question has no link. Instead, it was pasted as an OLE embedded object.

✦ A plus sign (+) next to a file name means that the external file has been updated since the file was placed or imported, and the internal element needs to be updated as well. Choose the **Update** or the **Update All** button to manually update the file. If you have set up automatic updating for the document in the Link Options dialog box, the internal element is updated automatically when the document is opened or printed.

✦ A minus sign (-) next to a file name also means that the external file has been updated and the internal element has not. But the minus sign also indicates that automatic updating has not been chosen for the file, and that you must choose the **Update** or the **Update All** button to update the internal element.

✦ An exclamation point (!) next to a file name means that not only the external file, but also the internal linked element, has been updated.

✦ A diamond means that the internal copy of the item has been modified.

✦ No status indicator means that everything is up to date with the file and no updates are required.

The type of file is listed under the Kind heading in the dialog box. Word processing files are listed as text, and graphics files are listed by the type of graphic (draw or image).

The Page column notes on which page the linked element was placed:

✦ A number in the Page column represents the page number where a file was placed, even if the file extends to more pages.

✦ **UN**—PageMaker doesn't know the location of the element. It's still in the Story Editor and hasn't been placed.

✦ **LM**—The element is placed on the left master page.

✦ **RM**—The element is placed on the right master page.

✦ **PB**—The element currently resides on the pasteboard.

✦ **OV**—Stands for overset text, and means that an in-line graphic is part of a text block that hasn't been placed on a page, or has been only partially placed.

Displaying Link Information

To display file information about the linked element, click the **Link Info** button in the Link dialog box, shown in Figure 10.22, or click the file whose link information you want to see. In the Layout Editor, you can also position the insertion point in the linked text and choose **Link Info** from the Elements pull-down menu.

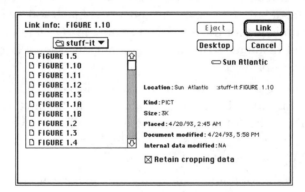

Figure 10.22 The Link Info dialog box.

The dialog box gives the following information about the linked element:

✦ **Location**—The name of the external file.

✦ **Kind**—The type of file this is, as described in the Links dialog box.

✦ **Size**—The current size of the external file.

✦ **Placed**—The date and time that the file was placed in PageMaker.

✦ **Document modified**—The date and time of the last modification to the external file.

✦ **Internal data modified**—The date and time of the last modification to the linked element.

To replace the current linked element with another external file, choose the file from the list box. Then click the **Link** button.

Linking Files versus Pasting Files

As stated earlier, any file that is physically accessible can be linked to a PageMaker document. However, when you paste text from the Clipboard into a document, it is not linked and will not be listed in the Link dialog box. This is because PageMaker must establish a direct connection from the linked element to the original file created by another application.

The Clipboard can paste embedded linked elements. You can cut linked text from one PageMaker document and paste it into another PageMaker document, and the link will transfer to the new document.

Setting Link Options

The Link feature has certain options for text and graphic files that determine how linked elements are updated and how elements are stored (an important consideration with very large graphic files). Choose one of the following ways of displaying the Link Options dialog box:

To set up or change default link options that will be in effect for all future links in PageMaker documents, without opening a document window, choose the **Link Options** command from the Element menu. You will see the Link Options: Defaults dialog box, shown in Figure 10.23. Use this dialog box to determine for both text and graphics how the linked element will be stored, whether the element will be updated automatically, and whether you will be alerted before updating. Click the appropriate option box to add an X to it.

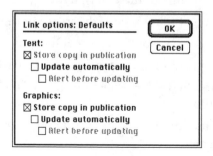

Figure 10.23 *The Link Options: Defaults dialog box.*

When a document has been opened or you have selected a text block, choose **Link Options** from the Element menu to display the Link Options dialog box, shown in Figure 10.24. This window is either the text or graphics half of the Default dialog box, depending on what you have selected. While you cannot change where the linked element is stored, you can request automatic updates. If you have selected a linked element in the Links dialog box, click the **Link Options** button to display the Link Options dialog box. The same options are available.

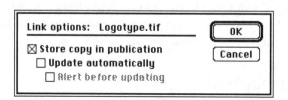

Figure 10.24 *The Link Options dialog box.*

Click **OK** or press **Return** to save the options and return to either the document or the Links dialog box.

COMPILING CHAPTERS INTO A BOOK

The **Book** command essentially takes the idea of linking one step further and links all the chapters of a book together—there is no single large document.

You still work with the chapters individually, but your individual documents become parts of a book. If you have ten chapters, two appendices, a glossary, and an introduction—each a separate PageMaker document—the **Book** command links them in the right order and even straightens out page numbering. And it compiles the book without ever creating a document of the combined files. As a result, you're not forced to work with a large, cumbersome document that is slow to use, save, and move around in.

Preparing the Book

Plan a little before rushing ahead with the creation of a book, manual, or proposal. How do you want to present information: topically or functionally? Who is the audience for this publication? How many chapters will cover the subject without discouraging the reader? What will be the unified look of the chapter layout? All of these questions and many more must be answered before the idea can be developed effectively.

Use the tools that PageMaker provides to help you produce a professional-looking publication. Chapters should have a uniform look—develop a chapter template for the page size, margins, headers, and footers. The book should have an understandable hierarchy of headings so that the reader will always know the relationship of the section currently being read to the preceding sections and the sections to come. Set up your headings as styles to make them consistent. Make each chapter a separate document. Make each appendix a separate document, as well as the introduction and preface or foreword. You can even create empty documents for the table of contents and the index—you'll need them eventually. When you have done all this (and, of course, finished the writing), you are ready to combine all of the separate documents into one book.

Combining the Chapters

To create the book:

1. Open the first document for the book (perhaps the introduction or table of contents).
2. Open the Utilities pull-down menu and choose **Book** to display the Book Publication List dialog box, shown in Figure 10.25.

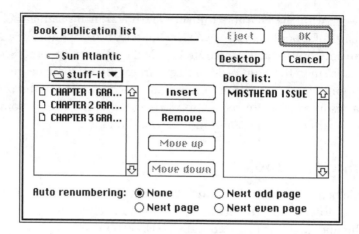

Figure 10.25 *The Book Publication List dialog box.*

3. Use the Book Publication List dialog box to select each part of the book (chapters, index, glossary, introduction, and so on) and insert them in order into the publication list.

4. Find the documents you want to add to the book list in the list box.

5. When the document names are displayed, click each document name and then the **Insert** button to add the name to the Book list.

6. Add to the Book list all of the document names that comprise the book. To change the order of the list, click a document name and click the **Move Up** or **Move Down** button to move the name up or down one position. To remove a document name from the book list, click the **Remove** button.

7. When you're finished, click **OK** to return to your document.

To perform book-oriented tasks such as building the index and table of contents, and printing the book, you must repeat steps 1 through 7 in each document you have just added to the Book list in the dialog box. Or, you can use this easy shortcut:

1. Choose the **Book** command again (if you are no longer working in the document to which you have added the first Book list, open that document and choose the **Book** command).

2. Before clicking the **Book** command, hold down the **Command/Ctrl** key. Instead of displaying the Book Publications List dialog box again, this opens a message box that shows the book list being copied to each of the documents in the list.

That's all there is to it! The Book list is added to each document in the list. Before leaving the Book Publications List dialog box, let's talk about page numbering.

 NOTE If you change the external file names or the document names of the internally linked files of any of the documents in the Book list, those documents will no longer be associated with the Book list. You must add the new document names to the Book list using the Book Publications List dialog box and recopy the Book list to each document in the list.

Numbering Pages

Do not attempt to add page numbers manually to the pages of your document. As I have explained earlier in this book, simply add the page number marker (**Command/Ctrl+Option/Alt+p**) to the master page(s)—PageMaker takes care of the rest. But what happens when the individual chapters of a book, each of which already has page number markers, are combined using the **Book** command? You choose among four page numbering schemes in the Auto Renumbering area of the Book Publication List dialog box. When used in conjunction with the **Restart Page Numbering** option in the Document Setup dialog box, the schemes cover virtually every condition that may be encountered in numbering the pages of a book, listed next.

✦ **None**—Choose **None** if you want the page numbers for each chapter and section of the book to begin with 1. Use the **Restart Page Numbering** option box in the Page Setup dialog box to start a particular chapter with a number other than 1.

✦ **Next page**—This option numbers the book consecutively from 1, or whatever number you enter in the Restart Page Number text box in the Page Setup dialog box.

✦ **Next odd page**—Choose this option if you'd like each section and chapter entered in the Book list to begin on an odd-numbered page.

Generally, books begin sections and chapters on right-hand pages, which usually are odd-numbered pages.

✦ **Next even page**—Choose this option if you'd like each section and chapter entered in the Book list to begin on an even-numbered page.

Restarting Page Numbering

Use the Restart Page Number text box in the Document Setup dialog box to restart the numbering of any section or chapter listed in the Book list. Here's how:

1. Open the document that is the section or chapter in the book list for which you'd like to restart page numbering.

2. Choose the **Document Setup** command on the File menu to display the Document Setup dialog box, shown in Figure 10.26.

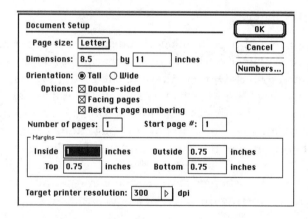

Figure 10.26 The Document Setup dialog box.

3. Click the **Restart Page Numbering** check box and enter the number to start with in the Start Page # text box. Normally you will enter **1** as the number to restart with, but you can enter any number you'd like.

4. Click **OK** or press **Return** to return to your document.

The page numbers for this section or chapter will now restart from the number you specified. For example, you could have four documents in the Book list representing the front matter of the book: the acknowledgment, dedication, preface, and table of contents. These four sections are numbered consecutively, but you want the first page of Chapter 1 to begin with the number 1. By opening the Chapter 1 document and choosing the **Restart Numbering** feature, Chapter 1 will be numbered the way you'd like.

Now, why don't we decide what style of page numbers to use.

Defining Numbers for Pages

You can choose a distinct numbering style for the whole book, or for individual sections and chapters of the book. For example, you can number the front matter with lowercase roman numerals (i, ii, iii, iv, and so forth), the chapters of the book with Arabic numerals (1, 2, 3, 4, and so forth), and the appendix pages alphabetically.

To change the style:

1. Open the document in which the numbering will begin. For example, if you are establishing numbering for the front matter, open the first document, such as the preface, in the front matter; if you are setting the numbering style for the chapters, open Chapter 1.

2. Open the Document Setup dialog box. Click the **Numbers** button to display the Page Numbering dialog box shown in Figure 10.27.

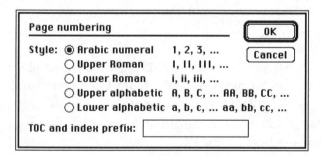

Figure 10.27 *The Page Numbering dialog box.*

3. Choose the numbering style you want for this part of the book.

The front matter of a book is usually numbered with roman numerals. The chapters are usually numbered with Arabic numerals.

NOTE

4. If you have added text to the page number markers (Page 14 instead of 14), you can add the same text to the table of contents and index page numbers by entering the text in the TOC and Index Prefix text box. Just type the text instead of a page number or the page number marker.

CREATING AN INDEX

Indexing books is a very complicated subject. There are people who make their living solely by indexing books for publishers. For an index to be useful, it should contain all of the subjects a potential reader will likely search for, as well as all of the page references and cross-references for each subject. These tasks are most suitable for a computer (with some advance planning). One of PageMaker's strongest features is its indexing capability.

To create a good index you must approach the book as if you were a first-time reader. Forget that you just finished writing it or contributed to its production. Now, you are the new reader thumbing through it for the first time. Ask yourself: If I wanted to find a certain subject, what indexed words would I want to see? What cross-referencing would be helpful? Which index entries are frivolous and which have substance? Work through the eyes of the reader, and you will build a good index. Work through the eyes of the writer, and you may wind up with some gaping holes in your index.

To create an index:

1. Mark each occurrence of the individual words and phrases you want to include in the index using the **Index Entry** command.

2. Edit the entries with the **Show Index** command, add second- and third-level subentries to further define the index entries. Add cross-references where necessary.

3. Build the index using the **Create Index** command.

To mark text as an index entry:

1. Switch to the Story Editor to mark index entries. (PageMaker shows you the index marks in the story view.)

2. Highlight the word or phrase you want to appear in the index.

3. Open the Utilities pull-down menu and choose **Index Entry** (or press **Command/Ctrl+Y**) to display the Add Index Entry dialog box, shown in Figure 10.28.

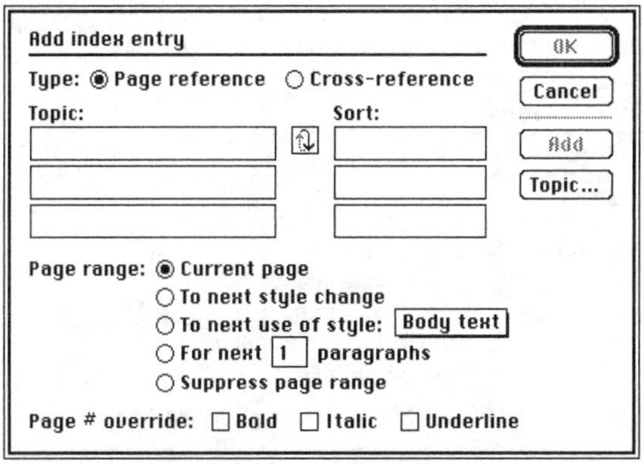

Figure 10.28 The Add Index Entry dialog box.

4. Use the Add Index Entry dialog box to enter, edit, and configure page-referenced and cross-referenced index entries. In the Type area of the dialog box, click the **Page Reference** radio button to enter a page reference.

Setting Up Page-Referenced Index Entries

Page-referenced index entries contain page numbers referring the reader to text concerning the entry—the normal entry you find in an index. To set up a page-referenced entry, do the following:

1. Enter the index topic and any subtopics for the entry. Notice three text boxes under Topic and three under Sort. These are first-, second-, and third-level areas in which you may enter up to three levels of topics. For example, an automotive repair manual might index the word *steering* as:

Level 1: FWD Steering

Level 2: Adjusting the rack and pinion system

Level 3: FWD minimum wheel clearance

These would be entered in the Add Index Entry dialog box as you see in Figure 10.29

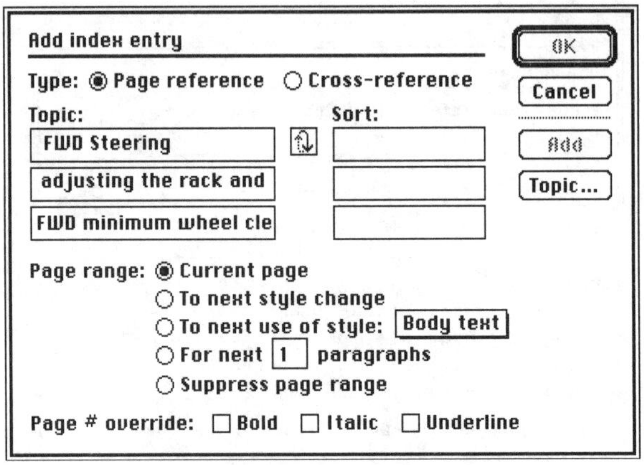

```
┌─────────────────────────────────────────────────────────┐
│  Add index entry                          ( OK )          │
│  ─────────────────────────────────────                   │
│  Type: ◉ Page reference   ○ Cross-reference  ( Cancel )   │
│  Topic:                    Sort:                          │
│  ┌─────────────────┐ ┌──┐ ┌──────────────┐   ( Add )      │
│  │ FWD Steering    │ │⬆⬇│ │              │               │
│  └─────────────────┘ └──┘ └──────────────┘   ( Topic... ) │
│  ┌─────────────────┐      ┌──────────────┐               │
│  │ adjusting the rack and│ │              │              │
│  └─────────────────┘      └──────────────┘               │
│  ┌─────────────────┐      ┌──────────────┐               │
│  │ FWD minimum wheel cle│ │              │                │
│  └─────────────────┘      └──────────────┘               │
│                                                           │
│  Page range: ◉ Current page                               │
│              ○ To next style change                       │
│              ○ To next use of style: [ Body text ]        │
│              ○ For next [ 1 ]  paragraphs                 │
│              ○ Suppress page range                        │
│  Page # override: □ Bold   □ Italic   □ Underline         │
└─────────────────────────────────────────────────────────┘
```

Figure 10.29 The Add Index Entry dialog box has room for each of the topics.

The three sort boxes allow you to specify a different word to sort that is different from the word in the topic box. For example, in Figure 10.29, you could enter the word **front** next to the level 1 topic FWD Steering, and the entry would be positioned alphabetically based on *f r-o*, not *f-w-d*.

2. Change the order of the topic and subtopics by clicking the looped-arrow icon. Each time you click the icon, the topics shift down one text box. Any sort terms shift with their associated topics.

3. Choose one of the **Page Range** option buttons:

    ✦ **Current page**—The page number for the current page on which the entry appears will be shown in the index.

    ✦ **To next style change**—Choose this option to show a range of page numbers that includes the current page on which the entry appears and on all subsequent pages until PageMaker encounters a style change. This usually means that the whole subsection from the current page number forward will be noted in the index. For example, if you have the word *steering* in a subsection called "Alignment" on page 151, and body copy continues for four additional pages until the next subhead, the index entry with this page-range option would look like: Steering 151–155. If the five pages offer a viable explanation of steering, or if this is a crucial area that discusses steering, assign the index entry this page-range option. However, if there is little relevant information about steering on the five pages, don't make the reader wade through the text by using a range of pages. Choose the **Current Page** option instead.

✦ **To next use of style**—Choose this option to note where the discussion of the index entry ends (at the change of a style). Choose the style by clicking the **Style** pop-up list to display the list of styles.

✦ **For next _ paragraphs**—Choose this option if you know that the discussion using the indexed entry continues for a known number of paragraphs. Enter the number of paragraphs in the text box.

* **Suppress page range**—Choose this to temporarily prevent the page number from being added to the index entry.

4. Choose one of the **Page #** override options to change the style of the page numbers. If the previously defined page number style is Normal, choosing one of these options will change the style to the option box style. If the page number style is already in one of the option styles, choosing the style here will cancel the style, and the page numbers will revert back to Normal. For example, if the previously defined page number style is Normal, an index entry might look like this:

Steering 151

If you click the **Bold** option box, the page number portion of the entry would change to:

Steering **151**

However, if the previously defined page number style is Bold, the entry would look like this:

Steering 151

If you then click the **Bold** option box, the page number portion of the entry would revert to the Normal style and look like this:

Steering 151

The same rules apply with the **Italic** and **Underline** option boxes.

5. Click the **Add** button to add another index entry without having to close and reopen the dialog box.

6. Click the **Topic** button to display the Select Topic dialog box.

Managing Page Reference Topics

The Select Topic dialog box gives you a concise view of all existing topics that have been added to the index, as well as the topic you are currently working on. Use the dialog box either to add additional topics or to add a second- or third-level subtopic to an existing topic. What follows are some of the ways in which you can use this dialog box.

✦ **Choose a topic**—Click the **Topic Section** pop-up list to open the pop-up list and scroll down the alphabetic list of letters to choose a topic. As you display a letter of the alphabet in the pop-up list, the topics scroll to that letter. Click the topic, and it and its associated second- and third-level subtopics (if any) appear in the Level 1, Level 2, and Level 3 list boxes.

✦ **Change the names of a displayed topic**—Edit the words in the pop-up list to make them consistent with other similar topics.

✦ **Add subtopics**—For a topic without subtopics, click in the **Level 2** or **Level 3** subtopic pop-up list and type a subtopic. Click the **Add** button to add the subtopic to the lists.

✦ **Capitalize the first letter of every Level 1 topic**—Hold down the **Command/Ctrl** key and click the **Next Section** pop-up list to capitalize the first letter of all first-level topics.

✦ **Import topics for other documents in the Book list**—Click the **Import** button to import the list of topics and subtopics for all other documents in the Book list of which the current document is a part. This ensures consistency across all of the sections and chapters in the book.

Click **OK** or press **Return** to return to the Add Index Entry dialog box.

Setting Up Cross-Referenced Index Entries

Cross-referenced index entries refer the reader to other page-referenced index entries. In the cross-referenced entry:

Steering wheel, see Hub assembly

Steering wheel is the index entry, *see Hub assembly* is the cross-reference. To set up a cross-referenced entry:

1. Enter the index topic and any subtopics for the entry described above.

2. Change the order of the topic and subtopics by clicking the looped-arrow icon.

3. Choose one of the **Denoted By** option buttons:

✦ **See [also]**—This is the default method of pointing out a cross-reference. If the topic also has a page reference, the wording "see also" is used for the cross-reference. If the topic did not contain a page reference, the word "see" will be used for the cross-reference.

✦ **See** simply refers the reader to another page reference.

✦ **See also** like the **See [also]** option, refers the reader to both the cross-reference and the page reference of the current topic.

✦ **See herein** refers the reader to a subtopic page reference within this topic. For example:

✦ **See also herein** refers the reader to page references for the main topic, plus a subtopic page reference within this topic.

4. Choose one of the **X-Ref Override** options to change the style of the cross-reference. If the previously defined cross-reference style is Normal, choosing one of the options will change the style to the option box style. If the cross-reference style is already in one of the option styles, choosing the style here cancels the style, and the cross-references revert back to Normal. However, if the previously defined cross-reference style is Bold and you click the **Bold** option box, the cross-reference portion of the entry reverts to the Normal style. The same rules apply to the **Italic** and **Underline** option boxes.

5. Click the **Add** button to add another index entry without having to close and reopen the dialog box.

6. Click the **Topic** button to display the Select Topic dialog box shown in Figure 10.30, to move to a different cross-reference topic.

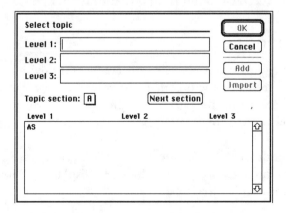

Figure 10.30 The Select Topic dialog box.

7. Click the **X-Ref** button to display the Select Cross-Reference Topic dialog box to mark a topic as a cross-reference to the current index entry.

Managing Cross-Referenced Topics

The Select Cross-Reference Topic dialog box, shown in Figure 10.31, gives you a concise view of all existing topics that have been added to the index, as well as the topic on which you are currently working. Use this dialog box to add additional cross-referenced topics or to add a second- or third- level subtopic to an existing cross-reference. You can also use this dialog box similarly to the Select Topic dialog box.

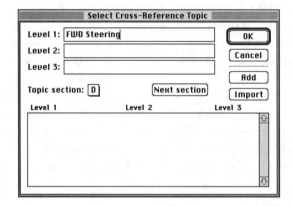

Figure 10.31 *Select Cross-Reference Topic dialog box.*

Click **OK** or press **Return** to return to the Add Index Entry dialog box.

Editing the Index

Once the majority of index entries and cross-reference entries have been made, the Show Index dialog box makes it easy to review and modify the list. You can see the entries for the current chapter, or for all the documents in the Book list. Follow these steps:

1. To see index entries for the entire Book list, open the Utilities pull-down menu and choose **Show Index** to display the Show Index dialog box, shown in Figure 10.32.

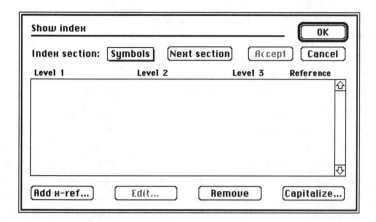

Figure 10.32 *The Show Index dialog box.*

2. Alternately, hold down the **Command/Ctrl** key while performing step 1 to see only the index entries for the current document.

3. Use the **Next Section** button to move alphabetically through the list of entries.

4. To change or add a cross-reference, click the **Add X-Ref** button. This opens to the Add Index Entry dialog box to add or change the reference.

5. To add or edit an index page reference, click the **Edit** button. Again, you'll see the Add Index Entry dialog box, in which you can add or change the reference.

6. Click the **Accept** button to accept the changes made in this dialog box.

7. Click **OK** or press **Return** to return to your document.

Automatically Marking Index Entries

You can use the **Change** command to search for exact in-text references and automatically mark them as index entries. Here's how:

1. In the Story Editor (use the Story Editor so that you can see the index entry symbols), choose **Change** to display the Change dialog box (see "Using the Change Feature," earlier in this chapter).

2. Enter the index entry you want to search for in the Find What text box.

3. In the Change To text box, enter the caret (**Shift+6**) and the semi-colon.

4. In the Options area, choose the **Whole Word** option box. To automatically add proper names to the index, enter the name as it appears in the text (for example, **John Doe**) in the Find What text box. Then enter **^Z** in the Change To text box. All instances of the name will automatically be marked as index entries and will appear in the index, last name first (Doe, John). If the name has a middle name or initial, add the characters **^s** between each of the first two names or between the first name and the middle initial (for example, **John^sQ. Public**). The name will appear in the index, last name first (Public, John Q.).

5. Click the **Find All** button to locate all entries and mark them with the index symbol.

Once the items are marked as index entries, they are displayed in the Show Index dialog box. Review the marked entries and edit or delete them as necessary.

Generating the Index

Now comes the best part: generating the index you worked so hard to develop.

Here's how:

1. Open the Utilities pull-down menu and choose **Create Index** to display the Create Index dialog box, shown in Figure 10.33.

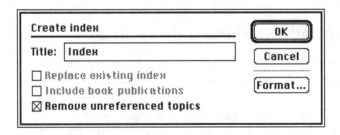

Figure 10.33 The Create Index dialog box.

2. In the Title text box, type the title for this index (the default title "Index" is displayed).

3. To replace an existing index with this new index, click the **Replace Existing Index** option box.

4. To include all documents in the Book list, click the **Include Book Publications** option box.

5. To remove any referenced topics, click the appropriate option box.

6. To generate the index, click **OK**. PageMaker compiles the index, returns you to your document, and displays a loaded-text icon. Move to the page you want for your index and click the mouse button to place the text block.

CREATING A TABLE OF CONTENTS

The table of contents is created automatically from the heading and sub-heading styles you marked using the **Include in TOC** option (see Chapter 6, "Setting Up Custom Styles"). To generate the table of contents:

1. Open the Utilities pull-down menu and choose **Create TOC** to display the Create Table of Contents dialog box, shown in Figure 10.34.

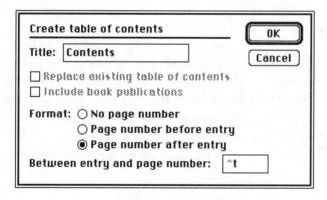

Figure 10.34 The Create Table of Contents dialog box.

2. Enter a title for the table of contents in the Title text box, or accept the default title "Contents.

3. If you want the table of contents you're about to generate to replace an existing table of contents, click the **Replace Existing Table of Contents** option box.

4. If you want to include heads from all the documents in the Book list, click the **Include Book Publications** option box.

5. Choose a format for the table of contents:

    ✦ **No page number**—Click this radio button to prevent page numbers.

    ✦ **Page number before entry**—Click this radio button to position the page number before the heading in the table of contents.

    ✦ **Page number after entry**—Click this radio button to position the page number after the heading.

6. Specify how you'd like to format the space between the table of contents entry and the page number. The default ^t tells PageMaker to insert a tab—see the table earlier in this chapter for a complete list of characters available to insert in the space.

7. Click **OK** or press **Return** to generate the table of contents. In a few moments, the mouse pointer changes to a loaded-text icon. Position the icon where you want the table of contents to begin, and click the mouse button.

To Sum Up

In this chapter, you have seen PageMaker's straightforward approach to creating professional publications with all the trimmings. Regardless of your publishing requirements, PageMaker can handle the layout and production with ease. If you use styles and templates and print to a high-resolution PostScript image setter, you will have a book ready for the printer.

In the next chapter, you will learn how easy it is to use PageMaker's powerful Help system.

CHAPTER 11

Using Photoshop Filters

- What are filters?
- Expanding PageMaker's filter options
- Using Photoshop filters
- To sum up

PageMaker 6.5's compatibility with Adobe Photoshop filters is just the tip of a new cross-application/cross-platform compatibility Adobe is incorporating into all its applications. Indeed, one of the most dramatic changes in PageMaker 6.5 is how smoothly the program works with other Adobe applications. You can drag-and-drop elements from Adobe Illustrator or Photoshop into PageMaker, export HTML pages from PageMaker that can be further fine-tuned in Adobe PageMill, and generally mix-and-match pieces from any of these applications as required.

That's great news for hard-working desktop publishers, as it makes it easier to use the tool best-suited for a task. Illustrator is your best source for sharp text effects and line-oriented objects that will be rendered at high resolutions in PageMaker publications. Photoshop is the tool of choice when you need to edit photographic images at the bitmap level. Output from either of these programs can be integrated into a PageMaker publication for precision layout.

Even so, it's useful to be able to apply some of Photoshop's filter effects to images that have already been placed in PageMaker. This chapter tells you why and offers some tips on how you can use these plug-ins more effectively.

WHAT ARE FILTERS?

Photoshop filters modify images by examining their pixels and making changes of some sort. Sharpening filters look at the contrast between adjacent pixels and, when sufficient difference is found, decide that an edge has been located. Increasing the contrast even more produces a sharpening effect. Alternatively, reducing contrast only between pixels where a contrast change is marked results in a blurry image.

Other filters change the hue of pixels, move them around to create a distorted image, or superimpose a texture on an image by combining the values of the existing pixels with those of an underlying pattern. Figure 11.1 shows an image that has been changed with three different filters.

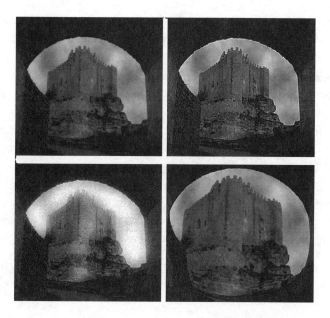

Figure 11.1 The original image is at upper left; at upper right is the same image sharpened; at lower left the image has been diffused; at lower right, the Spherize filter has been applied.

Photoshop 4.0 has nearly 100 filters, not all of which are useful or can be used within PageMaker. In Figure 11.1, the Spherize filter cannot be used within PageMaker, because it requires that you select part of an image to work with. Unlike Photoshop, PageMaker can't operate on a selection of an image. It has no image selection tools that would make that possible. So, in general, you must use Photoshop filters within PageMaker only on a full image. If you want to use a filter like Spherize, you must operate within the confines of an image editor.

Adobe provides you with a starter group of filters, but if you have Photoshop you can easily point PageMaker to the **Photoshop plug-ins** folder and make many more filters available to you. In general, certain types of filters will be of most use to you:

- **Sharpening filters** To improve the look of an image that is a little on the blurry side. You'll find sharpening, edge enhancing, and other filters in this group.

- **Blurring filters** To reduce unwanted artifacts, such as dust or scratches in an imperfect image. Photoshop's blur, Gaussian blur, and Dust & Scratches filters are examples of this type.

- **Diffusion/Grain filters** These also reduce dust and scratches, and add an arty effect. I like Diffuse Glow, but Photoshop also includes Grain and Photographic Grain filters.

- **Brush stroke filters** Photoshop has dozens of filters that can add a painterly effect to your images. Dry Brush, Watercolor, and other filters can salvage a bad image by making it look as if an artist has applied brush strokes to it.

As I mentioned earlier, you'll find that filters that require a selection or fine-tuning, such as the distortion filters, or rendering filters like Lens Flare, can't be used within PageMaker.

EXPANDING PAGEMAKER'S FILTER OPTIONS

Only Photoshop filters created for Photoshop Version 3.04 or later can be used with PageMaker, so if you have an earlier version you should consider upgrading. Photoshop 4.0 includes all the filters formerly sold separately as Adobe Gallery Effects, so the upgrade is well worth it simply for the new, free plug-ins you get. You can copy any Photoshop filters you want to use (and which are compatible) directly to your PageMaker folder's **RSRC>Plugins>Filter** folder, but it's more efficient to simply reuse the filters, and not have to create duplicates. To tell PageMaker how to find Photoshop's filters, just follow these steps:

1. Locate the **Photoshop Plugins** folder on your hard disk. It will usually be found within the Photoshop folder itself, but can be placed anywhere, as Photoshop includes a **Preference** option that can specify any folder for its plugins.

2. Inside the **Plugins** folder will be a folder named **Filters**. Depending on whether you have a Macintosh or a Windows PC, perform one of the following actions:

   • If you have a Mac, highlight the **Filters** folder, and press **Command-M** to create an Alias of it.

- If you have a PC, highlight the **Filters** folder, and right-click. When the context menu appears, choose **Create Shortcut**.

3. When the new alias/shortcut appears, locate your PageMaker folder's **RSRC** (**resource**) folder. Inside will be another folder called **Plugins**. Within that will be one named **Filters**. Open that folder.

4. Drag the alias/shortcut into the **PageMaker Filters** folder. Rename the alias/shortcut Effects.

5. Restart PageMaker, if necessary. The new filters will appear in the Element>Image>Photoshop Effects dialog box.

USING PHOTOSHOP FILTERS IN PAGEMAKER

Photoshop filters can only be applied to RGB and TIFF images you have placed in your PageMaker publication. If you want to apply filters to some other kind of bitmapped image, you'll need to use Photoshop, and then save as an importable image that you can place in your publication. This next section is a practice session you can use to learn how to apply Photoshop effects. Just follow these directions.

1. Create a new, empty PageMaker publication.

2. Use **File>Place** to put a TIFF image in the publication. You can use **Alarcon.tif**, found on the CD-ROM that accompanies this book, as we did. The publication will look like Figure 11.2.

Figure 11.2 *A TIFF image has been placed in the publication.*

3. Use **Element>Image** and find the **Photoshop Effects** menu choice, shown in Figure 11.3.

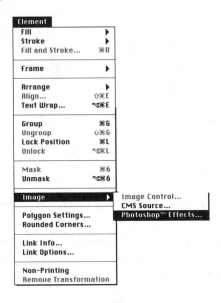

Figure 11.3 *Photoshop filters are available from the Element>Image menu.*

4. Select **Photoshop Effects**, and a dialog box will appear that allows you to select any of the available Photoshop filters from a drop-down list. In the Save New File As field, you should type in a new name for the modified file, so that PageMaker will not overwrite your original. You can click the **Save As** button to save the unmodified image immediately, or type in a new name and click **OK** to proceed. The dialog box is shown in Figure 11.4.

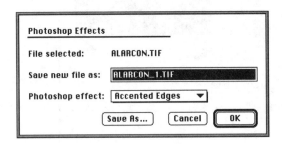

Figure 11.4 *The Photoshop Effects dialog box lets you apply available Photoshop filters.*

5. Now, choose the filter you want to apply from the drop-down list, shown in Figure 11.5.

```
▲
GE Rough Pastels
GE Spatter
GE Stamp
GE Sumi-e
Glass
Glowing Edges
Grain
Graphic Pen
Halftone Pattern
Ink Outlines
Mosaic Tiles
Neon Glow
Note Paper
Ocean Ripple
Paint Daubs
Palette Knife
Patchwork
Photocopy
Plaster
Plastic Wrap
Poster Edges
Reticulation
Rough Pastels
Smudge Stick
Spatter
Sponge
Sprayed Strokes
Stained Glass
Stamp
Sumi-e
Texturizer
Torn Edges
Underpainting
Water Paper
Watercolor
```

Figure 11.5 *The filters can be selected from a drop-down list.*

6. Next, a dialog box with the controls for that filter appears. If you have enough free memory, a preview of the original image with the filter's effect applied is shown. You can adjust the sliders or other controls until you achieve the effect you like. Then click **OK** to apply the effect. Figure 11.6 shows the Filter Control dialog box. We selected **Dry Brush**.

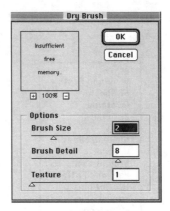

Figure 11.6 *Filter parameters can be adjusted in this dialog box.*

7. The final image has the effect applied. There is no Undo available for working with Photoshop effects, so proceed carefully, and remember to save each image file under an alternate name. If necessary you can delete an image you don't care for, and apply a different filter or parameters.

To Sum Up

Filters are useful for improving or modifying bitmapped images within PageMaker. While Adobe's layout program doesn't have the tools for doing extensive image manipulation, often you'll find that a filter applied to a graphic as a whole can improve it significantly. You can always use Photoshop for more complex image editing tasks, but PageMaker's ability to apply Photoshop effects can be a valuable time-saver.

CHAPTER 12

Creating HTML Pages with PageMaker

- ✦ What's HTML?
- ✦ What can HTML be used for?
- ✦ Configuring PageMaker to work with online files
- ✦ HTML styles and links
- ✦ Importing HTML pages and components into PageMaker
- ✦ Placing HTML pages
- ✦ Exporting HTML documents
- ✦ To sum up

The whole world is going Web-wacky, and the latest version of PageMaker is no exception. The World Wide Web has turned a bright spotlight of interest on HTML (Hypertext Markup Language), which is the major way of packaging instructions for displaying pages on Web sites. You'll find within your favorite page layout program tools for importing existing pages so you can modify them, and provisions for exporting existing PageMaker publications as fully formatted Web pages.

In this chapter, you'll learn a little about what HTML is—and only a little, since you don't need to learn all the complexities of HTML to take advantage of PageMaker's capabilities. We'll also look at ways in which you might want to use these pages in your own work. Some of the applications might surprise you.

WHAT'S HTML?

Don't be put off by the term Hypertext Markup Language. While HTML is a language, in many ways it functions just like PageMaker's internal system for formatting documents. In PageMaker, you create styles that determine how various levels of headings, body text, bulleted paragraphs, and so forth are displayed and printed. HTML includes styles like these, too, with some key differences that we'll look at shortly.

One thing that HTML does is allow the browser to control many of the parameters for displaying content. For example, you generally don't specify right and left margins for text. The browser automatically adjusts the line breaks so the text is shown correctly between the margins of the browser window. That makes it possible to display text in a variety of browsers, without worrying whether the user has a 1024 x 768- or 640 x 480-pixel screen. If all the text can't be displayed on a given screen, the user can move down the page using the browser's scroll bars.

HTML pages are simply plain text files like those you can create and edit with Windows 95's Notepad or WordPad applications, or the Mac's Simple Text. The pages consist of three main components, plus an optional external fourth component. These are:

✦ **Text content**. These are the words that will be displayed on the page. Your page can include text paragraphs, captions for images, and other plain text. Given no additional instructions, a browser like Netscape or Microsoft Internet Explorer will simply display this text using a default body text font, within the margins of the browser window.

✦ **Markup instructions.** These are special codes, placed between angle brackets (e.g., <code>) that provide the browser with instructions on how to display a particular piece of text, or image, or where to look for additional content to display or play back. A simple set of instructions might look like this:

```
<HTML>

<BODY>

<H1>Dave's World...</H1>

<P>You've reached the home page of David D. Busch, the world's
most successful unknown author. </P>

</BODY>

</HTML>
```

Note that each instruction in angle brackets, like <H1> (which indicates that the browser should start using the Heading1 style), is matched with a closing instruction using a forward slash, such as </H1> (which tells the browser to stop using the Heading1 style.) Everything within angle brackets is a markup instruction; everything between the instructions is text that will be displayed on the page.

The style names and their properties are defined by the rules of HTML itself, rather than by the person creating the document. In addition, HTML styles are much more limited in terms of the parameters you can specify: You may be able to specify the size of text relative to other text on the page (e.g., larger, smaller, smallest, etc.) and attributes like bold or italic, but not exact fonts or point sizes. To do that, you need to go behind simple HTML to a relatively new development called *cascading style sheets*, which give you greater control over these parameters. Cascading style sheets are currently beyond the capabilities of PageMaker and, therefore, beyond the scope of this book.

✦ **External content**. These are the components that will be shown on the page, or played back when you click on a button or link, but aren't included within the HTML text itself. Markup instructions point to where the browser should search for these pieces, whether that's on the CD-ROM or disk with the HTML page or somewhere on the Internet. Typical external content includes image files that are displayed on a page, plus audio files, movies, and so forth. These are often called *encoded* files, because they are not plain ASCII text, and require a special software module to decode them and play them back. The facility can be built into the browser itself (as is the case with the decoders for the two most common type of image files used on Web pages: JPEG and GIF format files), or included as a plug-in (an external module that becomes part of the browser) or helper application (a module that can be activated by the browser automatically when necessary.)

✦ **Comments**. The fourth kind of information that may be included on an HTML page are comments. These are just as you might expect: remarks about the page or its author that don't display, don't modify any of the text, or point to an external component. A comment is placed inside tags that include an exclamation point:

```
<! Please do not read this comment. Thank you.>
```

Like all languages, HTML is an evolving standard that changes over time. At first, HTML included only a few, limited instructions for formatting text and displaying graphics in a few standard ways. Then, as a way to jazz up sterile Web pages, extensions to the language were developed in somewhat haphazard fashion by vendors like Netscape and Microsoft. At first, these extensions were supported only by a particular browser, so Web sites began sprouting banners that said "Netscape Enhanced" or "Best Viewed with Microsoft Internet Explorer." Finally a truce of sorts was declared in the browser wars, with Netscape and Microsoft both supporting a more-or-less common set of extensions, adhering to the current release of HTML. At this writing, that's HTML Version 3.2.

Beyond the basics already outlined here, you don't need to learn the intricacies of HTML. PageMaker can import existing Web pages, or export its own documents as HTML pages. You'll need to learn HTML only to add special features beyond PageMaker's capabilities, such as scrolling frames. Even then you may be able to work with your exported PageMaker HTML pages within a WYSIWYG editor like Adobe PageMill, and never see a line of code at all.

WHAT CAN HTML BE USED FOR?

Even if you never plan to create a page that will be posted on the World Wide Web, HTML can still be a great tool. It can easily double as a multimedia authoring tool that you may use to quickly create training programs, databases, documentation, or many other kinds of publications. In truth, the real strength of HTML is its ability to format text and graphics into pages that can be linked to each other in creative ways, and viewed interchangeably on UNIX, Mac, PC, and other platforms. Consider the following applications for Web-like pages that you might not have thought of.

Catalogs

A catalog that can be viewed with any Web browser is a flexible, easily modified sales tool. Just create the catalog in PageMaker, dividing it into sections organized by product line. Hyperlinks can move customers quickly from one section to another, lead them to photos, audio files, or even QuickTime movies of products, and introduce them to a pricing page or order form at the appropriate time. Small catalogs without a lot of graphics can be easily placed on a floppy disk and mailed out with a brochure. Larger catalogs can be copied to a CD-ROM. As a bonus, you can take the exact same material and place it on your Web page for online access. A typical catalog-type application is shown in Figure 12.1.

Figure 12.1 Catalog pages can be attractively formatted using HTML.

Desktop Presentations

If you'd rather not learn a heavy-duty desktop presentation package, like Adobe Persuasion, you can easily create sophisticated desktop slide shows in

PageMaker, then export them as HTML files. The presentation can proceed in linear fashion like most such productions if you like. Just place Forward and Back buttons on the pages to link to preceding and subsequent pages. However, there's no reason why you can't include links to other branches of the presentation, allowing the presenter to jump around if he or she senses that the audience would be better served by viewing different sections, or seeing the material in a different order. This technique makes it possible to create one presentation that can be given to employees, customers, stockholders, new recruits, and other audiences, and customized on-the-fly.

Photo Galleries

While good albuming software exists, you might prefer to create your own image gallery for a CD-ROM by formatting HTML pages. Thumbnails can be displayed on some pages, with full-size images available for viewing with a click on a link. A whole disk full of images can be sorted, previewed, and presented with a well-organized set of pages. This is a good way for photographers to distribute portfolios. Images that have been compressed using the JPEG file format may amount to 20–30K of disk space each, so it's possible to include a fair number of pictures even on a floppy disk. Figure 12.2 shows a photo gallery formatted as an HTML page.

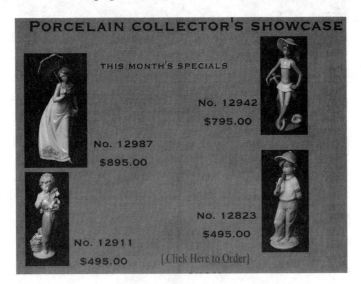

Figure 12.2 HTML pages can effectively present photographers' portfolios.

Corporate Intranet Information Systems

Create pages of information of interest to employees using PageMaker, just as you've always done. These can include personnel information, new job opportunities, product information, corporate backgrounders, bowling scores, company newsletters, memos—virtually everything you already distribute on paper.

Then, export them as HTML files and place them on the corporation's network, where they can be accessed by any user with a browser and access to the network. The cool part is that you don't necessarily need to set up fancy Web server software. Instead, just create a browser bookmark file pointing to the network file locations of the pages, or tell employees to use their browsers to access an HTML index page over the network (and then bookmark that so they can return to it.)

Your corporate intranet will then be available to any employee set up to look for it—without Internet access. Alternatively, you can copy the same corporate information to a CD-ROM and distribute it to branch offices for their network servers, or for use by individual employees.

Software Distribution

Place your software on a CD-ROM, then use PageMaker to create an HTML page that links to descriptions of the software, and which includes a link viewers can use to "download" the software to their hard disks. For security reasons, HTML doesn't allow you to execute installer programs directly, but is perfectly capable of opening a standard File Save window the user can activate to transfer software from your CD-ROM to their computer's hard drive.

CONFIGURING PAGEMAKER TO WORK WITH ONLINE FILES

At times, you may want to combine an existing HTML page with a PageMaker document you are creating. In those cases, it's useful to import the HTML file, make the changes you want, then export the file out as Web page again. PageMaker can also communicate directly with your Web browser to copy links and files from a local hard disk, or even over the Internet. (Just imagine someday creating a newsletter in PageMaker using clip art from the Internet!)

You can drag and drop text and graphics from your browser when the browser and PageMaker are both open and visible on the screen.

To perform all this magic, you need to set up PageMaker to communicate with your browser and the Internet. You'll need to tell PageMaker what browser you are using, where it should save files it downloads, whether to use a substitute or proxy server rather than a direct connection to the Internet, and some other small details.

Determining Proxy Servers, If Any

This first step is the only one for which you may need some help from a colleague or your network administrator. You need to determine the name whether your Internet connection uses a proxy server for some or all of its retrieval of Internet pages. As you might guess from the name, proxies function as a substitute for a direct connection. Corporations sometimes set up proxy servers on the "safe" side of a firewall, so its users only access World Wide Web pages that have been downloaded to the proxy first, instead of directly from the Internet. That gives the corporation an opportunity to filter out destructive or inappropriate material as it passes through the firewall.

More recently, some Internet service providers (ISPs) have been experimenting with proxy servers as a way to cut down on general Internet traffic. Frequently accessed pages can be viewed by the ISP's subscribers stored, or cached on its own proxy server, rather than retrieving the same pages over and over from the Internet. You can view your browser's preferences to determine whether or not your own connection uses a proxy server.

1. In Netscape, click **Options>Preferences>Network Preferences**. Then view the Proxies setting, as shown in Figure 12.3. If the **No Proxies** button is checked, you aren't using a proxy server. You have a direct connection to the Internet. If the **Manual Proxy Configuration** setting is checked, click **View** to see your current settings. Write down the HTTP Proxy URL shown, as well as the Port number next to it. Also note which areas your browser is authorized to contact directly, in the No Proxy For list. If the **Automatic Proxy Configuration** button is checked, write down the URL.

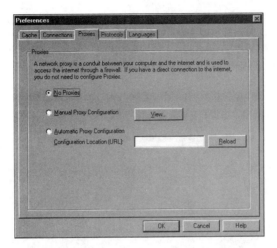

Figure 12.3 Netscape's Proxies dialog box shows your proxy connections, if any.

2. With Microsoft Internet Explorer, choose **View>Options**, and choose **Connections**, to view the dialog box shown in Figure 12.4. If the **Connect through a proxy server** box is not checked, you have a direct connection. If it is checked, click the **Settings** button, then write down the HTTP Proxy URL and its port. The exceptions will be noted in the box labeled Do not use proxies for addresses beginning with:. Write these down, too.

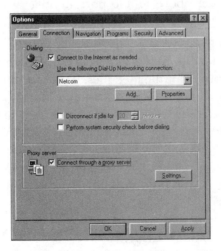

Figure 12.4 Microsoft Internet Explorer's Connections dialog box show similar information for that browser.

Entering Proxy Information

If you have determined you aren't using a proxy server, you can skip this step. Otherwise, follow these directions:

1. In PageMaker, choose **File>Preferences>Online Setup**. The dialog box shown in Figure 12.5 will appear.

Figure 12.5 The Online Preferences dialog box is used to set up PageMaker to work with HTML pages and Internet information.

2. In the URL Information box, type in the name of the proxy you wrote down in the step above, and its port number.

3. Next, write in the No proxies information in the middle field. Separate the entries with semicolons.

4. In the Download to folder field, enter the path to the folder where you want to place downloaded files. Windows 95 users may type in the subdirectory names if they choose, and Mac owners can also type in the folder hierarchy (using colons to separate the names of the nested folders). With either platform, it may be easier to just click the **Browse** button and search for the folder you want to use.

5. Finally, tell PageMaker where it can find your Web browser by typing in a path in the Web browser field, or by browsing to it.

HTML STYLES AND LINKS

While you don't need to learn all the special codes associated with HTML styles and links, you do need to learn what they are in order to use

PageMaker's HTML importing and exporting features. This section provides a quick introduction.

Styles

PageMaker offers equivalents for 15 HTML styles. Note that while you can apply fonts and type sizes to PageMaker styles, when they're translated back into HTML, they're turned into relative styles once more. That is, an HTML style applies whatever actual type size and font defined by the browser.

For example, there are six HTML heading styles, numbered Heading 1 (H1) through Heading 6 (H6.) With any browser, H1 will display as the largest heading (regardless of how large the type is), and H6 will be shown as the smallest heading (often barely larger than body text.) The actual sizes used are determined by the browser.

PageMaker styles for Web pages include HTML in their names (e.g., HTML H1) to let you know of their special status. Other supported HTML styles available in PageMaker include the following. Don't worry about learning how to do much more than enter or delete any of these, as you can't do more sophisticated HTML coding within PageMaker. The program's import and export filter can only convert back and forth between these styles. Other styles, such as those incorporating tables, frames, or image maps, are not displayed within PageMaker. Instead, they are preserved internally, then exported when you convert the PageMaker document back into HTML.

+ **HTML Address**—This marks the author's contact information and is displayed in italics.

+ **HTML Blockquote**—Used to mark long quotations and citations in a special way, by indenting both left and right margins relative to the rest of the page.

+ **HTML Body Text**—Defines text in the default style for the body of the page.

+ **HTML Menu List**—A list of items the user will select from.

+ **HTML Ordered List**—A numbered list of items.

+ **HTML Preformatted**—Used to mark text that will be displayed exactly as formatted, using fixed-width (monospaced) type.

+ **HTML Unordered List**—A bulleted list of items.

+ **HTML Directory List**—Unbulleted list of short items, each less than 20 characters, displayed in columns.

✦ **HTML Definition List**—Definition for a term in a glossary. This produces a two-column display, with terms on the left and definitions on the right.

Links

Links are controls within an HTML document that provide a location for the browser. That location can be one of the following:

✦ Another place on the same page that the browser should jump to.

✦ Another page stored elsewhere on that Web site or hard disk.

✦ Another page on a different Web site or hard disk (or somewhere on your computer network).

The location of an image, audio file, movie, executable file, or other component, either local or elsewhere on the Web or network, which the browser should download. If the browser has a plug-in, helper, or built-in support for that type of file, it can display or play it. If not (which will probably be the place in the case of executable files) the browser will offer to store the file on your hard disk.

As you can see, links are a powerful feature that enable HTML page browsers to build in jump-off points that visitors can use to navigate through multiple pages, view images, download files, and perform other functions. PageMaker can import links from existing pages so you can incorporate them into documents of your own.

IMPORTING HTML PAGES AND COMPONENTS INTO PAGEMAKER

There are two main ways to import HTML pages into PageMaker: using drag-and-drop and the **Place** command. These next exercises will show you how to import a page using both methods.

Dragging and Dropping a Whole Page

1. Copy the file **Import.htm** from the disk included with this book to your hard disk. You'll find it in the **Chapter 12** folder.

2. Open a new, blank PageMaker document. The specifications for the document don't really matter, as we're just experimenting with importing an HTML page.

3. Open your browser, and load the **Import.htm** file into it. With Netscape, you'd do that by using the **File>Open File In Browser** command (or just press **Command-O** if you have a Mac, or **Ctrl+O** if you have a PC). Microsoft Internet Explorer users can use **File>Open**, or press either **Command+O** or **Ctrl+O**.

4. Arrange your desktop so that both PageMaker and the browser's windows are visible at the same time. Your screen should look like Figure 12.6.

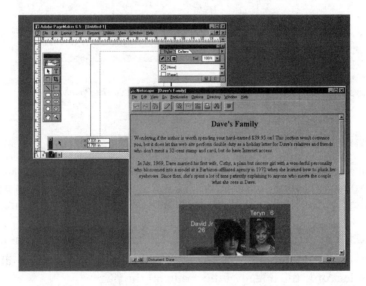

Figure 12.6 *Both PageMaker and your browser should be visible at the same time.*

5. In the PageMaker window, click the mouse to specify where you'd like to insert the HTML page in your document.

6. Go back to the browser window, and select the text for the whole page. You can also select only an individual graphic, link, or section of text if you want to import part of a page rather than the whole thing.

7. Drag the page from the browser window to the PageMaker document. The page is inserted in the document, as shown in Figure 12.7.

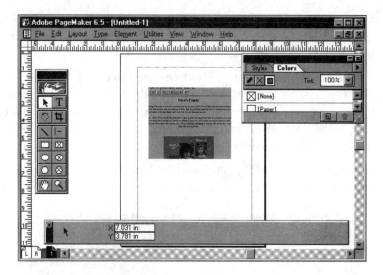

Figure 12.7 *The entire HTML page has been inserted in the PageMaker document.*

Dragging and Dropping Specific Elements

You can also drag only specific elements from a page into your PageMaker document. If you are creating your own HTML document and want to copy a graphic or hyperlink, it can be dragged from an existing page using the following steps:

1. Click in the PageMaker document to specify a new insertion point.
2. With the document from the last exercise and the browser still visible, select only the image of the castle on the page.

3. Hold down the **Option** key (if you have a Macintosh) or the **Alt** key (if you have a PC), and drag the graphic from the browser window to the PageMaker document. The HTML Import Options dialog box, shown in Figure 12.8, appears.

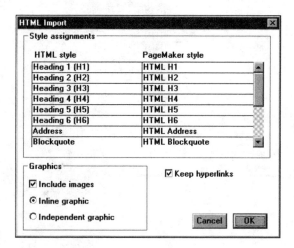

Figure 12.8 *You can specify parameters in the HTML Import Options dialog box.*

4. You'll notice that the Options dialog box has a scrolling list of HTML styles paired with the equivalent PageMaker styles they will be converted to. You can redefine any match by clicking in the right column, then choosing the new PageMaker style you want to use for that HTML style from the drop-down list, shown in Figure 12.9.

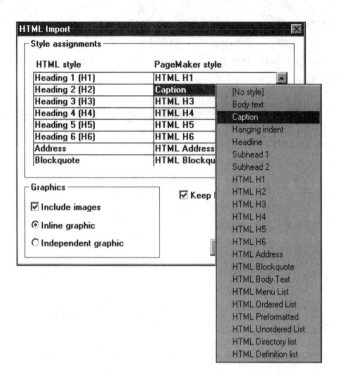

Figure 12.9 Any HTML style can be paired with a PageMaker equivalent of your choosing.

5. There are check boxes you can use to select whether hyperlinks should be preserved or ignored (in which case you'll have to type in new targets for the links), and others that let you include any graphics on the page or leave them behind.

6. Click **OK** to import the element into your PageMaker document.

Placing HTML Pages

You can also import HTML pages or links using the **Place** command. To experiment with this capability, just follow these directions:

1. As you did above, click an insertion point in your PageMaker document.

2. Choose **File>Place**. The Place dialog box, shown in Figure 12.10, will appear.

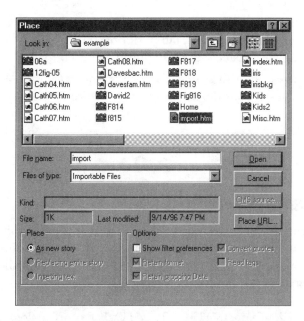

Figure 12.10 The Place dialog box is used for importing HTML files and links.

3. Locate the HTML file you want to place. It must end with an **.HTM** or **.HTML** extension. Or click **Open URL** to place a link. You must type the name of the link (or paste a previously copied link), as PageMaker is not able to browse for the link.

4. The Import HTML dialog box will appear, as in step 3 in the previous exercise. The dialog box is shown in Figure 12.8. Mark any options, as described earlier.

5. Click **OK** to place the document or link.

EXPORTING HTML DOCUMENTS

You can format any document with export as HTML pages in mind. The document can be one you've imported earlier, or one you create from scratch. Keep in mind the special rules of Web pages:

✦ You have no control over the size of the window in which the document will be displayed, so pages shouldn't depend on being a specific width.

◆ You have no control over other parameters, such as column width and type size or style. Indents, tab positions, line breaks, color, letter spacing, and word spacing are also outside your control.

◆ Web pages can display only GIF or JPEG images. PageMaker converts any images in your documents into these two formats automatically as you export.

◆ Try to use as many of the predefined styles as possible, as documents using them will export best.

Setting Export Preferences

Actual construction of a Web page is beyond the scope of this book. You'll want to consult one of the many guides to HTML and Web-site building for tips. We'll limit our discussion to actually exporting your finished document in HTML format. Just follow these directions:

1. Select **File>Export>HTML**. The HTML Export dialog box, shown in Figure 12.11, appears.

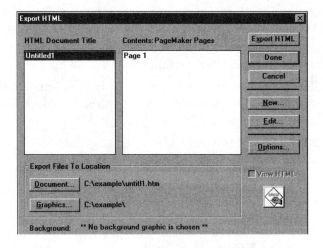

Figure 12.11 *The HTML Export dialog box allows you to make final settings before converting a document.*

2. You can provide an HTML document title for each separate page of your PageMaker document in the fields shown in Figure 12.11.

3. If you want to match different pages in the document to specific HTML pages, click the **Edit** button and assign the pages in the dialog box that pops up.

4. Click the **Document** and **Graphics** buttons to specify a special location to export the documents and graphics in a page.

5. If you've selected a background graphic for the pages, it will be shown at the bottom of the dialog box.

6. In the lower right of the dialog box is a **WWW** icon. Click this to specify a Web browser. Then check the box labeled **View HTML** if you want to view the page in the browser.

7. Click the **Options** button to produce the dialog box shown in Figure 12.12.

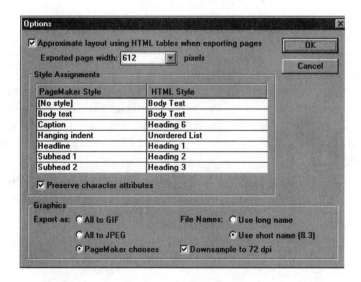

Figure 12.12 *The Options dialog box has some additional parameters you can modify.*

8. If you check the box at the top of the dialog box, layouts will be converted to HTML tables where appropriate.

9. You can specify a width for the exported page in pixels.

10. In the Style Assignments field, you can match your document's styles with the available HTML styles.

11. Check the **Preserve character attributes** box if you want boldface and italic to be preserved in the HTML document.

12. In the Graphics section, you can specify whether images included in the document are all converted to GIF, all to JPEG, or to either JPEG or GIF at PageMaker's discretion (photographs may look better as JPEG images; finely detailed graphics or those with few colors look better as GIFs).

13. Also in the Graphics section, you can specify whether Mac-style long filenames should be preserved (which will be fine if you're using the HTML page on a Mac) or if they should be converted to DOS-style eight-character/three-character-extension names.

14. Finally, you can click a check box to indicate that PageMaker should reduce images to 72-dpi resolution, which is the same as the resolution used to display them on most monitor screens.

15. Click **OK** to exit the Options box.

To Sum Up

While we didn't cover everything there is to know about HTML import and export, you should now know enough to experiment with these capabilities as you learn more about building Web pages. More importantly, we gave you a glimpse of some of the key uses for this kind of document beyond the World Wide Web.

In Chapter 13, we'll look at how PageMaker's Help system can be used to give you the support you need when working with complex features.

Using PageMaker Help

- ✦ Accessing Help
- ✦ About PageMaker
- ✦ To sum up

If you've read this far and have used PageMaker to work through some of the examples in this book, you realize PageMaker has a powerful Help system. Both Windows 95 and Macintosh Help systems are standardized across applications, so if you know how to use Help in another application, you'll find it very familiar in PageMaker.

ACCESSING WINDOWS 95 HELP

PageMaker's Windows 95 Help can be accessed through the Help menu. You can use the mouse to pull down the Help menu, or press **Alt-H** to view the entire Help menu, which includes **Help Topics**, **Shortcuts**, and the **About PageMaker** box. You can also press **F1** to jump directly to the Help Topics dialog box, shown in Figure 13.1.

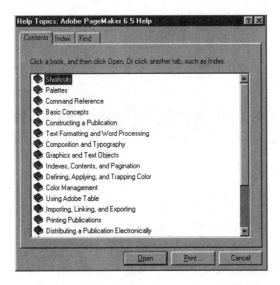

Figure 13.1 The Help Topics dialog box.

This dialog box has three tabs: *Contents*, *Index*, and *Find*. The Contents tab lists major topics that Adobe has set up to help you explore PageMaker's functions and features. The Index tab, shown in Figure 13.2, has two boxes. In the top box, you can type in the first few characters of the topic you're interested in.

The Help system will jump immediately to the index listing that most closely matches what you've typed in and display the available topics in the second box. You can also scroll through this box using the scrolling controls at the right of the box to browse through entries on your own. You might want to do this if you are looking for new and interesting features to learn about.

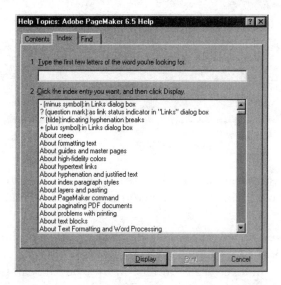

Figure 13.2 *The Help Index dialog box.*

The Find tab activates a Windows 95 wizard (but only the first time you use this feature) that can help you search through a large database of topics to find the exact subject you're interested in. When you click this tab, a dialog box like the one shown in Figure 13.3 pops up. You may check **Minimize database size** to create an optimized file of the most important words in PageMaker's Help files. The **Maximize search capabilities** button indexes every single word in the Help system, while the **Customize search capabilities** button makes it possible for you to specify which kinds of terms will be indexed.

Figure 13.3 *The Find Setup Wizard dialog box.*

Just follow the instructions on-screen to create your own database of terms, which Windows 95 will use again the next time you access the **Help Find** command from within PageMaker.

Once you've created the database, a dialog box like the one shown in Figure 13.4 appears. You can type in a few words for the search or select from a scrolling list of indexed terms to narrow the search. Searching takes place virtually instantly as you type in parameters. You can view available topics in the scrolling list at the bottom of the dialog box at any time. Double click on a topic to display its Help screens.

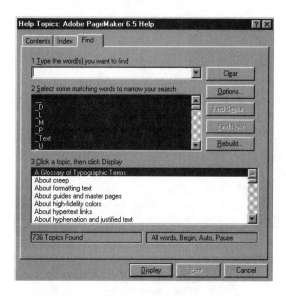

Figure 13.4 The Find dialog box.

The **Options** button produces the dialog box shown in Figure 13.5, which you can use to restrict your search in more sophisticated ways. For example, you can tell Windows 95 to look for entries that match all the words you type in any order or topics that match any one of those words. You may ask to see only topics that exactly match your entry. For example, if you wanted to see all help topics related to fonts, you might type **fonts typefaces kerning leading** and check the **At least one of the words you typed** radio button. However, if you wanted to learn how to edit styles, you would type in **Editing Styles** and click **The words you typed in exact order** button.

You can also specify where the words you typed may appear in the topics using the Show words that drop-down list. The choices include:

✦ **Begin with the characters you type**—Entering **kern** would locate topics that include *kern, kerned,* or *kerning.*

✦ **Contain the characters you type**—Entering **pag** would locate topics that include *paginate, repaginate,* and so on.

✦ **End with the characters you type**—Entering **setter** would locate topics like *image setter, typesetter,* and so on.

✦ **Match the characters you type**—Entering **<space>filter<space>** would locate only topics with the word *filter* included and would ignore *filters* or other variations.

The last two radio buttons on the Find Options dialog box let you specify whether Help should search immediately after you enter a character or wait for a pause. The Find Options dialog box is shown in Figure 13.5.

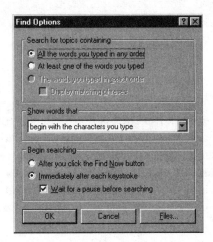

Figure 13.5 *The Find Options dialog box.*

ACCESSING MACINTOSH HELP

The Mac's Help system is just as easy to use. Choose the **System 7 Help** pull-down menu to reveal the PageMaker Help commands: **Contents**, **Search**, **Shortcuts**, and **Using PageMaker Help**. Select **Contents** to open the main Help window and its menu bar (since Help is a standalone application that remains active when you return to PageMaker). The main window provides help by function or topic. There is also specific help in using PageMaker's Help system.

Context-sensitive Help is available by pressing **Command+?**. A question mark replaces the mouse pointer or Toolbox tool you're currently using. Select any menu command to see Help messages relative to that command. For example, if you wanted to see Help concerning the Print dialog box, simply press **Command+?** and choose the **Print** command using the question mark icon.

Help from the Balloon Menu

To gain access to the PageMaker Help system, follow these steps:

1. Choose the **Balloon** pull-down menu to see the Help commands. Choose the **Contents** command to open the Help window.

2. Select one of the command buttons across the top of the window:

   ✦ **Topics**—Just like the table of contents of a book, the **Topics** command takes you to a functional listing of PageMaker's Help system.

   ✦ **Previous** takes you back to the previous window you were in. Using the **Previous** button, you can literally back out of the system.

   ✦ **Notes** allows you to add notes or annotation to specific help windows.

   ✦ **Keyword** lets you search through Help keywords, to quickly retrieve the Help text you want.

   ✦ **<<** and **>>** (the Forward and Backward arrows) move you quickly through the hierarchy of Help windows.

   ✦ **Search** is similar in ways to the PageMaker **Find** command. You use this command button to search for words or phrases in the Help system.

Using the Topics Command

The **Topics** command arranges Help by major and minor topics. For example, the major topics are presented in the Help Topics window.

Choose any step to move to more detailed help descriptions.

To see more details concerning this topic, double-click on one of the open folder items; for example, **Choosing an Importing and Updating Method**.

Click the **Previous** button to move backward through the windows of Help you've already seen.

Using the Notes Command

The **Notes** command button lets you add a note to yourself or anyone else using the Help system on your Macintosh. Regardless of where you are in the Help system, other than the main topics window, click the **Notes** button to open up a note window.

You can add anything you'd like to a note. For example, you could augment the Help steps with your own Help notes, or you could refer new users to pages in this book for additional information. Or, as the example suggests, you could add departmental rules to follow in conjunction with using PageMaker in your office.

Using the Keywords Command

The PageMaker Help system has thousands of words that are tagged as *keywords*, meaning that you can use the **Keywords** command to access them and their locations throughout the Help system. Just click the **Keywords** button to see the Keywords Help window.

Notice that there are subcategories of Help topics in the right-hand box that further break down the keyword in the left-hand box. Click on a Help topic to see specific Help windows. For instance, if you clicked on the **Align** keyword, you would see the Snap To Guides topic.

Using the Search Command

Sometimes you need some help, but you're just not sure under which topic the answers to your questions will be found. The Search feature in PageMaker's help system may be just the trick. Click the **Search** button to display the Search dialog box.

Here you can enter words to search by; however, make the search words as specific as you can. For example, if you're seeking help formatting text, but enter only the word **formatting** in the text box, the results of a very broad search would include many possible subtopics.

ABOUT PAGEMAKER: FOR BOTH MAC AND PC USERS

Just about every Macintosh or Windows application has an About window available, and PageMaker is no exception. On the Mac, it's available in the Apple menu, while Windows 95 users will find it as the last entry in the Help menu. The PageMaker About window displays the name of the registered user and the serial number of the software. The software's version number is also shown. Click anywhere in the box to return to your document.

Listing Installed Plug-Ins, Filters, and Dictionaries

The About PageMaker window also reports all of the currently installed plug-ins, import and export filters, and dictionaries. To see the list, hold down the **Command** key on the Macintosh or the **Ctrl** key on the PC while choosing **About PageMaker** from the Help pull-down menu. The plug-ins are displayed first. You may have to scroll down the list to see the import and export filters. Choose **OK** to return to your document.

TO SUM UP

PageMaker includes comprehensive Help you can access from a Contents, Index, or Find list. Using any of these systems, you'll find brief but helpful tips on most menu commands and functions right on your screen. You can even add notes to yourself that are incorporated into the Help system for later reference.

Improving Your System

If you have been chugging away on your Mac Plus or an old 386 PC, swearing one of these days you will surely throw your system out the window, now may be the time. PageMaker 6.5 will not run on a Mac Plus (nor will it run on an SE or Mac Classic). The Windows version requires Windows 95, which is surely too much of a resource hog for any computer slower than a 486/66. PageMaker 5.0 was the last version that could be run on older 68000-based Macintoshes, and Windows 3.1 users were left behind at Version 6.0.

Perhaps it's time for a quiet funeral and an upgrade to a computer with more refinement, breeding, and definitely more speed and memory. The Plus, with its slow processor and limited memory and the sluggish 386 have been the bane of high-end applications like PageMaker for years. Beware of

PageMaker 6.5's hunger for speed and memory: It is insatiable. The more memory the better; consider acquiring the fastest computer your credit card can afford.

ADDING MEMORY

On the latest computers, PageMaker 6.5 requires a minimum of 8 to 9 megs of memory to run (but just barely). Realistically, a minimum of 16 megs is more reasonable, and 24 to 32 megs is even better. Beyond that, performance improvements tend to diminish, unless you want (or need) to have more than two or three applications open at once, or often have a real memory hog like Adobe Photoshop operating at the same time.

Memory is, without a doubt, the least expensive upgrade you can make to your computer, if you measure the performance gains you get for the money. During 1996's outlandish RAM price wars, memory sank to incredibly low prices before they started nosing up again. Only a few years ago, I paid $600 for 16 MB of RAM, and was happy to get it for that amount. More recently, I snatched up some 16 MB SIMMs for $69 apiece—less than one-eighth the price. While RAM tariffs began to rise at about the time PageMaker 6.5 was introduced in November 1996, memory is still a bargain when you consider how dramatically performance can be affected by an extra 8 to 16 MB.

Also consider adding extra memory to your computer's video. PCs and many high-end Macs have PCI video cards that can be upgraded from the minimum (usually around 2 MB) to 4 MB or more. Upgrading to 4 MB of video RAM can bump the number of colors you can display at resolutions up to 1024 x 768 (or higher) from 65,535 (thousands of colors) to 16.8 million (millions of colors.) If you're laying out pages that include full-color images, these extra colors will help you evaluate how the picture looks when placed into your PageMaker publication. You'll also want better color when using PageMaker's ability to apply Photoshop-style plug-in filters to imported images.

Adjusting Virtual Memory

Virtual memory is a means of fooling PageMaker into thinking there is more memory in the system than there actually is. Virtual memory is actually a segment of the hard disk that is set aside to temporarily store information held in memory. Normally the data that has been held in memory the longest will be copied to the virtual memory segment of the disk, making room in

RAM for more data. If the information in virtual memory is needed, it's read back into memory and made available for PageMaker to use. The advantages of virtual memory is that you can cheat and open larger files than actual RAM allows (handy if you occasionally work with very large graphic files or scanned color photographs). The disadvantage is that virtual memory—being simply a very large file on the hard disk—runs much slower than RAM.

Windows 95 generally manages Virtual Memory all by itself with no help from you. Use the Start menu to access **Settings**, then choose the System Control Panel's **Device Manager**. Click the **Performance** tab and **Virtual Memory** button and make sure the **Disable virtual memory** check box is not marked. You can tell the operating system to manage virtual memory on its own, or specify a disk drive, minimum, and maximum amount of hard disk space to use.

Macintosh users will want to make sure they turn on the virtual memory feature of System 7. Just open the Memory Control Panel and click the **Virtual Memory On** radio button. Then choose the hard drive you want to use when creating the memory segment. Select the amount of space on the drive you want to designate for the virtual drive. Restart the Mac, and your system memory will equal the amount of RAM plus the amount of virtual memory. Add-in programs like Connectix' RAM Doubler 2 have their own virtual memory routines that not only simulate RAM on your hard disk, but create "more" real RAM by compressing the contents of memory to use it more efficiently. The latest version of RAM Doubler actually grabs unused memory back from PowerPC-native programs, so if an application has a preferred memory size of 10 MB (set in the Get Info dialog box) but only needs 6 MB at the moment, that's all it is allocated.

ADDING A LARGER-CAPACITY DISK DRIVE

A disadvantage of all applications these days seems to be their enormous size (PageMaker 6.5, fully installed, takes up 26 megs of space on your disk). Upgrading to PageMaker 6.5 may force you to seek a larger capacity drive. If the time is right for a larger hard drive, take heart—they've never been priced as low as they are now. There are some exciting new drives on the market that offer very high reliability, very low average access times, and very affordable prices.

Indeed, it's hard to find a hard drive that is smaller than 1080 megs these days, and 1.6 to 3.2 gigabyte drives have become increasingly common at prices that dip way below $500 even for the larger models. These 1-in. tall, 3.5-in. drives, available in both SCSI and IDE models, are very exciting. They sport access times in the 8- to 10-ms range and, because of their size, generate very little heat inside the computer's case (you might be surprised how hot the old, larger 5.25-in. disk drives can get). Heat is a real killer of disk drives, as well as of most other components inside the computer's case. As the drive heats up, the alignment of the heads to the spinning platters can change, resulting in misread data sectors. So the cooler a drive runs, the safer your data will be. New drives automatically compensate the head alignment based on the internal temperature of the drive.

No matter how large a drive you buy, the First Law of Computer Dynamics says that any drive, no matter how large, will quickly fill to within 90% of capacity. Programs you thought you'd never be interested in suddenly become irresistible after purchasing a larger drive. So go ahead and exceed your wildest estimates—in three months it'll probably be just about filled up! (The second law says that no matter how little you paid for the drive, you'll find a less expensive price advertised two days after buying it.)

SPEEDING UP YOUR SYSTEM WITH CACHING

Disk and instruction caching designates a portion of RAM to hold frequently used information that would normally be read repeatedly from the disk drive. Since it takes longer to read the information from the drive than it does to read it from memory, disk caching can improve the performance of your system at the expense of the RAM set aside for caching. Hard disks and CD-ROM drives often have built-in RAM, from 128K to 1 MB used for caching, but your computer's RAM can also be used for this purpose.

The disk cache is sorely ignored by many users, who may not even be aware that it is available. Windows 95 handles caching automatically, so the best way to improve your performance in this area is to simply add more memory. If your PC has an empty secondary, or level 2 cache slot, you may want to purchase a fast cache memory card to keep your CPU supplied with a continual diet of instructions and data, so you can avoid wasting precious clock cycles.

The Macintosh OS gives you a little more control over caching. To boost the cache size, click open the Memory Control Panel and set the disk cache size you want. In systems sporting the barest of memory it is best to leave the disk cache on a very low setting. However, if you have added RAM to your system—and hopefully added some extra RAM just for the disk cache—you can increase significantly the size of the cache and see a resulting improvement in your Macintosh.

Newer Macs also let you increase the amount of the secondary, or level 2 processor cache. Some Performas and low-end Power Macs are furnished with no level 2 cache at all, but can be upgraded with reasonably priced 256K and 512K cache boards that fit in a slot on the motherboard.

COMPUTER VIRUSES

Computer viruses are hidden programs that reside in your computer (stored on a hard drive or floppy diskette) and do something that shouldn't be done. Some viruses are simply mischievous, others do physical damage to files, or even erase or reformat your hard disk. Each time PageMaker starts, it looks for any changes a virus may have made to the program. If it finds anything different, it warns you and gives you a chance to cancel starting the program. Some of the ways to prevent viruses include:

✦ Purchase a program that identifies and eradicates viruses, like Symantec's Norton AntiVirus.

✦ Back up your data files onto floppies, tape cartridges, or one of the newer ZIP, SyQuest EZ, or magnetic-optical disk systems on a regular basis. Important files should be backed up daily.

✦ A computer virus isn't transmitted through the air. It gets into your computer as part of a program. Be very careful downloading shareware from bulletin boards and electronic mail systems.

✦ Be cautious about shareware. I suggest getting your software only from reputable companies and online sources whose success demands quality control and rigid testing.

✦ Be discriminating about whom you allow to use and work on your computer. If you deal with reputable companies, you shouldn't have any problems.

✦ Insure your hardware and software against loss. Many business insurance policies now offer riders for such protection.

* In an office environment, set up password protection for your computer so that only you can gain access. Password protection not

only keeps a potential hacker from fooling around, but in the event that the computer is stolen, it offers little resale value if no one can use the system.

TRANSFERRING PAGEMAKER FILES BETWEEN MACINTOSH AND WINDOWS COMPUTERS

PageMaker 6.5 files are interchangeable between the Macintosh and Windows versions of the application (both Macs and PCs were used in the development of this book). All you have to do is transfer them via a medium common to both, or modem or a null modem cable.

There are a number of programs on the market that handle computer-to-computer transfers. My favorite is MacLink Plus, by Dataviz, Inc. MacLink runs in the Macintosh that is connected to the PC with a serial cable. The files are transferred in either directory.

Another way of transferring files is by using the Apple SuperDrive that comes in all currently available Macs. The SuperDrive can read Windows 1.44-MB floppy disks, so you can transfer files to and from the disks in the Mac with ease. Support for reading Windows-format files is built right into Mac OS 7.5 and higher.

You can create a SuperDrive equivalent on a PC by using one of several available utilities for Windows, including Mac-in-DOS software, by Pacific Micro (1-415-948-6200). The program, which costs around $60, lets you read Macintosh files on any Macintosh-formatted double-density floppy with your PC's 1.44-MB, 3.5-in. floppy drive. Not only can you copy any file on the Mac floppy onto your system, you can just as easily copy PageMaker for Windows files onto the Mac floppy. You can even start the program, insert a blank floppy in your drive, and format the floppy as a Macintosh floppy!

 If you want to transfer earlier versions of either PageMaker for Windows or PageMaker for the Macintosh across platforms, you must first convert the file to the current version of PageMaker. In other words, if you have a PageMaker for Windows 4.0 file that you wish to open in PageMaker 6.5 for the Macintosh, you must first open the file in PageMaker 6.5 for Windows, save the file as a PageMaker Windows 4.0 file, and then transfer it to the Macintosh computer. The same is true for moving files from the Macintosh to Windows.

Appendix B

This appendix is designed to give you the basics of how each command in PageMaker works. Often, you will have read much more involved explanations in the preceding chapters, but this appendix can give you a quick reminder of what a particular command does. The commands are presented in the order that they appear on PageMaker's menus. I'll include sample dialog boxes for some of the commands, where I think they will help you understand the menu item.

NOTE Before a document is opened, any menu command not dimmed means you can choose the command, open the dialog box, and adjust the settings, which then become the new default settings for PageMaker.

THE FILE MENU

Use the File menu, shown in Figure B.1, for all file-management chores, including opening and closing documents, importing and exporting documents, and defining linked files. You also print files with this menu, and you can exit the program.

```
┌─────────────────────────────┐
│ File                        │
├─────────────────────────────┤
│ New...                  ⌘N  │
│ Open...                 ⌘O  │
│ Recent Publications      ▶  │
├─────────────────────────────┤
│ Close                   ⌘W  │
│ Save                    ⌘S  │
│ Save As...             ⇧⌘S  │
│ Revert                      │
├─────────────────────────────┤
│ Place...                ⌘D  │
├─────────────────────────────┤
│ Acquire                  ▶  │
│ Export                   ▶  │
├─────────────────────────────┤
│ Links Manager...       ⇧⌘D  │
├─────────────────────────────┤
│ Document Setup...      ⇧⌘P  │
│ Printer Styles           ▶  │
│ Print...                ⌘P  │
├─────────────────────────────┤
│ Preferences              ▶  │
├─────────────────────────────┤
│ Quit                    ⌘Q  │
└─────────────────────────────┘
```

Figure B.1 The File menu.

New

Choose the **New** command to open a new document in PageMaker. Selecting the command opens the Document Setup dialog box, where you can set up the parameters for the page. When you close the Document Setup dialog box, a new page is created and displayed in the Fit in Window view.

Open

Choose the **Open** command to open an existing PageMaker document or template. PageMaker displays the Open Publication dialog box, so that you can select a document to open. The opened document is displayed in the same view size as when it was closed. In the Open Publication dialog box, choose the existing PageMaker document or template from the list of files and folders. Choose the **Original** radio button to open the original document.

Choose the **Copy** radio button to open a copy of the document, leaving the original intact (see Save and Save As).

Recent Publications

Place the cursor on the **Recent Publications** command to activate a fly-out submenu with a list of the last publications you worked with. You can select one directly from the submenu, without having to search your hard disk folders for them.

Close

Choose **Close** to close the current document. If changes have been made to the document since the last time it was saved, PageMaker asks if you'd like to save the document before closing. If you choose **No**, you lose the work you have done to the document since the last time you used the **Save** command.

You can also close any document by clicking the **Close** box, located in the upper-left corner of the document window on a Mac or in the upper-right corner on a Windows 95 machine. Again, if you haven't saved your work, PageMaker reminds you to do so (see Save, Save As, and Revert).

Save (Command/Ctrl+S)

Choose the **Save** command whenever you want to save your work. The first time you choose **Save** with a new document, PageMaker displays the Save Publication As dialog box, shown in Figure B.2. Enter a name for the new document.

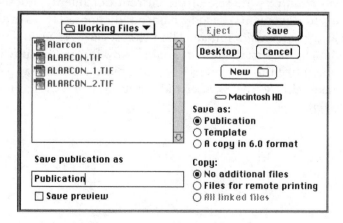

Figure B.2 *The Save Publication As dialog box.*

If you are creating a publication, choose the **Publication** radio button. If it is a template, choose the **Template** radio button. In the Copy area of the dialog box, click the **No Additional Files** button if you do not want to save an additional copy of the linked external files to the same folder that the new publication is saved to (see Links). If you'd like to include copies of all external files with your document, click the **All Linked Files** option, and the linked files will be copied to the same folder as the new document. PageMaker will warn you if there is not enough room in the folder for all the files.

If you will be printing this document at a service bureau or if you have selected a floppy to save the document to, click the **Files Required for Remote Printing** option to ensure that all necessary linked files or special files (e.g., **Track-Kerning Resource** file) are included with the document. You can also save a publication in the older PageMaker 6.0 format if you need to exchange files with someone who is still using the previous version.

Save As

When you'd like to save a copy of an existing document or template as another document or template with a different name, choose the **Save As** command. PageMaker displays the Save Publication As dialog box for you to enter a different name. The **Save As** command also reduces the size of the document, which can grow in size as revisions, spelling corrections, resizings, and so on are made. **Save As** eliminates that excess baggage and compresses the file, making it smaller, faster, and more efficient.

To simply compress the size of the current document, choose **Save As**, give the current document a second name, and choose **OK** to save the first document as the second document. Then choose **Save As** again and give the second document the first document's name. Now the first document is compressed. If you'd like this compression to take place each time you select the **Save** command, choose the **Smaller** radio button in the Preferences dialog box (see Preferences).

Revert

Use the **Revert** command to revert to the last-saved version of the document. In other words, if you save changes you make to your document, begin working on a new page or alter an existing page, and then choose **Revert**, PageMaker changes the document back to the way it was when you last saved it.

PageMaker has its own internal back-up scheme to offer some protection between times that you choose the **Save** command. The program saves a miniature version of the current document whenever the following actions occur: printing, copying, inserting, or deleting one or more pages, moving from one page to another, switching between the Story Editor and the Layout Editor, clicking the **current page** icon, or changing parameters in the Page Setup dialog box. If you choose the **Revert** command while holding down the **Shift** key, you restore to the last *mini-saved* version of the document.

Mini-saved versions of the document are made even before you save a new document the first time. Until you name and save the document, PageMaker gives it a temporary name. You will find the file in the **Rescued Items** folder inside the Trash Can. If you lose power to your Macintosh while working in a newly created but yet-to-be-saved document, open the folder, click on the temporary file, and once PageMaker has started, use the **Save As** command to give the file a proper name.

Place (Command/Ctrl+D)

While working in the Layout Editor, choose the **Place** command to import a text or graphic file and place it on the page (or pages) of the document. When you choose this command, PageMaker displays the Place Document dialog box, shown in Figure B.3 (even though the dialog box is titled *Place Document*, it works for placing both text and graphics). Locate the name of the word processing, database, spreadsheet, or graphics file you'd like to import.

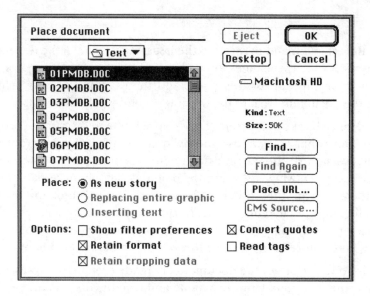

Figure B.3 *The Place Document dialog box.*

If you have not selected a text block with the Pointer tool or clicked the Text tool insertion point in a text block, the **As New Story** (or **As New Graphic**) radio button will be checked. To replace the current text in the text block with the new text, select the text block with the Pointer tool and choose **Place**. The **Replacing Entire Story** (or **Replacing Entire Graphic**) radio button will be checked. To insert new text or place a graphic as an in-line graphic, position the Text tool insertion point in the text block where you'd like the new text or graphic to be inserted. Choose **Place**, and the **Inserting Text** (or **Inserting Graphic**) option will be checked.

Click the **Retain Format** box to retain the file's formatting and style sheet (if applicable). For example, if the file was formatted in WordPerfect in 12-point Helvetica, checking the option box would format the file in PageMaker in 12-point Helvetica. If you do not check the option box, the default PageMaker formats and specifications will be added to the file. The **Convert Quotes** option box, when checked, converts word processor–style quotation marks to the "curly" quotation marks found in real typesetting and converts double dashes to the em dash.

Some fonts may not have curly quotation characters. In that case, PageMaker will not attempt to convert the characters. Also, word processor–style quotation marks following numbers (indicating feet or inches) are not converted to curly quotes.

NOTE

If you check the **Retain Tags** option box, PageMaker looks for style names enclosed at the beginning of paragraphs in angled brackets (<>) that match named styles in the PageMaker document. If the names match, the paragraphs will be formatted in the PageMaker style. If PageMaker cannot find a matching style, it adds the file's style name with an asterisk to the styles in the Style palette. The text will still be formatted in the default style for the document. Edit the style name (see Type:Define Styles) to add the attributes you'd like for the style.

When you have selected the options you'd like, choose **OK** to return to your document. The pointer changes to a different "loaded" icon depending on what kind of file you are placing. Position the icon on the page and click the mouse button to place the text or graphic.

In the Story Editor, the **Place** command places the current story in the document. When you choose the command from the File menu, the mouse pointer changes to a loaded-text icon and the document in the Layout Editor is displayed. Position the icon and click the mouse button to place the text on the page (see Layout:Autoflow).

Acquire

The **Acquire** command allows you to select a TWAIN image source (such as a scanner) and to grab images directly from the source and place them in PageMaker.

Export

Choose the **Export** command to save elements of your PageMaker document in one of these forms:

- An Adobe Portable Document Format (PDF) file.
- An HTML file.
- As a graphic file in JPEG, TIF, GIF, or DCS format.
- As text in a word processing format, such as WordPerfect or Word.

Simply select the element you want to export within PageMaker, then choose the appropriate export mode from the Export submenu, shown in Figure B.4.

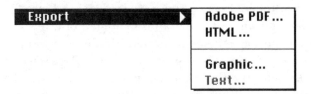

Figure B.4 *The Export submenu.*

Choose the folder for the exported document from the list box. Choose the type of export file in the File Format pop-up list. (The formats displayed in the pop-up list reflect the export filters you have currently loaded with the PageMaker installation program.) If you have selected some text from a document to export, the **Selected Text Only** option will be checked. Otherwise, the **Entire Story** option is checked. To export style tags that carry the PageMaker style names, click the **Export Tags** option box.

N O T E   Using the **Export Tags** option, if you export your PageMaker document as a Microsoft Word document, index markers in the PageMaker document will be converted to Word index markers. This means that you can edit index entries in Word, and when the document is imported back into PageMaker the new index markers will be in place. It also means that you can add Word's index markers in your word processor and convert them over to PageMaker index markers when the document is imported and placed.

Links Manager

Choose the **Links Manager** command to see all the current links in your document. Whenever you place text or graphics in PageMaker, a link is created to the external application's file. You can see the status of the document's links with the Links dialog box (see Figure B.5). This dialog box displays the name of the linked file, the type of file, and the page number the file starts on. A status indicator and a status explanation line indicate whether or not there is a problem with the link (the external file can't be located, for example) and whether the external file or the internal linked element needs to be updated.

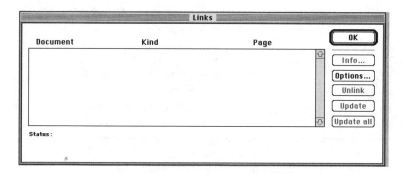

Figure B.5 *The Links Manager dialog box.*

The Links Manager dialog box leads to two other dialog boxes: the Link Info dialog box and the Link Options dialog box. Choose the **Update** button to update only the selected file in the dialog box. Choose the **Update All** button to update all files that need to be updated.

Link Info

Choose the linked file in the Links dialog box you want and click the **Link Info** button to display the Link Info dialog box, shown in Figure B.6. The Link Info dialog box shows pertinent information about the file, including its size and location, the date and time it was placed, and the date and time the original or internal copy was last changed. You can select a different linked file to see its link information. You can also choose a new, unlinked file in the list box and link the file by clicking the **Link** button. Choose **Cancel** to move back to the Links dialog box.

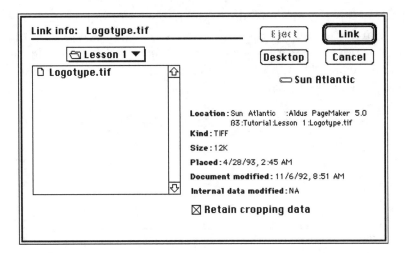

Figure B.6 *The Link Info dialog box.*

Link Options

Choose the **Link Options** button in the Links dialog box to display the Link Options dialog box. In this dialog box, you can set the options for the linked file highlighted in the Links dialog box.

You can store a complete copy of the linked element inside the PageMaker document by checking the **Store Copy in Publication** check box (this is the default option for text files and encapsulated PostScript files, in which case the option is checked and dimmed). Storing a copy inside the publication increases the size of the publication. For graphic files, especially full gray-scale or color TIFF files, this option could drastically increase the size of the document (PageMaker warns you if the file exceeds 250K in size).

If the externally linked file has changed, clicking the **Update Automatically** option means the internally linked file will be updated automatically whenever the PageMaker document is opened. Once checked, if the document is opened and PageMaker cannot locate the externally linked file, you'll see the Cannot Find dialog box, informing you that the file in question cannot be found. Use the list box to choose the file to link. Click the **Link** button to reestablish the link to this file. To unsuccessfully end the search for the file, choose the **Ignore** button. Choose the **Ignore All** button if more than one file cannot be located.

Checking the **Update Automatically** option allows you to choose to be alerted before the updating occurs. Check the **Alert Before Updating** option box if you'd like to be notified before the linked element is updated. Choose **OK** to return to the Links dialog box.

Document Setup

Choose the **Document Setup** command to establish the page size, page orientation, margins, and related parameters for the document. This command opens the Document Setup dialog box, shown in Figure B.7.

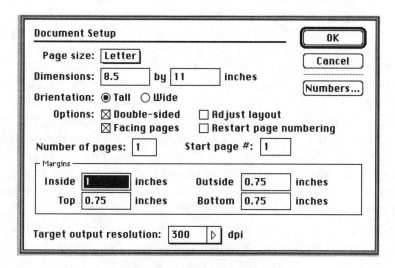

Figure B.7 *The Document Setup dialog box.*

First, set the page type by clicking the **Page Size** pop-up list and choosing the page type from the list. Different printers, depending on what size paper they can handle, will demand different page type settings in the pop-up list.

The Page Dimensions boxes for width and height will reflect the size of the selected page type. Enter different dimensions if the listed page types don't suit your job requirements. The Page Size pop-up list will reflect your nonstandard dimensions by saying *Custom*. Choose **Orientation:Wide** if you want to print landscape. The dialog box defaults to the **Tall** option, which prints portrait. If you change the dimensions after you begin laying out your page, PageMaker does not adjust text or graphics to the new dimensions. The text or graphics on the pages may overlap onto the pasteboard.

N O T E   You can enter dimensions smaller than the selected printer can handle. If you enter larger dimensions, the printed page has to be reduced to fit on the maximum-size paper the selected printer can handle, or you have to use the **Tile** option (in the Print Document dialog box).

To start page numbering with a number other than 1, enter the starting number in the Start Page # text box. If you have built a Book list using the **Book** command and have selected the **Next Page** option to number the pages of the book consecutively, entering a starting number of **1** in this text box renumbers the book from this document forward.

Increasing the starting page number by an odd-numbered amount forces left-hand, odd-numbered pages to become right-hand, even-numbered pages. Increasing the starting page number by an even-numbered amount forces the opposite. If you have *double trucks* (layouts that continue across the break between facing pages), changing the odd/even orientation changes the pairing of facing pages. The double trucks may overlap onto the pasteboard.

When you create a new document using the **New** command, PageMaker starts you off in the Document Setup dialog box. You are free to set up as many pages as you think you need for the publication. Once you have created the document, you can no longer use the # of Pages text box to adjust the number of pages in the document. Instead, use the **Insert Pages** or **Remove Pages** commands on the Layout pull-down menu.

In the Options area of the dialog box, choose whether you want double-sided pages (printed on both sides) or facing pages (think of an opened book, the two pages facing each other with the binding in the middle). If you choose **Facing Pages**, increasing the inside margin size adds a wider binding width to the right margin of left-hand pages and to the left margin of right-hand pages. The **Adjust Layout** option tells PageMaker to automatically modify the layout of the page to accommodate any changes you make to the underlying master pages.

Set margins to the values you want. The left margin changes to the inside margin when you choose the **Facing Pages** option. Press **Tab** to move the insertion point to each margin text box. When you are finished, choose **OK** to return to your document.

Numbers

Before returning to your document, you can set up how page numbers will be handled in your document by clicking the **Numbers** button. You'll see the Page Numbering dialog box, shown in Figure B.8.

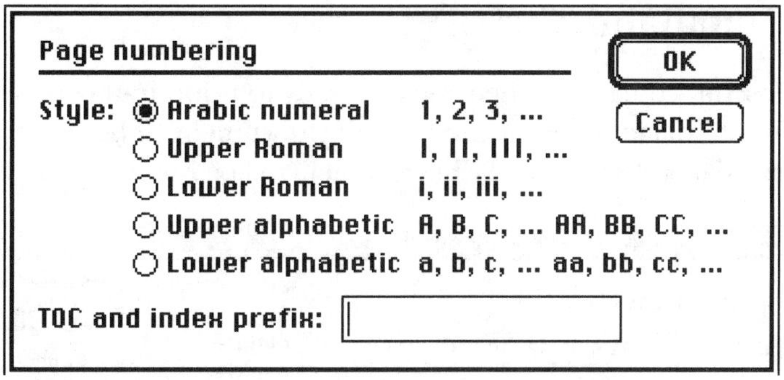

Figure B.8 *The Page Numbering dialog box.*

Use this dialog box to set the numbering style for your document. Please note that if you choose roman numerals, PageMaker changes to Arabic numerals after the 5000th page. If you choose alphabetic letters, PageMaker changes to Arabic numerals after the 52nd page.

The page number is created automatically by inserting page number markers where you want the page numbers to appear. The markers are created by pressing **Command/Ctrl+Option/Alt+p**. On right-hand pages you'll see the marker *RM* (for right marker), on left-hand pages there will be an *LM* (for left marker). You can add the marker individually to each page, but a faster way is to add the marker to the master page (or, if you have selected **Facing Pages**, to both the left and right master pages). When the document is printed, PageMaker adds the actual page number wherever it encounters a page number marker.

To add text to page numbers in the table of contents and index, type the text in the TOC and Index Prefix text box. When you are finished, choose **OK** to return to the Document Setup dialog box.

Printer Styles

The Printer Styles fly-out submenu lets you save and retrieve printer settings from among printers you have already installed and defined for PageMaker or to create a new printer style. This option lets you switch quickly among available printers and to create a document set up specifically for one printer. It stores most of the settings available from the printer dialog boxes in the previous section, except for page ranges (which must be specified for each job) and parameters like spot ink angle and frequency settings.

Print (Command/Ctrl+P)

Choose the **Print** command when you are ready to print draft copies, print to a high-resolution image setter, or prepare your document to be sent to a service bureau. PageMaker displays the Print Document dialog box, shown in Figure B.9.

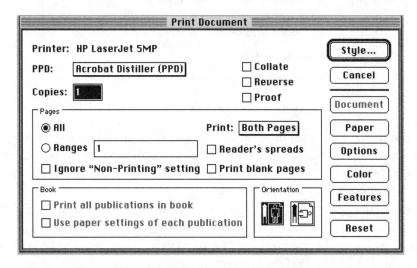

Figure B.9 *The Print Document dialog box.*

Use the Print Document dialog box to set the parameters you want for your print job. For example, at the top of the dialog box, open the two list boxes and select the printer and the PPD you want to use for this print job. Then enter the number of copies you'd like printed and whether you'd like them collated or printed in reverse order. To print quick copies of pages without graphics, click the **Proof** check box. Click the **Reverse Order** check box to reverse the order in which your printer prints. To print selected pages of your document, enter the range of inclusive page numbers in the Ranges text box. Click the **Ignore "Non-Printing" setting**, **Reader's Spreads**, or **Print blank pages** boxes to activate these options. Click the **Paper**, **Options**, **Color,** or **Features** command buttons to move to additional dialog boxes of parameters and features you can invoke to customize your print job. You can read about these dialog boxes in detail in Chapter 7, "Printing."

Preferences

The **Preferences** command allows you to set certain preferences for PageMaker's operation. The preferences may be changed at any time without affecting the layout of the document. Preferences are divided into four sections: *General, Online, Layout Adjustment,* and *Trapping.* The general Preferences dialog box is shown in Figure B.10.

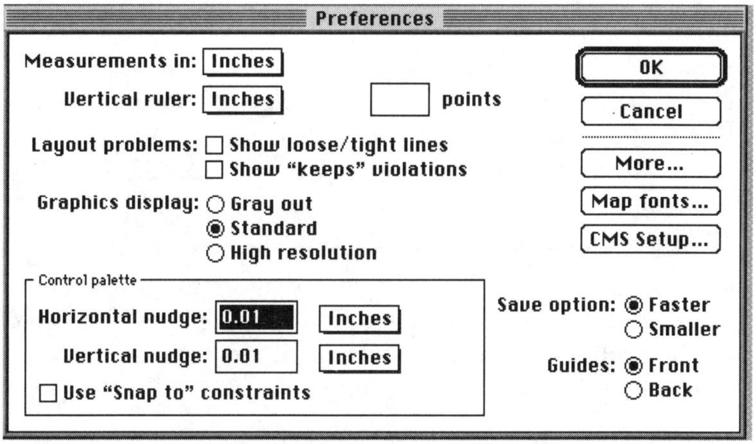

Figure B.10 Preferences.

Changing the measuring system affects all text boxes in the system that require or display measurement values (like the Margin text boxes in the Document Setup dialog box). The rulers also display the currently selected measurement system. If you set the Vertical Ruler pop-up list to **Custom**, you can specify the amount of leading in the Points text box. By choosing **Snap To Rulers** in the Options menu, the baselines of your text line up with the tick marks on the vertical ruler.

In the Show Layout Problems area, checking the **Loose/Tight Lines** option displays any lines that are either under or over the spacing parameters established in the Spacing Attributes dialog box (accessed by choosing the **Paragraph** command in the Type menu, then choosing **Spacing** from the Paragraph Specifications dialog box). The lines will be highlighted with a gray background. Checking **Keeps Violations** highlights any lines of text that do not adhere to the widow and orphan controls or the Keep with Lines control (set up in the Paragraph Specifications dialog box). PageMaker sometimes violates these controls to compose the page. When PageMaker highlights the inconsistencies, it's easy to find and correct them manually.

If you choose the **Guides:Front** option, the guidelines will be seen in front of text and graphic elements. If you choose **Guides:Back**, the text or graphics will partially cover the guidelines. Choose the level of resolution at which you want to display graphics. **Gray out** shows a gray shape the size of the graphic. **Normal** renders an accurate display of the graphic but without the fine detail of the high-resolution setting. The **High** setting takes the most time for the screen to redraw.

In the Save Option area, the **Faster** option means that mini-saved versions of the file are included when you choose the **Save** command. **Smaller** means that each time the file is saved with the **Save** command it is compressed the same way it is with the **Save As** command (see Save As). Choose **OK** to return to your document.

If you click the **More** button, PageMaker displays the More Preferences dialog box, shown in Figure B.11. To ensure all text is autoflowed into the pages (using the **Place** command), click the **Turn pages when autoflowing** check box. Normally, with the box unchecked, the Autoflow option only displays the final page that text is flowed onto.

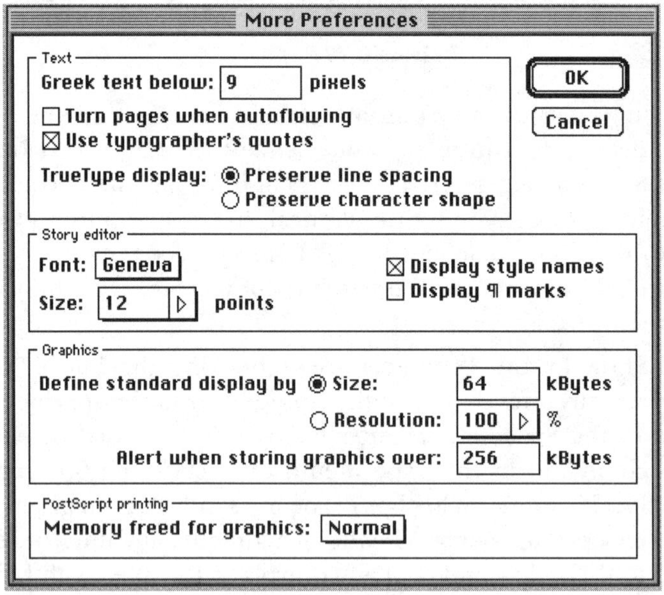

Figure B.11 *The More Preferences dialog box.*

The **Use Typographer's Quotes** check box substitutes typographer's curly quotes instead. You have to uncheck the check box if you'd like to enter " or ' for inch or foot symbols. The two TrueType options preserve the shape and leading of TrueType fonts used in your document. Set the size, in pixels, below which text will be *greeked* (the text is displayed as a shaded bar). The higher the resolution of your monitor, the more pixels it has, and the smaller the type size will be before it is greeked. Greeking the text speeds the rate at which the screen redraws its image.

Finally, set the font and size you want to use in the Story Editor with the Font and Size list boxes. Click the **Display Style Names** check box to display styles assigned to text in the Story Editor. To display invisible paragraph, tab, and space marks, choose the **Display ¶ marks** check box. You can define whether the standard graphics display is determined by size or resolution and limit the size of graphics stored with your file before PageMaker will warn you in the Graphics area. You can also allocate the amount of memory used for graphics in the PostScript printing area. Choose **OK** to return to the Preferences dialog box.

Choose the **Map Fonts** button to display the Font Matching Preferences dialog box, shown in Figure B.12. This dialog box allows PageMaker to look at the fonts in your document and determine how closely they match the fonts on your system. To disable the feature, click **Allow Font Matching** to remove the *X* from the **Panose** and **ATM** font matching check boxes. Additional dialog boxes below this one let you specify special font name spellings and exceptions that should be included in the font matching routines.

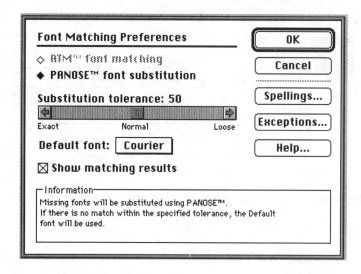

Figure B.12 *The Font Matching Preferences dialog box.*

Color Management System

The **CMS Setup** button lets you choose one of several color management systems (CMS) to calibrate your monitors and printers for use within PageMaker. A CMS translates colors from one set, or *gamut*, used by, say, a scanner or other source for a file with color information, into the gamut used by another device, such as a monitor or color printer. Since not all colors can be reproduced exactly by all devices and color systems (not all colors that can be printed using a CMYK color model can be represented on your CRT screen, which uses RGB colors, for example) a color management system can optimize your colors when you move them from one color system and device to another. The Kodak Precision Color Management System is furnished with PageMaker, as well as other Adobe products, such as Photoshop. It lets you do things like import Kodak Photo CD images using automatic CMS color correction and convert bitmap images from RGB to CMYK or high-fidelity ink separations.

The Color Management System Preferences dialog box, shown in Figure B.13, allows you to set parameters for these calibration systems.

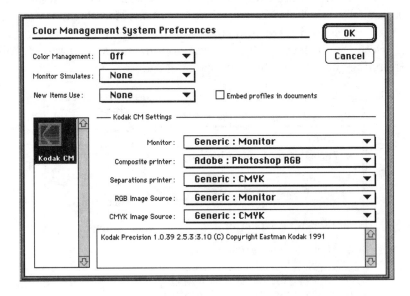

Figure B.13 *The Color Management System dialog box.*

Use the Color Management drop-down list to turn color management on and off, and to select which CMS to use (only the Kodak system is provided with PageMaker 6.0 at this writing.) The **Monitor Simulates** option lets you specify whether you want your monitor to emulate the color balance of your composite printer, separation printer, or neither. The New Items Use list determines whether a color management system should be automatically applied to new publications. You can check the **Embed profiles in documents** box to include the color calibration profile within the document itself, to ensure that it accompanies the publication at all times.

Specific to the Kodak Color Management System are a series of five boxes that let you choose profiles for your monitor, color composite printer, separations printer, RGB image source such as a scanner or monitor, and CMYK image source.

Online Preferences

This dialog box allows you to set up preferences for manipulating HTML files. It was discussed extensively in Chapter 12.

Layout Adjustment Preferences

This dialog box, shown in Figure B.14, lets you set parameters for PageMaker 6.5's automatic Layout Adjustment features. Click the **OK to resize groups and imported graphics** if you want to give PageMaker the freedom to change the size of these objects when it adjusts a layout automatically. Click the **Ignore object and layer locks** button to allow PageMaker to free up components that were locked down as it changes the layout. The **Ignore ruler guide alignments** option will let PageMaker realign objects without using the rulers and guides you have set up. The **Allow ruler guides to move** button lets PageMaker actually move these alignment aids for you to correspond with the new layout. The **Keep column and margin alignment** button tells PageMaker to retain the same columns and margins you had set up before the layout was changed.

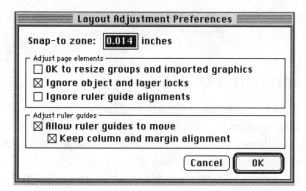

Figure B.14 Layout Adjustment preferences.

Quit (Command/Ctrl+Q)

Choose the **Quit** command to close the application and return to the Macintosh desktop. PageMaker prompts you to save the current document.

THE EDIT MENU

The Edit menu (see Figure B.15) handles a variety of editing chores, including copying, cutting, and pasting; finding and changing words and phrases; checking spelling; and toggling between the Layout Editor and the Story Editor.

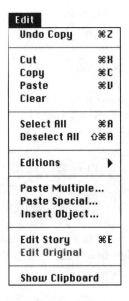

Figure B.15 *The Edit menu.*

Undo (Command/Ctrl+Z)

Basically, the **Undo** command undoes whatever you did most recently. Although the **Undo** command doesn't work with some functions (for example, you can't undo scrolling or changing the page view size), there are many things that can be undone. You can undo the resizing of a text block or graphic element. If you change the size of a text block, then immediately choose the **Edit** menu; you will see that the **Undo** command has changed to **Undo Stretch**, meaning PageMaker knows that the last action you took can be undone and so labels the command with the reverse of the action. The secret to the **Undo** command is that if the action can be undone, the command will tell you.

Cut (Command/Ctrl+X)

Cutting text or a graphic element removes the element from its present position and transfers it to the Clipboard. The cut element remains in the Clipboard until you cut or copy something else to the Clipboard, which copies over the element.

When you highlight text with the Text tool and cut the text, the text following the cut reflows to fill in the gap. When you select text with the Pointer tool and cut the text, the gap remains where the text had been.

All applications have **Cut**, **Copy**, and **Paste** commands—they are fundamental to the mutual functionality of the Macintosh. You can cut text or graphics from PageMaker and paste it into another application, like Word or WordPerfect, and you can cut text from Word and paste it into PageMaker.

Copy (Command/Ctrl+C)

Copying is similar to cutting, except the element that is copied remains, and a copy of it is transferred to the Clipboard. You can then paste the copied element anywhere else in PageMaker or into another application. Again, remember that the Clipboard holds only the most recent text or graphics cut or copied.

Paste (Command/Ctrl+V)

The **Paste** command moves whatever is currently in the Clipboard to the document or pasteboard in PageMaker. You can see what you are about to paste by choosing the **Clipboard** command from the Window menu.

If you have the **Pointer** tool selected when you paste, the position of the pasted element will be slightly offset from its original position, if the original position is known or centered on the page. Text and graphics pasted with the Pointer tool become independent text blocks or independent graphics.

If you have the **Text** tool selected when you paste, and you click an insertion point in a text block, the pasted text is threaded into the text block. A graphic is inserted as an in-line graphic (part of the text block). Text pasted onto the pasteboard or a new area of the page, but not in an existing text block, assumes the maximum width it can. In other words, pasting a word at the insertion point of the left margin creates a text block that extends across the column or page (the text block seeks the right margin). To create a more reasonably sized text block, first drag-place the text (hold down the mouse button and drag a box the preferred width). Then choose the **Paste** command—it fills the box that you dragged open with the mouse.

Clear

Using the **Clear** command is the same as pressing the **Delete** or **Backspace** key: The selected text is deleted, but not copied to the Clipboard. You can undo cleared or deleted text or graphics by immediately choosing the **Undo** command.

Select All (Command/Ctrl+A)

In the Layout Editor, the **Select All** command selects all elements, text, and graphics on the page. In the Story Editor, **Select All** selects the entire story. To select all threaded text blocks on all pages of one story, choose the **Text** tool and click the insertion point anywhere in the story that has text blocks you'd like to see. Choose **Select All**, and all the threaded text blocks for the story are highlighted. To deselect the elements, click anywhere in any selected element.

If you have selected all of the text and graphic elements on the page and wish to selectively deselect them, hold down the **Shift** key while you click the elements you don't want selected.

Deselect All (Shift+Command/Ctrl+A)

This command unselects everything.

Editions (Macintosh Only)

The **Editions** menu choice opens the door to PageMaker's implementation of Mac OS's standard Publish and Subscribe features, which allow you to place text or graphics from one application into another and then have the operating system automatically update the copy of the text or graphics when the original is changed. The facility lets you use text or graphics—say, boilerplate or a logo—in more than one publication, then update them once and see the changes reflected in all the publications that use them. For example, if you create many different forms, letterheads, and other documents for a single company, if a logo, address, or phone number is embedded using **Publish and**

Subscribe, you can update the logo or text information and have the update "published" in each "subscriber" document simultaneously. The **Editions** submenu includes **Subscribe To**, **Subscriber Options**, and **Stop all Editions**, choices common to other applications that support Publish and Subscribe.

Paste Multiple

Use the **Paste Multiple** command to repeatedly paste the same contents of the Clipboard a number of specified times. Choose this command to display the Paste Multiple dialog box. Enter the number of times you'd like to paste the contents in the Copies text box.

Paste Special

Paste Special presents a dialog box (see Figure B.16) that allows you to select the type of object you want to paste. Some OLE servers present different types of OLE objects for you to select from. Choose the file type you'd like from the list presented in the dialog box. It also includes the **Paste Link** command. Unlike the **Paste** command, **Paste Link** pastes the contents of the Clipboard as an OLE object. The command is dimmed unless you have copied an object from an OLE server application. Use the command exactly like **Paste**, with the exception that you can double-click on the pasted object to automatically open the application that created it.

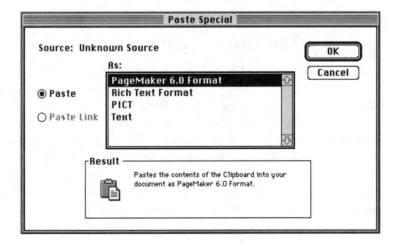

Figure B.16 The Paste Special dialog box.

Insert Object

When you want to embed an OLE object rather than paste an OLE object, choose the **Insert Object** command. You will see the Insert Object dialog box (see Figure B.17). The dialog box lists all of the OLE server applications currently installed in your system. Scroll down the list to find the application you want. Click the application to start it and create the object you'd like to insert. When you are finished, save the object in the server application and close it. The object is inserted in your PageMaker document.

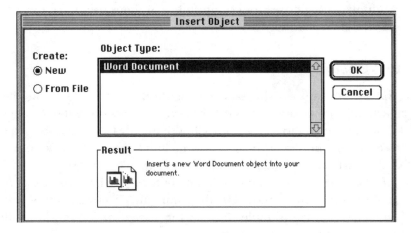

Figure B.17 *The Insert Object dialog box.*

Edit Story and Edit Layout (Command/Ctrl+E)

PageMaker has two editors and offers two views of your work. The *layout* view is what you see when you start PageMaker and open a file or create a new file. In this view, you are working in the Layout Editor. The page is laid out before you: Stories, headlines, and graphics are all visible. If you choose the **Edit Story** command from the Edit menu, you switch to the story view. In this view, you are working in the Story Editor. You can see only one story at a time, but you have available many word processing tools not accessible in the Layout Editor. When you are in the Story Editor, the command on the Edit menu reads **Edit Layout**. When you are in the Layout Editor, this command reads **Edit Story**. Choose the view and editor that suits the work you need to do.

Edit Original

Choose the **Edit Original** command when you wish to edit text or graphics you have added to your pages either with the **Place** command or through an OLE link. For example, if you have placed a WordPerfect 2.0 story in your document, click the story to select it, open the Edit menu, and choose **Edit Original**. WordPerfect will start, the WordPerfect document will be opened, and you can make any changes to the story you want. When you move back to PageMaker and update the link for the story placed in your document, you'll see the changes you just made to the original document in WordPerfect.

Show Clipboard (Macintosh Only)

Displays the contents of the Clipboard.

THE LAYOUT MENU

Use the Layout menu (see Figure B.18) to establish the basic layout for your document.

Figure B.18 *The Layout menu.*

Go to Page (Command/Ctrl+G)

The **Go to Page** command is an easy way to move to a specific page in your document; choosing it displays the Go to Page dialog box. Use this dialog box to enter the page number to which you'd like to move. Or, choose the appropriate radio button to move to the master pages. Choose **OK** to move to the page you want.

Insert Pages

You can add pages to your document at any time. Choosing this command displays the Insert Pages dialog box, shown in Figure B.19.

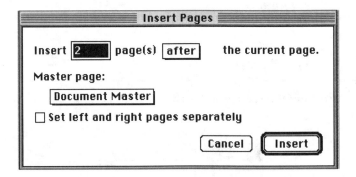

Figure B.19 *The Insert Pages dialog box.*

Enter the number of pages you'd like to add to your publication in the Insert Pages text box. Then decide whether you'd like the pages added before the page you are currently on, after the current page, or, if you are working with facing pages, between the current pages. You can also select which Master Page to use for the new pages. Choose **OK** or press **Return** to add the pages. The specifications of paragraphs and type for the current pages will be carried over to the newly added pages. Threaded text that is split by the inserted pages remains threaded.

 If you are working with a double-sided publication, adding pages between the current pages or adding an odd number of pages can change the left/right orientation of the document's pages. If the left and right margins are not the same measurement, you may have to realign text and graphics to the new margins.

Remove Pages

You can remove pages just as easily as you can insert them. Choosing this command displays the Remove Pages dialog box. In the two text boxes, enter the beginning and ending page numbers for the pages you want to remove. Choose **OK** or press **Return** to remove the specified pages. If you are working with double-sided pages, you may have problems with unequal width margins, depending on how many pages are removed. Text and graphics may have to be realigned on some pages.

Sort Pages

This choice lets you rearrange the order of your document pages; page 3 can become page 7, or pages 1 and 2 can be swapped, for example. The Sort Pages dialog box shows you icons representing the pages, and you simply click and drag the icons to reorder them. Choose this command to see the Sort Pages dialog box, shown in Figure B.20.

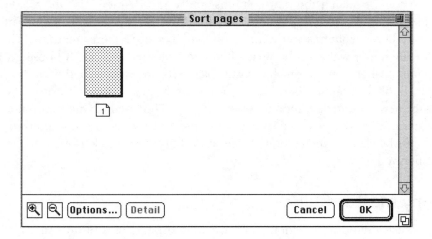

Figure B.20 The Sort Pages dialog box.

You can vary the size of the page icons by clicking the **Plus** or **Minus Magnification** buttons. If the icon pages are grayed, you can show true thumbnail sketches of your document pages by clicking the **Options** button and choosing **Show Detailed Thumbnails**.

When you have rearranged the icons the way you want them, choose **OK** to return to your document, and the real pages will be sorted to reflect the arrangement you set up in the addition.

Go Back (Command/Ctrl Page Up)

Goes back one page in your document.

Go Forward (Command/Ctrl Page Down)

Moves ahead one page in your document.

Column Guides

The **Column Guides** command displays the Column Guides dialog box, which lets you enter the number of columns for a page, the amount of space between them, and check an **Adjust layout** box if you want PageMaker to modify the layout of the page to match the new columns you've just defined. Use the Column Guides dialog box to set up multiple columns for the page or document. Enter the number of columns you want in the Number of Columns text box. Then enter the gutter width in the Space Between Columns text box. Choosing the command when you are on the master page sets the column definition for all pages in the document. Choosing the command from any page in the document sets the new column definition for only that page. The **Column Guides** command automatically creates equal-width columns. You can create unequal-width columns by clicking the column guides and dragging them left or right to the position you want.

Copy Master Guides

If you have established guidelines on the master pages of your document, and you move one or more of the guidelines on a specific page, the **Copy Master Guides** command becomes available. Later, if you want to return the moved guide to its original position, choose the command, and the guides will be reset to their master page positions.

Autoflow

When the **Autoflow** command is checked, text placed on a document page automatically flows to as many consecutive pages in the document as the size of the text file dictates. You do not have to have the pages available; Autoflow creates the pages as it needs them. Choose the checked command again to turn off Autoflow.

THE TYPE MENU

The Type menu contains commands and dialog boxes that control precisely how type is displayed on the page. To change the default type values for the document, make your choices without positioning the Text tool insertion point in the document. To have the settings you choose affect only selected text, highlight the text first with the Text tool. To have the settings affect text you are about to type, click the insertion point, then choose the command from the Type menu, shown in Figure B.21.

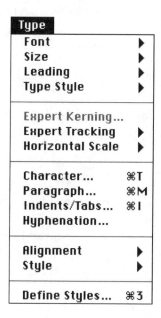

Figure B.21 *The Type menu.*

Font

Choose the **Font** command to display a submenu of all the fonts you currently have installed.

Size

Choose the **Size** command to display a submenu of preset sizes from 6 to 72 points. If you don't see the size you'd like, choose **Other** and enter the size in the dialog box. You can enter type sizes as small as 4 points, or as large as 650 points, in 0.1-point increments.

Leading

Choose the **Leading** command to display a submenu of selected leading sizes based on the size currently selected in the Size submenu. For example, if you select **10 points** as the type size, the leading selections will range from 9 to 30 points. Choose **Auto** to allow PageMaker to calculate automatically the correct amount of leading, based on the size of the type. Choosing **Other** allows you to enter a leading value that is not displayed. You can enter leading values from 0 to 1300 points, in 0.1-point increments.

Type Style

Choose the **Type Style** command to display a submenu showing the different available styles that can be applied to the selected typeface.

Expert Tracking

While PageMaker's type specifications allow you to adjust tracking for any group of selected text, the Edit Tracks addition modifies tracking values for specific fonts in specific sizes and styles—whenever you add text in the modified font, the changed tracking values will apply. Choose the **Edit Tracks** addition to display the Edit Tracks dialog box, shown in Figure B.22.

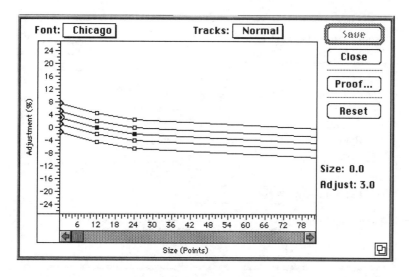

Figure B.22 *Edit Tracks dialog box.*

The five lines in the graph represent (from top to bottom) very loose, loose, normal, tight, and very tight tracking values. The curve of the line is the default tracking, represented along the vertical axis as percentage adjustments and in font sizes along the horizontal axis. Any part of the curve rising above zero on the Adjustment axis adds positive tracking; any part dropping below the zero point creates negative tracking. To change the track value for a font, first choose the font from the Font pop-up list. Then choose the line you'd like to modify from the pop-up list. For example, to modify the tight line, choose **Tight** from the pop-up list.

Click the line where you want to add a point. Then drag the point up or down to modify the tracking value. Once you have modified the tracking values for the fonts you want, you can see printed proofs of your changes by clicking the **Proof** button. You then see the Create Proof Sheet dialog box (see Figure B.23).

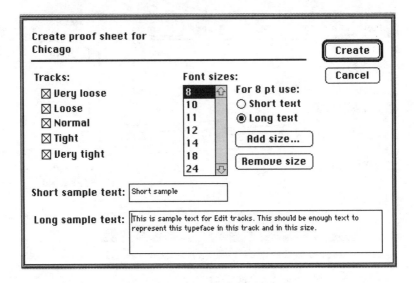

Figure B.23 *The Create Proof Sheet dialog box.*

Expert Kerning

This module lets you add expert kerning to PostScript Type 1 fonts that contain kerned-pair values. It will not kern Type 3 or TrueType fonts. The module is generally used for small amounts of text you wish to kern more precisely. You will see the dialog box shown in Figure B.24.

Figure B.24 *Expert Kerning dialog box.*

In the Kern Strength text box, enter any value from 0.0 to 2.0, indicating the kern strength you'd like to apply to the highlighted text. The higher the value, the tighter the kerning. Then choose the source of the original design of the font (describes how the font designer intended the font to be used or the original size of the font) by selecting the **Design Class** option applicable to the font. If you don't know the design class, choose **Text**. The text will be kerned based on the parameters you have entered. Once you add expert kerning

Horizontal Scale

This submenu allows you to expand or contract type on a given line by a set percentage.

Character Command/Ctrl+T)

Choose the **Character** command to display the Character Specifications dialog box, shown in Figure B.25.

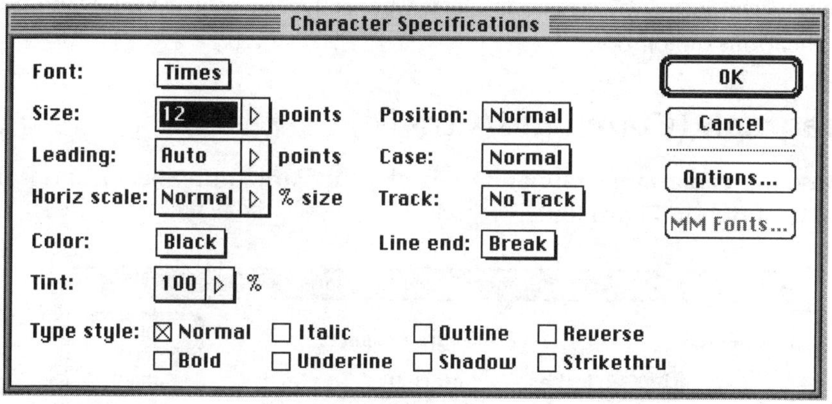

Figure B.25 *Character Specifications dialog box.*

Instead of using the other Type submenus, you can make your selections in this dialog box. In addition, you can specify the position (normal, subscript, or superscript) of the type by clicking the **Position** pop-up list, and the case (normal, all caps, or small caps) style by clicking the **Case** pop-up list.

Options

Choose the **Options** button in the Character Specifications dialog box to display the Character Options dialog box, shown in Figure B.26.

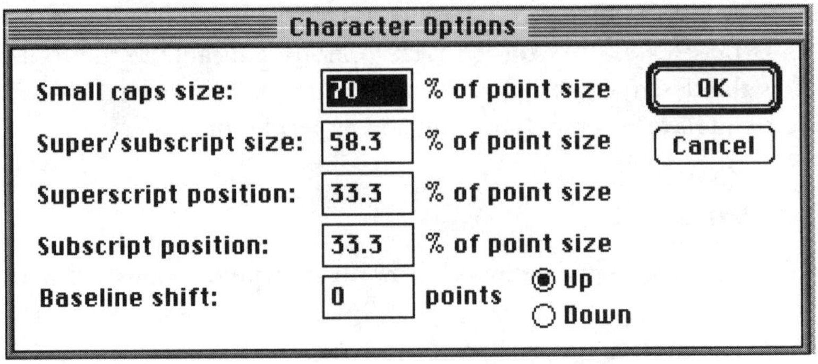

Figure B.26 *The Character Options dialog box.*

Use this dialog box to enter different values for the proportional size of small caps and superscript and subscript characters and the proportional positioning of superscript and subscript characters. Choose **OK** to return to the Character Specifications dialog box.

Paragraph (Command/Ctrl+M)

Choose the **Paragraph** command to display the Paragraph Specifications dialog box, shown in Figure B.27.

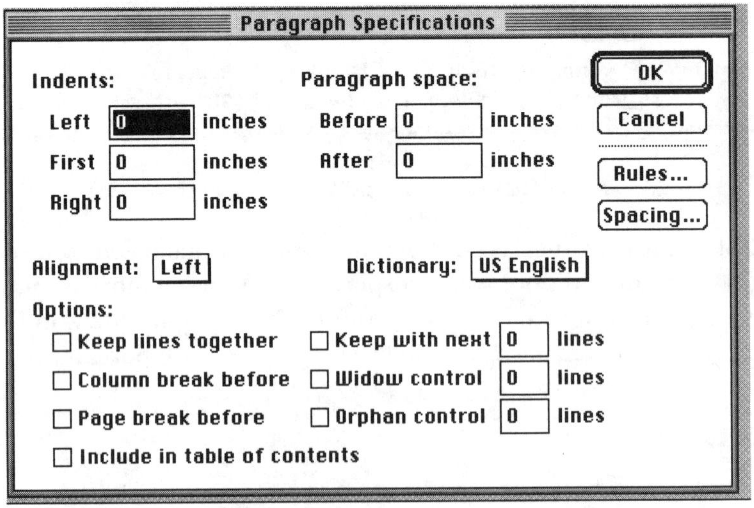

Figure B.27 *Paragraph Specifications dialog box.*

All the information about how paragraphs will be handled is included in this dialog box and the two dialog boxes that branch from it. In the Indents area, specify how left, right, and hanging indents will be arranged. The Paragraph space area determines the amount of space before and after paragraphs. Type alignment can be set in the Alignment pop-up list (which is the same as setting the alignment with the Alignment submenu). In the Options area, you can determine exactly how the beginning and ending lines of the paragraph will be handled with respect to page and column breaks. Check the **Include in Table of Contents** option box to mark headings and chapter titles for inclusion in the table of contents.

Rules

Choosing the **Rules** button opens a dialog box, shown in Figure B.28, that sets parameters for adding lines (rules) to your paragraphs. For rules either above or below the paragraph, you can decide the weight of the line, its color, and its width. Press the **Options** button to determine how far above or below the baseline the line will be positioned. Choose **OK** to return to the Paragraph Specifications dialog box.

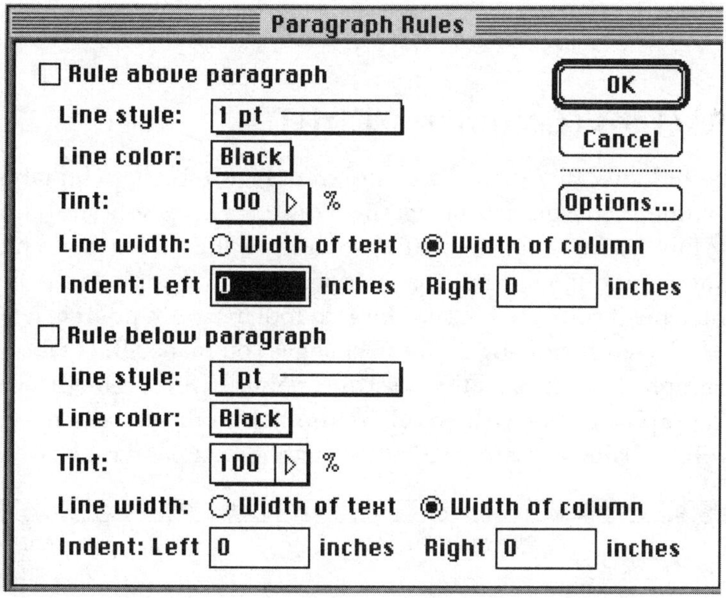

Figure B.28 The Rules dialog box.

Spacing

Choose the **Spacing** button in the Paragraph Specifications dialog box to open the Spacing Attributes dialog box, shown in Figure B.29. This dialog box sets minimum, desired, and maximum spacing values for letter spacing and word spacing. You can also decide whether leading is calculated proportionally or by the top of caps method. Press the **Reset** button to reset the default values in the text boxes. Choose **OK** to return to the Paragraph Specifications dialog box.

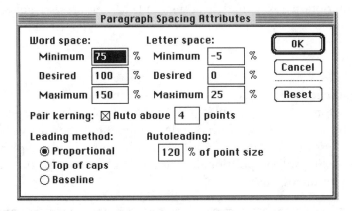

Figure B.29 *The Spacing dialog box.*

Indents/Tabs (Command/Ctrl+I)

Open the Indents/Tabs dialog box, shown in Figure B.30, to set tab stops for your document. If you are using the Pointer tool when you choose the Indents/Tabs dialog box, the settings made to the dialog box change the default indent and tab settings for the document and apply to the next paragraph you type. If you have clicked the Text tool insertion point in a text block and have selected the dialog box, the changes you make affect tab settings in the paragraph that contains the insertion point. If you highlight more than one paragraph of text with the Text tool, the tab settings made in the Indents/Tabs dialog box affect all of the highlighted paragraphs.

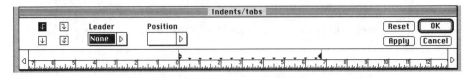

Figure B.30 *The Indents/Tabs dialog box.*

To set a tab stop, click the **tab** icon you'd like to move and drag it to a new position. To remove the tab stop, drag the tab icon off the ruler. To add a new tab, click the **tab** icon in the left corner to highlight it, then click the pointer where you'd like the tab to be placed. Alternatively, choose the **Tab Action** button to add, delete, move, or repeat a tab stop. Select a leader character by choosing the **Leader** button. To reset the tabs to their default positions, choose **Reset**. You can see the results of your settings by pressing the **Apply** button, which affects the text in view (if the Indents/Tabs dialog box is partially blocking the text, click the title bar of the dialog box and drag it to another part of the screen). Choose **OK** to return to your document.

Hyphenation (Command/Ctrl+H)

Choosing the **Hyphenation** command opens the Hyphenation dialog box, shown in Figure B.31. In it you can turn hyphenation on or off and specify how words should be hyphenated. Choose the **On** or **Off** radio button to toggle hyphenation on or off. Select **Manual Hyphenation** if you want to decide how to hyphenate words in the publication based on discretionary hyphens you have inserted. Choose **Manual Plus Dictionary** to find words with discretionary hyphens and words in the hyphenation dictionary. If you choose **Manual Plus Algorithm**, PageMaker uses the discretionary hyphens, the dictionary, and a mathematical formula to determine how words should be hyphenated. You can also decide how many consecutive lines can end with a hyphen, and you can set the hyphenation zone. Choose the **Add** button to display the Add Word to Dictionary dialog box.

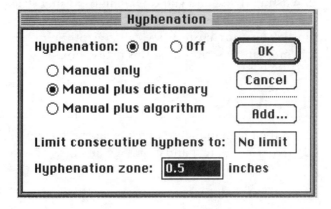

Figure B.31 *The Hyphenation dialog box.*

You can use the **Hyphenation** command to help repair corrupted files. Simply hold down the **Command** and **Shift** keys while choosing the command, and PageMaker tries to fix the file. If the file is OK, you will hear one beep; if the problem is identified and corrected, you'll hear two beeps; if the problem can't be fixed, you'll hear three beeps.

Alignment

Choose the **Alignment** command to display the Alignment submenu, in which you can select an alignment configuration for your text: align left, align center, align right, justify, or force justify.

Style

Choosing the **Style** command displays the Style submenu, listing the default or custom styles established for the current document. Highlight the text you'd like to mark with a style, then choose the **Style** command and select the style from the menu. You can also choose styles from the Style palette.

Define Styles

To create new styles, change existing styles, or remove styles, choose the **Define Styles** command to display the dialog box (see Figure B.65).

The Define Styles dialog box lists the styles defined for the current publication. Choose the **New** button to define a new style. You can base new styles on elements of existing styles, and you can change existing styles, which will change characteristics of all text marked with the style. You can also remove styles from the list or copy custom styles from other publications. See Chapter 6 for a complete description of this dialog box.

THE ELEMENT MENU

The commands on the Element menu, which is shown in Figure B.32, control the display and orientation of text and graphic elements.

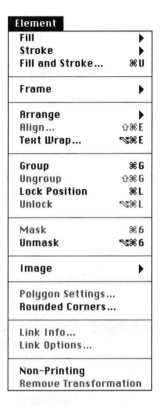

Figure B.32 *The Element menu.*

Fill

Choose the **Fill** command to display the Fill submenu. If the shape you have drawn with one of the drawing tools is selected, the choice you make in the Fill submenu affects only the selected element. If you choose a different fill pattern without first selecting an element, the choice becomes the default style for shapes that will be drawn. **Paper** is a solid fill pattern the color of the paper. **Solid** is normally black. The percentage shades represent screens of 100% solid (black).

Stroke

Choose the **Stroke** command to display the Stroke submenu. If the line or shape you have drawn with one of the drawing tools is selected, the choice you make in the menu affects only the selected element. If you choose a line style without first selecting an element, the choice becomes the default style for shapes and lines that will be drawn.

Fill and Stroke... (Command/Ctrl+U)

This dialog box lets you set the characteristics of both Fill and Stroke properties simultaneously.

Frame

This submenu, shown in Figure B.33, has seven items that allow you to move between frames, break threads between frames, and enter frame options.

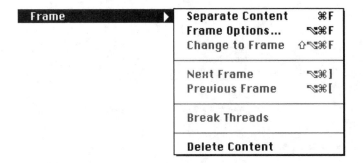

Figure B.33 *The Frame submenu.*

The **Separate Content** choice lets you detach the contents from the frame to move it elsewhere, while **Delete Content** removes what's in the frame while leaving the frame itself in place. **Change to Frame** converts a text box into a frame, while **Next Frame** and **Previous Frame** move from the currently selected frame to either the following or preceding one, according to the links you've set up. **Break Threads** removes the links from the selected frame to others (before and after) in the chain. **Frame Options** produces the dialog box shown in Figure B.34, which you can use to specify alignment of text within a frame, along with margins inside the frame.

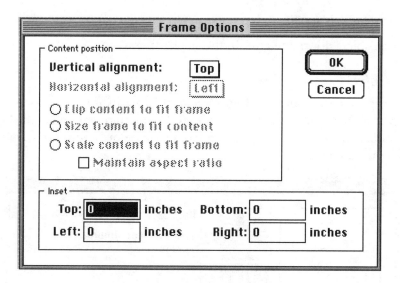

Figure B.34 The Frame Options dialog box.

Arrange

This submenu includes several commands you can use to change the stacking order of objects on your layout. They include the following five options.

Bring to Front (Command/Ctrl+F)

When two or more elements are stacked on top of one another, select each element by holding down the **Shift** key and clicking the elements. Each in turn will be selected. To move the selected element to the top of the stack, choose **Bring to Front**.

Bring Forward

This command moves an object in front of the object immediately on top of it. It may still be underneath other objects in "higher" layers.

Send to Back (Command/Ctrl+B)

In a stack of two or more elements, send the top element to the bottom of the stack by selecting the element and choosing **Send to Back**.

Send Backward

Moves an object down one layer in the stack's hierarchy.

Align Objects

Select two or more objects, then choose this menu item to produce the dialog box shown in Figure B.35, which lets you align the selected objects horizontally or vertically by choosing from icons representing the available alignment schemes.

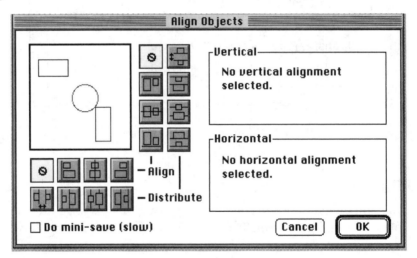

Figure B.35 *The Align Objects dialog box.*

Text Wrap

The **Text Wrap** command controls the way text flows around an independent graphic element. Select the graphic with the Pointer tool and choose the command to display the Text Wrap dialog box, which is shown in Figure B.36.

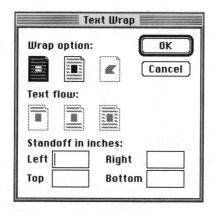

Figure B.36 *The Text Wrap dialog box.*

Pick the **Wrap** option you want by clicking the icon. The first icon represents text flowing over the graphic. The second flows text around the graphic's boundary. If you have modified the boundary to mask the shape of the graphic, then the third icon will already be selected.

To change the area and shape of the boundary, click the graphic to select its boundary. Notice the diamond-shaped handles. Drag a handle to change the shape of the boundary. You can create more sizing handles by clicking along the boundary where you want them to appear.

Choose the **text flow** icon you want. The first icon is called the *column-break* icon; choose it and text stops flowing when it encounters a graphic and begins again on the next column. The second icon is called the *jump-over* icon; choose it and text stops when it encounters a graphic but starts again immediately following the graphic (it jumps over the graphic). The third icon is called the *wrap-all-sides* icon; choose it and text flows around all sides of a graphic. Finally, enter the amount of *standoff* around the graphic. The standoff is the margin between the graphic and the wrapped text. Choose **OK** to return to your document.

Group/Ungroup (Command/Ctrl+G, Shift+Command/Ctrl+G)

Select several objects and choose **Group** to lock them together as a unit. Thereafter, moving one of the grouped objects moves all of them together. Choosing **Ungroup** breaks your group apart.

Lock Position/Unlock (Command/Ctrl+L, Shift+Command/Ctrl+L)

Choose **Lock** to force an object to remain solidly fixed in its position. You'll need to select the object again and use **Unlock** to free it if you want to move it again later.

Mask/Unmask (Command/Ctrl+6, Shift+Command/Ctrl+6)

These choices let you cover up or reveal part of an object with a shape tool (rectangle, ellipse, polygon.) Place the object you want to use as a mask on the object it will be masking, then choose the **Mask** option. Use **Unmask** to reverse the process.

Image

The Image menu includes submenus for Image Control, specifying a Color Management System, and a Photoshop Effects filter submenu.

When you select a graphic, the **Image Control** command becomes available. Choose this command to display the Image Control dialog box, which is shown in Figure B.37. Use this dialog box to alter the image of black-and-white and full gray-scale TIFF files and paint-type files. The slide bars adjust the lightness, which lightens or darkens the image, and contrast, which changes the contrast of foreground to background images.

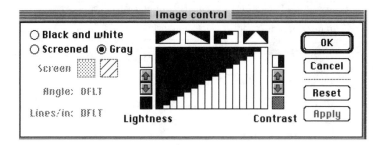

Figure B.37 *The Image Control dialog box.*

Choose either the **dot** or **line screen pattern**. The dot pattern is used for most images, while the line screen creates special effects.

Change the screen angle and lines-per-inch frequency of the image. PageMaker normally sets the screen angle at **45˚**. However, you can choose any angle from 0˚ to 360˚. The more lines per inch, the finer the resolution and detail. The *screen frequency* is a factor of the printing device, a 300-dpi laser printer can print only 53 lines per inch (lpi); a Linotronic L330 image setter can output screens at 200 lpi.

Choose **Apply** to test your choices on the image. Press **Default** to change the settings back to the default values. Choose **OK** to return to your document.

The Image menu's Photoshop Effects submenu lets you use many common Photoshop filters on TIFF images that have been placed in your document.

Polygon Settings...

Use this dialog box, shown in Figure B.38, to set the number of sides and inset value for a regular polygon you've drawn with the Polygon tool.

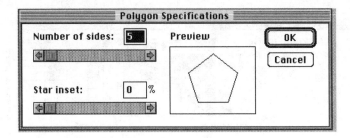

Figure B.38 The Polygon Settings dialog box.

Rounded Corners

Choose this command to display the Rounded Corners dialog box, which is shown in Figure B.39.

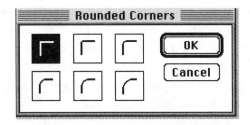

Figure B.39 The Rounded Corners dialog box.

To change the radii of round-cornered rectangles and squares, select the shape and choose the **Rounded Corners** command. This opens a small dialog box in which you can choose among the different corners. Click the one you want and choose **OK** to return to your document. Selecting a different radius in the dialog box without selecting a round-cornered shape changes the default corner radius for the document.

Link Info

The **Link Info** command displays the dialog box described in the File menu's **Links** command.

Link Options

Use the **Link Options** command to set up certain parameters concerning linked text and graphic files. If neither a linked text or graphics file is selected, choosing the command displays the Link Options: Defaults dialog box, which is shown in Figure B.40.

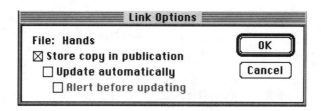

Figure b.40 The Link Options: Defaults dialog box.

First choose how text and graphic links will be stored: as a separate file or internally as part of the PageMaker file. Then select for both text and graphics whether or not you want PageMaker to update the internally linked files automatically whenever you open the document. The **Alert Before Updating** option means that PageMaker will ask if the files should be updated before performing the update.

If you select a linked text file and choose this command, the dialog box will contain only the text options. Select a linked graphic and you'll see the graphics options in the dialog box.

Non-Printing

This option lets you mark a selected object as nonprinting. It will be displayed on your screen, if the **Display Non-Printing** option has been activated, but it will not print unless you choose the **Print Non-Printing** option from the Print Setup menu.

Remove Transformation

Use this command to remove skewing, rotation, or reflection applied to an object. Once you invoke the command you can't undo it with the **Undo** command.

However, save the document before choosing the command, then if you don't like what you've done, you can choose the **Revert** command on the File menu to revert to the transformations you just removed.

UTILITIES MENU

The Utilities menu (see Figure B.41) holds a number of vital tools and utilities for controlling text. It includes plug-ins, find/replace commands, dialog boxes for creating long document indices and tables of contents, and trapping options.

Figure B.41 The Utilities menu.

PageMaker Plug-ins...

Choose the **Plug-ins** command to open the Plug-ins submenu, shown in Figure B.42.

```
Add Cont'd Line...
Balance Columns...
Build Booklet...
Bullets and Numbering...
Change Case...
Create Color Library...
Drop Cap...
EPS Font Scanner...
Expert Kerning...
Global Link Options...
Grid Manager...
Keyline...
Pub Info...
Publication Converter...
QuickTime Media...
Running Headers & Footers...
Save For Service Provider...
Update PPD...
Word Counter
```

Figure B.42 *The Plug-ins menu.*

Add Continued Line

The Add Continued Line plug-in automatically inserts *continued to* and *continued from* notices that show to where a text block jumps. Click the Text tool in the text block that jumps to another page and choose the command to display the Continuation Notice dialog box, which simply consists of two radio buttons. To add a jump notice to the top of the jumped text block (the *continued from* notice), click the **Top of Textblock** radio button. Likewise, to create the continued to notice at the bottom of the text block, click the **Bottom of Textblock** option. Click **OK** and the addition adds the appropriate *continued to* and *continued from* notices with the correct page numbers.

Balance Columns

Aligning the top and bottom of multiple text columns is an on-going requirement as you develop the pages of your document. Often, we let the bottoms of multiple columns seek their own alignment to accommodate for widows, orphans, and graphics. However, the tops of the columns should generally be aligned to the same common baseline. The Balance Columns Plug-in does the alignment for you. To use the addition, **Shift**-click the number of columns on the page you want to align (normally you will select all the columns). Then choose the addition to see the Balance Columns dialog box, shown in Figure B.43.

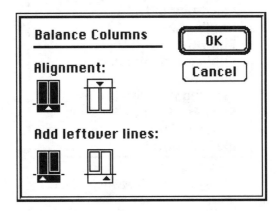

Figure B.43 *The Balance Columns dialog box.*

To align the column tops, select the upper-left icon; to align to the bottom of the columns, select the upper-right icon. To add the remaining lines starting with the left column, click the lower-left icon; to add the remaining lines starting with the right column, click the lower-right icon.

Build Booklet

This addition creates arrangements of pages needed for a commercial printer to print your document. Choose the command to see the Build Booklet dialog box (see Figure B.44).

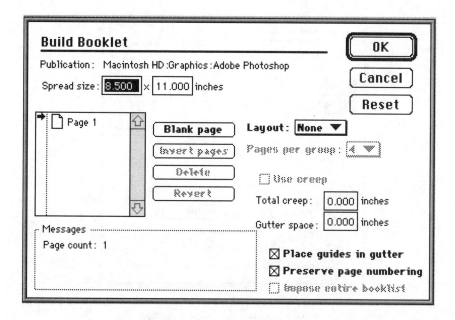

Figure B.44 *The Build Booklet dialog box.*

Enter the spread size in the Spread Size text boxes. If, for example, you want to have 8.5 x 11-in. pages printed two-up, set the spread size up to be 11 x 17 in. The messages box will analyze your layout and tell you if you need more pages. If so, you can add the pages with the **Blank Page** button; they will be inserted where you click and drag the right-facing arrow. Choose the layout for this booklet by opening the Layout pop-up list and choosing the appropriate layout. The selection you choose changes the spread dimensions in the Spread Size text boxes. Finally, enter the amount of creep on the press in the appropriate text boxes.

Bullets and Numbering Plug-in

The Bullets and Numbering addition automatically adds bullets or numbers to the paragraphs in the text block. Choose the command to open the Bullets and Numbering dialog box, shown in Figure B.45.

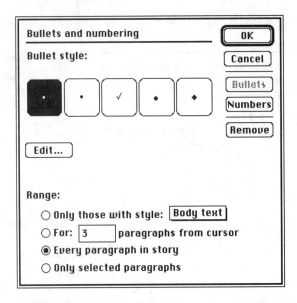

Figure B.45 *The Bullets and Numbering dialog box.*

To add bullets or numbers to each paragraph in the entire text block, click the **Every Paragraph in Story** radio button. To add bullets or numbers to only selected paragraphs based on the style assigned to the paragraph, click the **Only Those with Style** radio button. Then open the Style pop-up list and choose the style to which you want to add bullets. To add bullets or numbers to certain paragraphs in relation to the paragraph the insertion point (cursor) is currently in, choose the last radio button and enter the number of paragraphs in the text box. To add numbers, click the **Numbers** button; to add bullets, click **Bullets**. To edit bullets, click the **Edit** button. You will see an Edit Bullet dialog box, shown in Figure B.46.

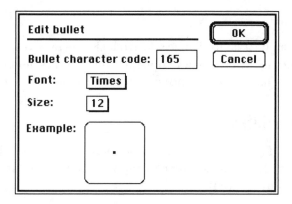

Figure B.46 *The Edit Bullet dialog box.*

You can set up any character in any font to be a bullet with this dialog box. First decide which font you want to use by choosing it from the Font pop-up list (you can choose **TrueType Wingdings** or **Zapf Dingbats** if they are installed on your system). Then select the ASCII code for the character you want.

N O T E   With a Mac, an easy way to see characters paired up with their codes is to use the Key Caps desk accessory. Click on the **Apple** icon and select **Key Caps** to open it and select the font whose characters you'd like to review. The code for the character you click on is shown at the bottom of the dialog box.

Finally, enter the size of the character you want in the Size pop-up list; an example of the bullet will be displayed in the example box. Choose **OK** to accept the parameters of the bullet you select and return to the Bullets and Numbering dialog box.

Change Case

This command can be used to change selected text to all uppercase, all lowercase, toggle text (upper to lower/lower to upper), title case (first letter of each word in uppercase), or change to sentence case (capitalize first words of sentences).

Create Color Library

This plug-in allows you to save a group of colors you've assembled on your Colors palette for reuse at a later time in another publication, using the simple dialog box shown in Figure B.47.

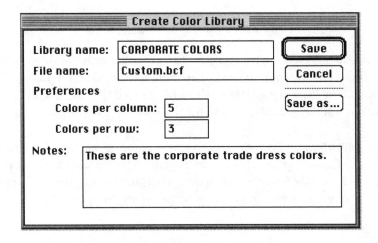

Figure B.47 *The Create Color Library dialog box.*

Drop Cap

The Drop Cap plug-in negates all the trouble PageMaker usually is to create a drop cap. Click the text insertion point at the beginning of the paragraph that you want to add a drop cap to and choose the plug-in to display the Drop Cap dialog box, shown in Figure B.48.

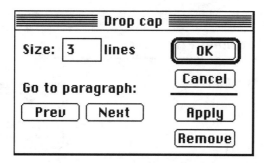

Figure B.48 *The Drop Cap dialog box.*

Simply enter the number of lines deep that you'd like to align to the drop cap (the number of lines determines the size of the capital letter). Click **OK** and the addition builds the drop cap. Unlike the drop cap you create from scratch, the addition's drop cap is part of the text block.

To see a preview of what the drop cap will look like in the paragraph, click the **Apply** button. You will see the drop cap added to the paragraph. To move to another paragraph to add a drop cap, press the **Prev** or **Next** button. You can remove a drop cap by clicking the **Remove** button.

EPS Font Scanner

Choose this plug-in to turn on and off PageMaker's automatic EPS *font scanning feature,* which will examine your encapsulated PostScript graphics for fonts to make sure your system has the corresponding screen fonts installed. If no matching font is found, a dialog box alerts you when you try to print the file and gives the options of printing the font anyway (using an outline font on your hard disk, if available, or with Courier, if not) or not printing the font. EPS graphics don't print if the **Proof** option is selected from the Printing Options dialog box, so this warning will not appear. Figure B.49 shows the EPS Font Scanner Preference dialog box.

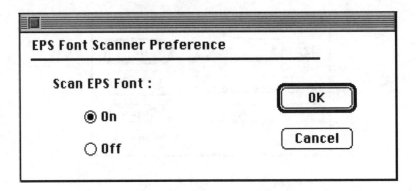

Figure B.49 *The EPS Font Scanner Preference dialog box.*

Expert Kerning

This is the same dialog box as Expert Kerning, described previously under the Type menu.

Global Link Options

Provides options for changing links in the current page or all pages.

Grid Manager

Grid Manager is the new utility for creating libraries of grids and guides you can apply to Master Pages in your publications. You can define a page grid, including number of rows, columns and gutters, margins, and whether a set of guides should appear on odd or even pages. The Grid Manager is shown in Figure B.50.

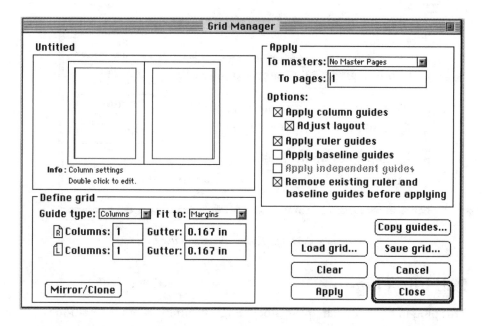

Figure B.50 *The Grid Manager plug-in.*

Keyline

The Keyline plug-in provides a quick way of creating a thin border around objects on your page. The dialog box, shown in Figure B.51 lets you specify whether the keyline should be placed in front of or behind an object, whether the portion of the page under the object should be knocked out (so it won't print or overprint). Click on the **Attributes** button to bring up the Fill and Line dialog box, which can be used to define the width, color, tint of the line, and its fill, as well as whether it should be transparent or if it should overprint the background.

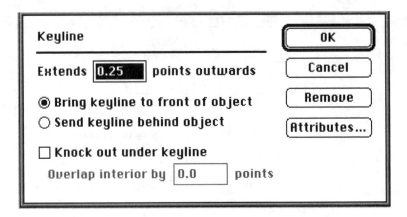

Figure B.51 *The Keyline Plug-In dialog box.*

Pub Info Plug-In

This plug-in gives you a helpful, albeit lengthy, summary of information you'll need prior to sending the document to your service bureau. Click this plug-in to display the Pub Info dialog box (see Figure B.52).

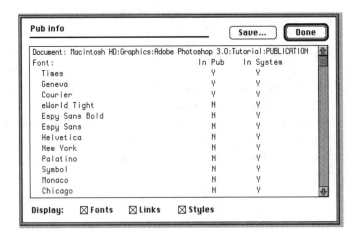

Figure B.52 *The Pub Info Plug-In dialog box.*

In the Display area, click the appropriate check boxes to show the status of fonts links and styles used in the document. The report can be saved as a text file (that you can print later) by clicking the **Save** button. Click the **Done** button to return to your document.

Publication Converter

This plug-in converts publications between PageMaker 6.5 and 6.0 versions.

QuickTime Media

This plug-in is used to convert frames of imported movie files into images for PageMaker.

Running Headers/Footers

Running headers and footers are a little different from what we usually think of being headers and footers. True running headers are at the top of the pages, like regular headers, but running headers normally reflect changing text that is current to the page on which the header appears. For example, the header lines of dictionary pages are considered running headers because they show the first word and the last word on each page. The Running Header/Footer addition does the same thing. Choose this command to display the dialog box shown in Figure B.53. In the Find area of the dialog box, choose the **First Instance** option to select the first word or reference on the page; or the **Last Instance** option to choose the last word or reference. Then use the Left pages or Right pages area to indicate where on the page you want to place the header or footer.

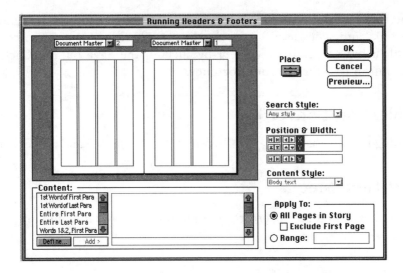

Figure B.53 *The Running Headers/Footers Plug-In dialog box.*

Save for Service Provider

This plug-in saves the publication in a format that can be used by service bureaus.

Update PPD Plug-In

The Update PPD plug-in lets you create a custom PPD file if you can't find one for your printer or to create an updated version of the one furnished with your printer if you add memory, another paper tray, or some other accessory. The utility can actually poll a PostScript printer to obtain the information it needs, so all you need to do is click the **Update** button in some cases. The **Option** button lets you specify additional paper sizes, add fonts from the hard disk attached to the printer, and add entries for fonts in the printer's RAM.

Word Counter

This plug-in counts the words in your publication.

Find (Command/Ctrl+8)

The **Find** command is a powerful feature that searches for words, phrases, text attributes, and hidden characters and codes. The **Find** command and its cousin, the **Change** command, can be used only in the Story Editor. Choose this command to display the Find dialog box, shown in Figure B.54.

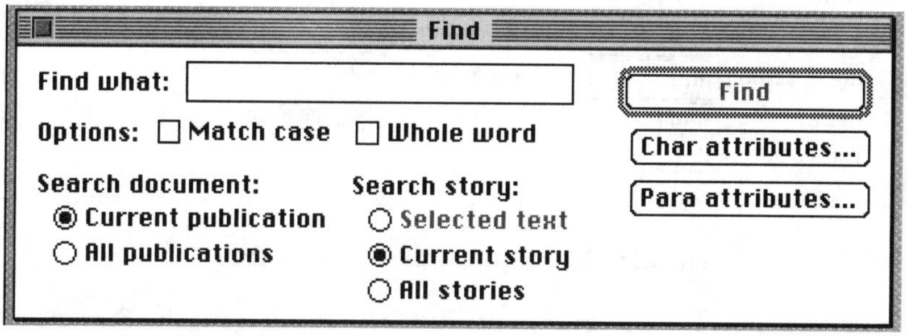

Figure B.54 *The Find dialog box.*

Enter the word or phrase (searched-for words are sometimes called the *search string*) in the Find What text box. Choose **Match Case** to match the uppercase or lowercase presentation of the word. Choose **Whole Word** to prevent PageMaker from identifying partial word matches (such as searching for *ring* and locating *string*). You can enter a wildcard character to replace specific characters in the search string; wildcard characters are useful if you are not sure of the spelling of the word for which you are searching. The wildcard character is the caret and the question mark together (^?). You can also enter a number of special characters to search for, including hard return codes, discretionary hyphens, and so on.

The **Find** command normally searches the entire story, from the insertion point forward. When it reaches the end of the story, PageMaker asks if you want the **Find** command to wrap back to the beginning and search from the beginning up to the insertion point. To search selected text, highlight the text with the Text tool and choose **Find**. To search all stories in a document, choose the **All Stories** radio button.

Choose the **Find** button to start the search. After the first occurrence of the search string, the **Find** button changes to **Find Next**. To find the next occurrence, choose **Find Next**. The **Find Next** command on the Edit menu also becomes available after finding the first occurrence of the search string.

Attributes

To add text attributes to your search string, click the **Char Attributes** button, which opens the Find Character Attributes dialog box, shown in Figure B.55.

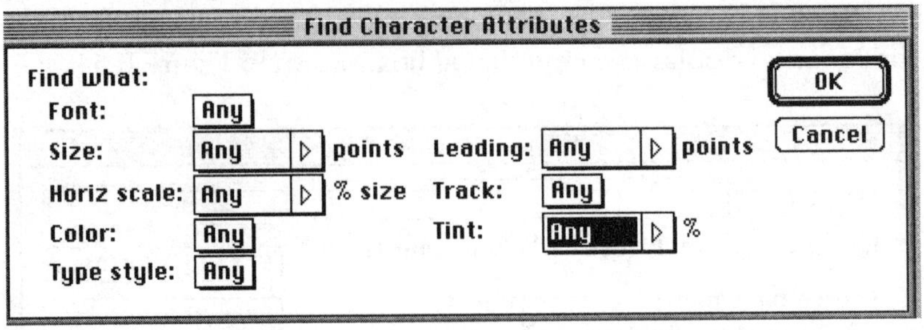

Figure B.55 The Find Character Attributes dialog box.

You can also search for paragraph attributes by clicking on the **Para Attributes** button, producing the dialog box shown in Figure B.56. To search for a specific style defined for the document, open the Para style pop-up list and click one of the styles. The **Find** command then searches for all occurrences of the search string in the style specified.

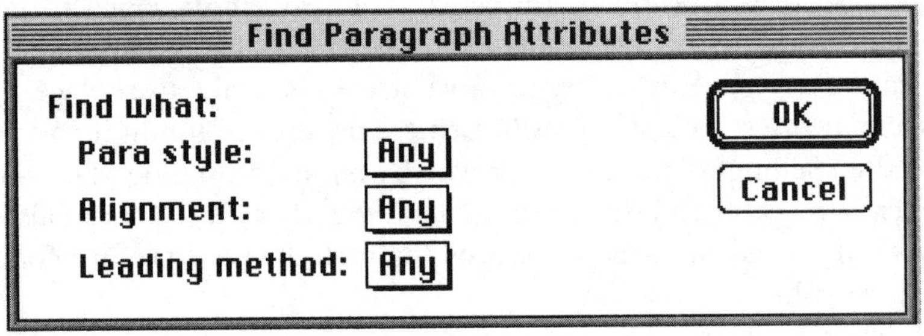

Figure B.56 The Find Paragraph Options dialog box.

To further define the search criteria for the search string, you can add a specific font in the Font pop-up list or a specific size in the Size pop-up list. You can also choose among the type styles by checking the appropriate option box. Text may also be copied from your document and pasted into the Find and Replace boxes. When you are finished, choose **OK** to return to the Find dialog box and begin your search.

Find Next

Also available only in the Story Editor, the **Find Next** command is dimmed until after the **Find** command has found the first instance of a searched-for word or phrase. You can then choose the **Find Next** command to search for more occurrences of the same word or phrase.

Change (Command/Ctrl+9)

The **Change** command is also available in the Story Editor. It is really an extension of the **Find** command: After you find what you are searching for, the **Change** command lets you change it to something else or delete it. The **Change** command's dialog box is very similar to the Find dialog box. Enter the search string in the Find What text box. Enter into the Change To text box what you'd like to change the search string to. The remaining options are the same as the Find dialog box.

Choose the **Find** button to find the first occurrence of the search string. Choose the **Change** button to change that occurrence to what you entered in the Change To text box. Choose **Change & Find** to make the change and immediately find the next occurrence of the search string. Choose **Change All** to find all occurrences and change them all. Be careful with this one! Choosing the **Type Attributes** and **Para Attributes** buttons takes you to dialog boxes very similar to those used in the **Find** command.

Spelling (Command/Ctrl+L)

PageMaker's speller, available only in the Story Editor, works much like any spelling program—if you have used one before you will find this one familiar enough. It is remarkable not so much in its functions but in its speed. Choose the **Spelling** command to display the Spelling dialog box, shown in Figure B.57.

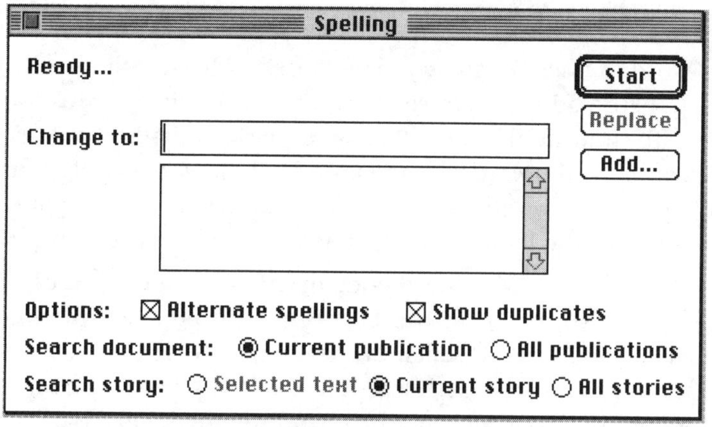

Figure B.57 The PageMaker Spelling dialog box.

If you'd like to spell check only part of a story, highlight the text with the insertion point and choose **Spelling**. Otherwise, the speller begins checking at the location of the insertion point and continues forward to the end of the story. When it reaches the end, PageMaker asks if you want the speller to wrap back to the beginning and spell check from the beginning up to the insertion point. To spell check all the stories in the PageMaker document, click the **All Stories** option.

Add Words

If you'd like to add or delete words from the spelling dictionary, choose the **Add** button, which opens the Add Word to User Dictionary dialog box, shown in Figure B.58.

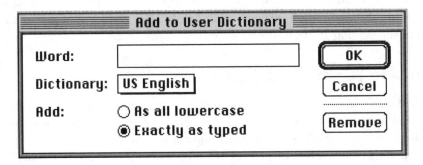

Figure B.58 *The Add Word to User Dictionary dialog box.*

The Add Word to User Dictionary dialog box is shared with the Hyphenation function. Use it to add or remove words or to hyphenate words for the User Dictionary. To indicate the most favorable place to hyphenate the word you are entering, break the word with the tilde symbol. One tilde signifies the best place to hyphenate, two tildes signify the next best place to hyphenate, and three tildes signify the least desirable, but acceptable, place to hyphenate.

If you have purchased other dictionaries from Adobe, you can select the dictionary you wish to use in the Dictionary pop-up list (dictionaries are installed using the Adobe Installation program). To add the word in all lowercase letters, or to add it exactly as entered in the Word text box, choose the appropriate option. To remove a word from the dictionary, type the word in the Word text box and click the **Remove** button. Choose **OK** to return to the Spelling dialog box.

Book

Choose the **Book** command to create a list of PageMaker documents, that, when combined, comprise a book. For example, if you have PageMaker documents called CHAPTER 1, CHAPTER 2, CHAPTER 3, CHAPTER 4, INTRODUCTION, TABLE OF CONTENTS, and INDEX, the **Book** command puts them together, in the proper order. Choosing this command displays the Book Publication List dialog box, shown in Figure B.59.

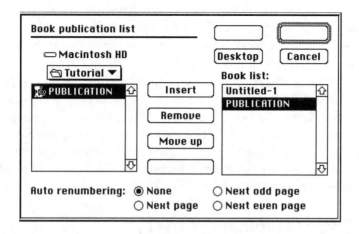

Figure B.59 The Book Publication List dialog box.

For each document you'd like to include in the book, find the document in the list box, click the document name, and choose the **Insert** button to add it to the Book list. After you have inserted all the documents into the Book list, use the **Move Up** or **Move Down** button to adjust the order of the documents in the list, if necessary. If you'd like to remove a document from the list, click the **Remove** button.

If, for some reason, you move a document included in a Book list, the Book list will still include the name of the document, even though PageMaker won't be able to find it. You'll be notified of the missing document when you perform any book-oriented tasks, like printing the book or compiling the index or table of contents. To fix the problem, go back to the Book Publication List dialog box, remove the document name that cannot be found from the Book list, find the document in the list box, and re-insert it using the **Insert** button.

The Book Publication List dialog box also controls how PageMaker numbers pages in the book. For example, if you choose the **None** radio button in the Auto Renumbering area of the box, PageMaker does not number the pages of the documents in the Book list in consecutive order. Each document has its own independent numbering.

Check the **Next Page** option to provide consecutive numbering throughout the book. If the last page of Chapter 1 is 38, then the first page of Chapter 2 will be 39, and so forth. If you'd like the page numbering to restart at a particular point (for example, to number the front matter sections consecutively), then restart the page numbering for the chapters, open the Document Setup dialog box, and choose **Restart Page #** for the first chapter receiving the new number (see Document Setup).

If you'd like all new chapters or sections to start on an odd page number, check the **Next Odd Page** radio button. If the chapter or section would normally fall on an even-numbered page, PageMaker will add a blank page to the end of the previous chapter or section, to force the next chapter to start on an odd page. Likewise, if you'd like the chapters or sections to start on even pages, check the **Next Even Page** radio button. When you are finished with the dialog box, choose **OK** to return to your document.

Index Entry (Command/Ctrl+Y)

Choose the **Index Entry** command to create entries for a publication's index, to edit existing entries, and to add cross-references to the entries. The command displays the Add Index Entry dialog box (see Figure B.60).

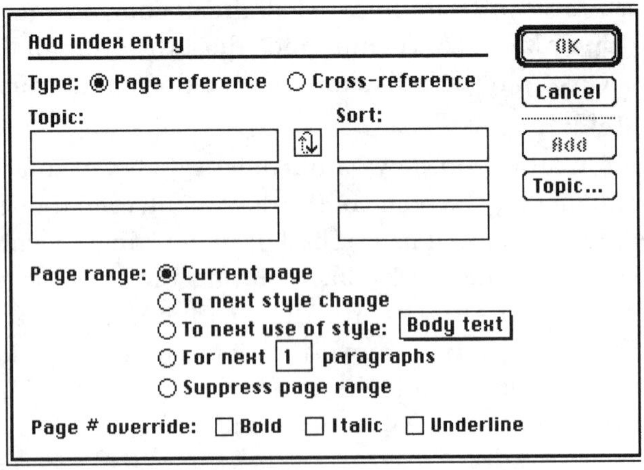

Figure B.60 *The Add Index Entry dialog box.*

Use this dialog box for a variety of activities, including marking text as index entries or as cross-references, adding second- and third-level subentries to the entry, and choosing the page range for the page number of the entry. Choose the **Add** button to add the entry to the list of index entries without closing the dialog box. Choose the **Topic** button to see a second dialog box that allows you to enter and edit index topics. If the entry is a cross-reference, you can also display a special Cross-Reference dialog box.

Show Index

Choose the **Show Index** command to display a very useful dialog box, as shown in Figure B.61, which lists, alphabetically, all current entries for the document. The Show Index dialog box is a handy way to review your index entries, check for consistency, and spot any potential problems. You can add cross-references to entries directly from this dialog box by clicking the **Add X-Ref** button. You can also edit entries by choosing **Edit**, and remove them with the **Remove** button. See Chapter 10 for complete details about the **Show Index** command.

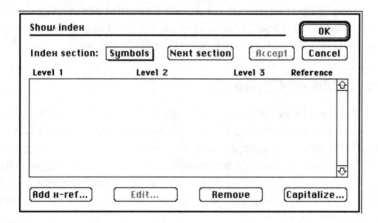

Figure B.61 *The Show Index dialog box.*

Create Index

This command actually generates an index by gathering the entries and cross-references, compiling the page numbers, and arranging everything in alphabetical order. Choosing this command opens the Create Index dialog box, shown in Figure B.62.

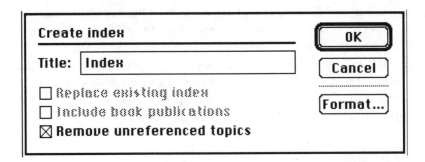

Figure B.62 *Create Index dialog box.*

You may enter the title for the index in the Title text box. If you have already generated an index, and this index supersedes it, choose the **Replace Existing Index** option. If you are working with documents in a book list, choose the **Include Book Publications** option to create an index that includes all the publications in the Book list. If you are not working with a Book list, the option will be dimmed. If you check **Remove Unreferenced Topics**, the index removes any topics that aren't tied to index references or cross-references. Choose **Format** to display the Index Format dialog box, which is used in setting the actual format of the index pages. See Chapter 10 for complete instructions about formatting and generating the index.

Create Table of Contents

Chapter titles, headings, and subheadings can be marked as table of contents entries by so specifying in the Paragraph Specifications dialog box. (Since PageMaker defines a paragraph as text followed by a hard return, chapter titles and headings are considered paragraphs.) You can mark each heading manually by opening the dialog box and checking the **Include in Table of Contents** option box, or you can add the option to the style specification for chapter titles and headings.

Once the headings are marked, choose the **Create Table of Contents** command to generate the table of contents. You will see the dialog box in Figure B.63.

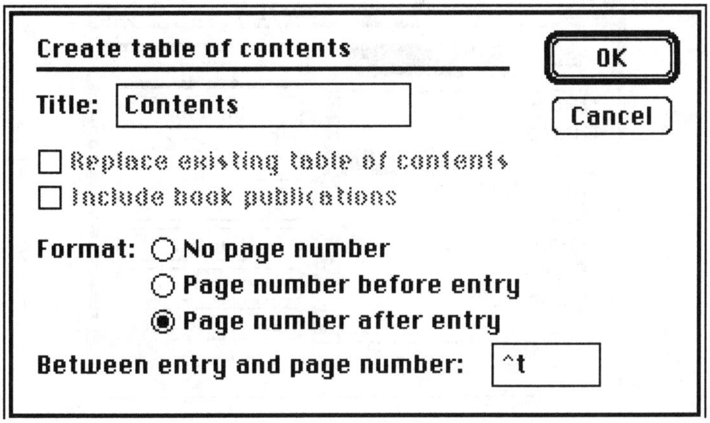

```
┌─────────────────────────────────────────────────────────────┐
│  Create table of contents              ┌───────────────┐     │
│                                         │      OK       │     │
│  Title: │Contents              │        └───────────────┘     │
│                                         ┌───────────────┐     │
│         □ Replace existing table of contents│  Cancel   │    │
│         □ Include book publications     └───────────────┘     │
│                                                               │
│  Format: ○ No page number                                     │
│          ○ Page number before entry                           │
│          ● Page number after entry                            │
│  Between entry and page number:  │^t        │                 │
│                                                               │
└─────────────────────────────────────────────────────────────┘
```

Figure B.63 *The Create Table of Contents dialog box.*

The Create Table of Contents dialog box is very similar to the Create Index dialog box. Choose whether you want to replace an existing table of contents or whether to include all book publications entries in the table of contents by clicking the appropriate options. You can format the table of contents without page numbers or with numbers to the right or to the left of the entries. Finally, you can specify a character other than the default tab character to be inserted between the entry and the page number. See Chapter 10 for complete information about creating a table of contents.

Define Colors

The **Define Colors** command displays the first of several dialog boxes, which are shown in Figure B.64. This dialog box is used in editing existing colors and creating new ones. You can choose from any of three color models and up to five color-matching libraries to define a new color, or you can copy a custom color from another document.

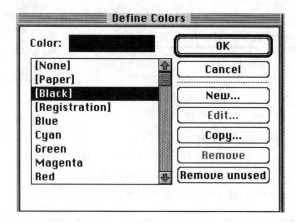

Figure B.64 The Define Colors dialog box.

THE STORY MENU

The Story menu, shown in Figure B.65, is available in the Story Editor only.

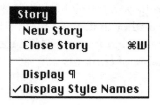

Figure B.65 The Story menu.

New Story

The **New Story** command opens a new story window labeled *Untitled*. You can stack up a number of new stories—each will be numbered. Move between the story windows by choosing the window you'd like in the Window pull-down menu.

Close Story

To close a story, choose the **Close Story** command. If the story has not yet been placed on the document page, PageMaker warns you with a small dialog box. Choose **Place** to place the document, and the story window closes, the Layout Editor is displayed, and the mouse pointer changes to the loaded-text icon. Click the loaded-text icon to place the story.

Display

While working in the Story Editor, you can display several hidden symbols, including paragraph marks, spaces between words, and tab marks. Choose the **Display** command to display the symbols. Choose the command again to hide them.

Display Style Names

To open a left margin in the story view window (called the *sidebar*) and display the style names of all paragraphs marked with a style, choose the **Display Style Names** command. You can click the style name to highlight the entire paragraph. Paragraphs without names will be marked with a small bullet in the margin. Clicking the bullet highlights the paragraph. To close the sidebar, choose the checked command again.

VIEW MENU

The View menu, shown in Figure B.66, offers controls for viewing and controlling your document windows.

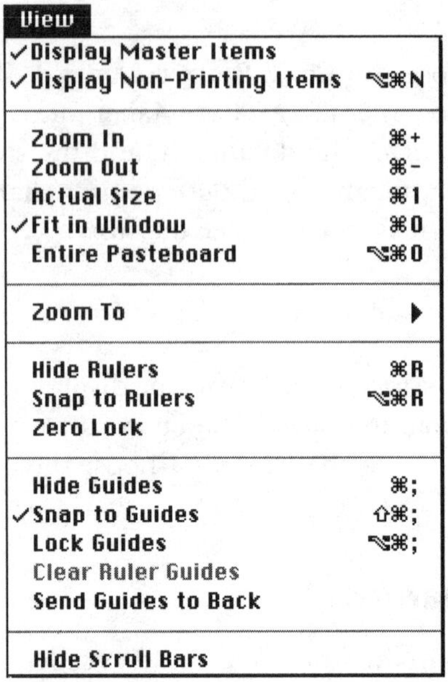

```
 View
✓Display Master Items
✓Display Non-Printing Items    ⌥⌘N

  Zoom In                        ⌘+
  Zoom Out                       ⌘-
  Actual Size                    ⌘1
✓Fit in Window                   ⌘0
  Entire Pasteboard            ⌥⌘0

  Zoom To                         ▶

  Hide Rulers                    ⌘R
  Snap to Rulers               ⌥⌘R
  Zero Lock

  Hide Guides                    ⌘;
✓Snap to Guides                 ⇧⌘;
  Lock Guides                  ⌥⌘;
  Clear Ruler Guides
  Send Guides to Back

  Hide Scroll Bars
```

Figure B.66 *The View menu.*

Many of the controls in the View menu are designed to let you show or hide various elements of the screen and your document. Their functions are too self-evident to require separate explanations. These include:

- **Display/Hide Master Items**
- **Display/Hide Non-Printing Items**
- **Display/Hide Rules**
- **Display/Hide Guides**
- **Display/Hide Scroll Bars**

Others change the size of your image. They include:

- **Zoom In (Command/Ctrl+Plus Sign)**
- **Zoom Out (Command/Ctrl+Minus Sign)**
- **Actual Size (Command/Ctrl+1)**
- **Fit in Window (Command/Ctrl+0)**

The Fit in Window Page view size reduces the page, regardless of how large it is, to a size that fits in the document window. If you reduce the size of the window, the view of the page reduces an equal amount. The Fit in Window view gives a good overall view of the page layout.

- **Entire Pasteboard (Option/Alt+Command/Ctrl+0)**

The Entire Pasteboard view shows the entire pasteboard. It is useful when you've temporarily placed an element on the pasteboard and can't locate it in a larger view. **Zoom To** allows you to zoom to from 25% to 400%.

Snap to Rulers

When the **Snap to Rulers** command is checked, text, graphic elements, and guidelines are pulled to the nearest tick mark on the ruler. Change the definition of the ruler by changing the page view size (the larger the view, the finer the definition of the rulers). Choosing the checked **Snap to Rulers** command turns off the command.

Zero Lock

Choose the **Zero lock** command to lock the zero points of the vertical and horizontal rulers. Once locked, the zero points cannot be moved until you choose the command again, unlocking the rulers.

Snap to Guides

Choose the **Snap to Guides** command to have text and graphic elements accurately align with (snap to) the nearest guideline. Turn off the **Snap** feature by choosing the checked command again.

Lock Guides

Once guidelines have been established, choose the **Lock Guides** command to lock them in place so they cannot be moved inadvertently. You can unlock them at any time by choosing the checked command again.

Clear Ruler Guides

Removes all guides from your document

Guides in Front/Guides in Back

Use these check options to position guides in front of or behind objects.

Clear Ruler Guides

Use this option to remove all ruler guides from a page.

INDEX